Persuasion
a latter-day tale

Persuasion

a latter-day tale

REBECCA H. JAMISON

Bonneville Books
An Imprint of Cedar Fort, Inc.
Springville, Utah

ISBN 13: 978-1-59955-947-6

Published by Bonneville Books, an imprint of Cedar Fort, Inc.
2373 W. 700 S., Springville, UT 84663
Distributed by Cedar Fort, Inc., www.cedarfort.com

LIBRARY OF CONGRESS CATALOGING-IN-PUBLICATION DATA
Jamison, Rebecca H. - author.
 Persuasion / Rebecca Jamison.
    pages cm
 Summary: When Anne broke off her engagement years ago, she thought she'd
never see Neil Wentworth again. But when Neil's brother buys the house she
grew up in, it seems fate has other plans.
 ISBN 978-1-59955-947-6
 1. Mormon women--Virginia--McLean--Fiction. I. Title.

 PS3610.A56645P47 2012
 813'.6--dc23

                         2011046588

Cover design by Rebecca Jensen
Cover design © 2012 by Lyle Mortimer
Edited and typeset by Michelle Stoll

Printed in the United States of America

10 9 8 7 6 5 4 3 2

Printed on acid-free paper

*H*ow much should I ask for the chocolate fondue fountain? Five dollars? Twenty? I haven't got a clue. This is my first garage sale, and I have to admit, I'm nervous. It's true—I'm not much of a salesperson. When I was nine, I sold a box of Girl Scout cookies to an old lady down the street. She said they were too expensive and would only pay half the price. I paid the other half out of my allowance. That's how my career in sales started. And that's how it ended.

I'm trying to convince myself that garage sales are different. People actually want to come to garage sales. Why else would they be up at 8:00 a.m. on a Saturday morning? I write $15 on the sticker and place the fondue fountain on the table beside the pasta machine. I set up the artificial Christmas tree, and I'm about to arrange Dad's collection of old sunglasses on a card table when I hear my older sister, Liz, opening the garage door.

Liz is one of those women who counts calories (she has an app on her cell phone), exercises at least an hour a day, and keeps a weekly appointment at the beauty salon. With her carefully highlighted hair and slim figure, she looks as if she's my younger sister. But she's actually eighteen months older. That's right—she's about to turn thirty. Liz walks over to the Christmas tree, touches a branch with a French-manicured finger, then sighs. "Oh, Anne, do we have to sell the Christmas tree?"

"There's another one, you know. We haven't used this one for years."

Liz steps back with her hands on her hips and looks at the top of the tree. "Oh, you're right. This is the old one . . . Poor Dad. I can't believe he has to move. Couldn't we do something to help him?"

I take my eyes off Dad's sunglasses to look at Liz. Couldn't we do something to help him? I thought I was helping. "Maybe the garage sale will make enough to pay down a credit card bill." I don't say what I'm thinking—that maybe she could help me with the garage sale, or, better yet, get a job. She's capable of working. She's just never had to. Dad doesn't seem to mind that Liz hasn't moved out of the house. He also thinks it's funny when people mistake him and Liz for husband and wife. That's because, although Dad is pushing sixty, he takes pride in looking to be around thirty-nine years old.

Liz stares at me, a look of horror on her face. "I thought we agreed that we would call it an estate sale. 'Garage sale' sounds so tacky."

"We can call it an estate sale if you want. It just makes it sound like Dad's dead."

"So, you'll change the signs and everything? I'd hate to have a bunch of garage sale people coming to our house."

I'm about to say that I've already put up all the signs when Dad joins us. He's a tall man who still has a full head of blond hair. His few gray hairs blend in so well that they give him a slightly sun-bleached glow. He stands looking at a rack of his old designer clothes, smiling and shaking his head, apparently amused that such clothing was ever in style. Then he turns and smiles like he did once when he brought a puppy home for us. "Greg Shepherd just called. Should be here any minute. He's already found someone who wants to look at the house."

Liz moans. "But we don't even have a sign up yet."

"Greg said that with a house like ours in a neighborhood like ours, we shouldn't be surprised to have people interested already. Real estate is doing well all over northern Virginia, but especially here in McLean. And June is a good month for selling."

I'm going to miss this old, redbrick colonial with its big, wide front porch. I love the slippery, old, creaky floorboards and the tall staircase that's perfect for sliding down. I'll miss the way the sun streams in through the tall windows in the living room, lighting up Dad's dark leather furniture and oriental rugs; the crystal ceiling lamps that sparkle in the bedrooms; the pink bathtub where I took all my childhood baths and the cabbage rose wallpaper that lines the bathroom walls. Most of all, I'm going to miss the yard with all its overgrown azaleas and boxwoods. As a child, I spent long hours there, walking along the mossy pathways, learning the names of the trees—oak, hickory, maple, dogwood, redbud—and watching birds playing in the birdbath.

Dad walks over to the side of the garage where I've stacked his old golf clubs, ski equipment, tennis racquets, and exercise gadgets. He picks up a racquet and swings. "You know, Liz, I think it's going to be great to start over. With a smaller place, I can afford a few luxuries, maybe a better car. It'll be a better social climate for you too."

Liz giggles. "We'll need to find a place with lots of doctors and lawyers."

The truth is that my father is so far in debt that even if he sells the house for the asking price, he will barely pay off the home equity loans he's taken out. Plus, he'll still have eight credit cards to pay off and two car loans. Although he is an accountant, Dad is always a little too optimistic about his financial situation. Maybe it's because he's used to dealing with the larger debts involved in running businesses. Whatever it is, I'm not about to remind him of how bad his situation really is. That would be too shameful, too embarrassing for both of us. It's hard enough that he has to move out of the home where he's lived ever since the year I was born.

"If we get what we're asking for the house," Dad is saying, "we might be able to afford a nice condominium. There are some new ones down in Fredericksburg right beside a golf course."

Liz fumbles with some of her old jewelry that's lying out on a card table. "Daddy, we couldn't possibly move to Fredericksburg. That's so far away."

"I don't see that it matters, Liz. I'm about to reach retirement age, and you're flexible." He clears his throat and holds up one of the old skis. "Anne, I don't think you're asking enough for these. I must have paid $300 for this set. And that was just a few years ago."

Knowing we couldn't get more than twenty-five dollars for them, I'm glad our conversation is cut short by Greg Shepherd's arrival. Greg Shepherd is a short, stocky man who, if dressed up properly, would make a perfect Santa Claus. He's an old friend of Dad's—they've known each other since Liz and I joined the Church. Actually, he's our home teacher, which doesn't matter a bit to Dad—he doesn't have strong feelings about religion one way or another. He pretty much left it up to Mom to freak out over us joining The Church of Jesus Christ of Latter-day Saints. Even though Mom allowed us to join, she still thinks it's a cult. I guess I probably would too if I hadn't read the Book of Mormon and listened to the missionaries. Living without the gospel was like driving in the rain without windshield wipers. When I learned about the gospel, things cleared up for me.

I know, joining the Church isn't really a normal way for a teenage girl to rebel. And what teen wants to join a church whose teachings include abstinence from alcohol and sex? It sometimes amazes me that Liz and I ever even wanted to visit the church. But Liz had a huge crush on a Mormon boy, so when one of our girlfriends invited us to an activity, she was all about going to church.

At first, we went for the boys and the activities, then we started to see that those kids had something we didn't. For the most part, they were happier, they had a sort of inner confidence, and they actually knew what they believed. For me, who had never really known what to believe, that was enticing.

When our friends invited us over to hear the missionaries, I'll admit I was scared, but I shouldn't have been. I learned I had a purpose for being on earth. And I came to know God as someone who loves me. When I kneeled down to pray about getting baptized, joy wrapped around me, and I knew I wanted to follow Jesus Christ.

I've tried to explain it all to Dad, but he doesn't seem to care. What matters to Dad is that his home teacher, Greg, is one of the most successful real estate agents in the county. Greg waves to us as he walks up the driveway toward the garage and calls out, "I forgot to tell you, Walter, I think you might actually be acquainted with this couple who's coming to look at the house. The man used to go to your country club. His name's Wentworth."

Am I hearing right? Did he say Wentworth? I dive down behind the table beside me and pretend to arrange a box of Liz's old paperback novels as my face grows red—and it isn't from the pictures on the covers of all those historical romances.

Greg puts a finger to his lips—another Santa Claus move. "That's funny. I just talked to him on the phone, and I can't seem to remember his first name. A tall man—red-haired. He's one of the doctors up at the hospital." This at least is a relief—it's his brother, not him. I let out my breath slowly.

Dad shakes his head.

After an awkward silence, I interrupt, "You mean Jack Wentworth. He was the pool manager a few years ago."

Dad slaps his thigh. "That's why I couldn't remember him. I was thinking he was one of the members."

Liz shrugs. "I don't remember him either." I'm relieved to hear her say it. That, at least, will spare me a tiny bit of embarrassment.

Greg enthusiastically rubs his hands together. "So, when can I show them the house?"

I put the box of books up on the table and sort through them. I'm not really sorting anything, though, except the feelings that are coursing through me. The one overwhelming feeling is that I don't want to see Jack. I'm sure he'll remember me, and I don't want to stir up unpleasant feelings. Just hearing the name "Wentworth" mentioned again is enough to make me want to hide like a shy cat.

Conveniently, Dad decides to show the house tonight instead of in the morning when I'm running the garage sale. While they're showing the house, I'll be relaxing in my apartment with a book. To make sure of this, I decide to finish setting up for the garage sale in the morning. If some of the items don't get priced, so be it. I've heard that people prefer to haggle at garage sales anyway.

Once Greg leaves, I say good-bye and head for my car. But even as I'm walking out of the house, I'm thinking that in a month or two, he could be walking on this same pavement.

My mind is so preoccupied that I get to my apartment complex with hardly any idea of how I arrived here. I live on the fifth floor of a seven-story building. It's a modern complex with new, beige carpets in the hallways and two elevators that never stall—the perfect choice for single professionals. Yes, it's expensive—everything in northern Virginia is expensive—but I make up for it by driving an old car, a car that embarrasses my father. I also skimp a little on my retirement savings.

My roommate, Marcy, is standing at the stove in the kitchen when I walk into the apartment. She's wearing a big white apron and has her hair up in a high ponytail.

Marcy is the only African-American woman in the singles ward. She is also, by far, the tallest woman in the ward and a divorcee, but that doesn't hold her back at all. She has plenty of dates. It helps that she's a great cook. Guys like that, even if she is a vegetarian.

Marcy has, in fact, pretty much taken over the kitchen, which she's decorated in her own retro style. The curtains, pot holders, flowerpots, and dishes are all shades of yellow and orange. Glossy-leafed succulent plants grow in pots along the tops of the cabinets. She claims the warm colors help her relax after working long hours as a congressional aide.

Marcy calls out to me as soon as I step in the door. "I'm making eggplant Parmesan. Do you want some?"

I put my purse down on the kitchen table. "No thanks. I'm having a chocolate day." I open the freezer.

"What's wrong?"

I dig to the back of the freezer for the emergency pint of Ben & Jerry's Brownie Batter ice cream. "Did I ever tell you about Neil Wentworth?"

"I don't remember. Do you work with him or something?"

"No, I knew him eight years ago when I was in college. We were engaged for a day or so."

Marcy looks at me with her mouth wide open. If I wasn't so nervous about the whole thing, I'd feel triumphant—there isn't much that gets past Marcy. She shakes her wooden spoon at me. "You didn't ever tell me you were engaged. What happened?"

I stick a spoon—a silver-plated one Marcy got for a wedding present—in the ice cream. "I got scared. My mom and dad both disapproved. They said we were too young. That we would turn out divorced like they did. I was worried that I didn't know how to be a good enough wife. He was right off his mission. He wanted to be a police officer. I didn't want to be a police officer's wife. It's so dangerous, and I would have always been worrying. I thought I couldn't handle it. I thought it would be better for him if I didn't marry him. Back then, I was so insecure about everything. Maybe it was because of my parents' divorce." I take a bite of ice cream.

Marcy opens the oven door. "So, did you see him?"

"His brother is going to come look at Dad's house tonight." I push the ice cream away from myself. "I really need to go on a diet."

"You do not need to go on a diet. You look great." Marcy puts a casserole dish in the oven, dries off her hands, and comes to sit down across from me at the table. I feel like I'm talking to my mom. Not my real mom, but the mom I wish I had. "So you're worried you'll see this guy. Do you want to see him?"

I lean back and comb my hands through my hair. "I don't know. I was really in love with him. We were so comfortable together. I've never felt that way about anyone else. Do you remember when I was dating Charlie? I couldn't get excited about him. I mean, we had fun together, but it was like something was missing."

"I remember how relieved you were when you finally broke up with him . . . I still can't believe he married your sister . . . So is this Neil guy still single?"

"I haven't seen him since the day we broke up. It was the same day I went back to college, and he moved up to Maryland. All I've heard is that he's up in Baltimore, and he's a police officer."

Marcy reaches for her laptop at the other end of the table. "Well, there's one way to find out."

"You're not going to Google him."

"You gave me enough information. If my search doesn't work out, I have a friend up in Baltimore." Marcy is one of those people who seems to have connections in every city on the East Coast.

I'm too nervous to sit at the table while Marcy searches. "I think I'll take a bubble bath." Grabbing the ice cream, I head for the bathroom. I always thought it was too late to find him again. He's probably happily married with two or three children. Eight years is a long time. It's certainly long enough for Neil to forget all about me.

I shut the door and turn on the water. The noise of the water rushing out of the bathtub faucet slows my thoughts. I pour in half a container of vanilla scented bath salts. (The directions said to use a tablespoon; but what the heck, they're supposed to be relaxing.)

Why am I so worried about Neil? What are the chances I'll ever see him again? If I do see him, he'll probably introduce me to his cute, little wife—and that will be the end of it. No matter what, my journal from 2002 is going to stay unopened under my bed.

Sinking my body down into the hot water, I feel my sore muscles begin to relax—my feet, legs, back, arms, neck, head. Guys like Neil always get married. It's too late. There's nothing to worry about—nothing at all to worry about, nothing, nothing. I'm repeating it to myself like a mantra when Marcy knocks at the door. "Still single," she calls.

2

Thursday, May 9, 2002

I think I'm dating someone—it's hard to tell because he's never really said the word "date." He hasn't kissed me either. So I guess I should say we're just friends (but I'm crossing my fingers.) His name is Neil, and he just got back from his mission. (He went to England.) Last Sunday, he asked me to a fireside. Since then, we've eaten lunch together every day, but maybe that's because it's only a mile to walk from his work (the country club) to mine (the library.) The wonderful thing about him is that he understands me, no matter what I talk about. He can be really insightful about spiritual things and still understanding about the problems I have with my family.

Speaking of my family, Mom has a new boyfriend. She brought him over to our house last night. He's an antique dealer. He went all over the house, looking for something valuable, the way they do on television. He said he couldn't find anything more than twenty years old, as if that was a very bad thing. I think Dad was jealous, but he tried not to show it.

It's 9:30 a.m. and I've already sold almost all of Dad's furniture, the Christmas tree, and half the exercise equipment. I can't believe how successful this sale is. People have been coming and going since we started at 8:00 a.m. I'm inside the garage, talking to a man about the lawn mower when I see Neil getting out of a car with his brother. He could have just as well been stepping off the page of an L.L. Bean catalog. He looks the same as I remember him—the dark hair, strong shoulders, confident smile. The police work has obviously kept him in top condition. His clothes fit him perfectly. His brother, Jack, must have brought him to help inspect the house. While Jack points to the roof, Neil stands with his hands on his hips and nods. He's wearing dark glasses.

It's as if I'm frozen. The lawn mower man offers fifteen dollars. I say that will be fine, forgetting that I promised Dad to sell it for at least fifty. I take the money, stick it in my fanny pack, and pull the baseball cap further down on my head. Neil has to remember this is my house. He'll expect to see me.

I wish I'd spent a little more time dressing this morning. I should have guessed this would happen. The worst thing is there's nowhere to hide. Being the only family member in the garage, I'm stuck. If I'd known they were coming, if Dad had only told me, I could have worn something other than baggy sweatpants and a T-shirt covered with paint stains. And makeup—did I even put any makeup on before I left the apartment? I didn't curl my hair either. I have the type of hair that always has to be curled. Hairdressers call it wavy, which for me means some of my hair is straight and some is curly—you can never tell how it will look in the morning.

A woman carrying a pasta machine, some video tapes, and a curling iron hands me a twenty. It takes longer than usual to calculate the change. The whole time I'm wondering if Neil has noticed me. While I'm fumbling for a five-dollar-bill in my fanny pack, I'm surrounded by several other people wanting to buy things. I see Dad talking to Jack in the driveway. Neil is staring down at the boxwood bushes, his hands still on his hips.

We stood next to those boxwoods the first time he kissed me. The bushes have a way of reminding me of it with their deep, woodsy scent. Neil and I rode our bikes and had a picnic at the park. By the time we'd gotten back, he was in a hurry to get to work. We were both sweaty, me especially. He wrapped his arms around me and gave me a kiss that melted away every unhappy thought lurking in my body. Then he said good-bye and headed off to work. I remember standing there, unable to move, feeling as if my spine had turned to Jell-O.

I wish I could feel a little of that peacefulness now. My hands are shaking as I fumble with money. I hope Dad isn't being too rude.

It doesn't seem that he's recognized Neil at all. He's only looking at Jack. It's now inevitable. I'm going to have to say something to Neil. I don't want him to feel rejected all over again. On the other hand, I'm glad to be so busy with the garage sale that I don't have to go out and greet him right now. I wonder what I should say. Well, at least it will be over soon.

Within a few minutes, Neil, Jack, and Dad disappear to the other side of the house. The crowd of customers is thinning out, so I run inside to put some of the money from my hip pack in a change box. While I'm at it, I run into the bathroom for a second to borrow a little blush and mascara from Liz. But I can't find any of Liz's makeup. She must have already packed it. When I return to the garage, my sister Mary is pushing her double stroller around the boxes and tables. Mary has the softened body of a woman who's borne two children and is now a few weeks into her third pregnancy. Her hair is brown, like mine, and permed. She's wearing jeans and a loose, pink T-shirt. Her features are smaller and more delicate than mine. I used to be a little jealous about that.

I maneuver around the shoppers to greet her. "Hi, Mary, am I ever glad to see you. We've been so busy. I haven't had a moment to myself."

Mary looks around. "Where's Liz?"

I shrug my shoulders. "I don't know. She's probably around back at the pool. She told me she's trying to save money by tanning outside instead of at the salons. I thought she was going to help with—"

"I've gotta run to the store," Mary interrupts. "We're out of milk and there's nothing to eat for breakfast. My morning sickness is out of control. I can't face taking the kids to the store. They're always so hard to shop with, and I'm really not feeling well today. I can see you're busy, so I'm gonna see if Liz will watch them." She parks the stroller at the back of the garage and pulls the squirming boys out. "Make sure no one runs off with the stroller." I open the door to the house while Mary drags the kids through.

To be honest, I'm a little worried about Liz watching the boys beside the pool. I don't want to make a 911 call on top of everything else that's happening. But I shouldn't have worried. Not five minutes after Mary leaves, Liz drags the boys back out to the garage. She puts one hand on a hip and points to the boys with the other. "I can't watch these kids. They won't do anything I say. You've got to tell Mary to take some sort of discipline class. You're the only one who can give her advice."

By this time, there isn't much left in the garage and fewer people are getting out of their cars to look at the merchandise. The boys, an eighteen-month-old and a three-year-old, are climbing on the one remaining sofa. I've pulled them off at least ten times. I'm pulling them off again when Jack and Neil walk into the garage. Neil's face is the same: smooth and tanned with clear blue eyes that are so disarming. All the angles are just right: the straight nose, the determined chin, and the intelligent brow. He could have been a politician. Except for that little piece of hair that sticks up at the crown of his head, he could go on television right now. Back when we were dating, I took the trouble to carry gel in my purse to plaster down that piece of hair.

Jack looks at Neil, who looks at me. Because I can't seem to say anything, Neil has to be the first to speak. "Hi, Anne. It's nice to see you." He reaches his hand out to shake mine. But I'm holding the toddler who is now kicking and screaming.

I try to smile. I remember hearing somewhere that a smile is the most important accessory. That's good because it's all I've got. "Oh, hi, Neil. It's good to see you too." The toddler continues to scream.

Neil cocks his head and looks at the little boy in my arms. He isn't going bald at all. His hair is still dark and thick on top. "Do you need some help?"

I can hardly believe that he is still so handsome, and I'd forgotten how his voice is so gentle and deep. "Oh, no, I'm fine."

He puts his hands in his pockets and rocks back on his heels. "So, are these yours?"

I smile. "Yeah." Then I realize he's asking about the children. I guess he hasn't been Googling my name lately. "I mean, they're mine, but they're not mine. I mean, they're my sister's kids. They're my nephews. I'm watching them for her."

There's a long pause. I'm trying to think of something to say. Should I ask about his job or his family? Maybe I should offer him a drink or something to eat. A man who has been testing out the exercise cycle comes toward us. Neil steps back. "Well, I guess you're busy. Nice seeing you again." He turns and walks over to where Jack is staring at a small crack in the garage floor. The two of them look around the garage for a while, then walk back outside. They're heading toward their car as Mary comes in.

I'm helping the man to get the exercise cycle out of the garage and telling myself that the worst is over. I saw him. We spoke. Now I have nothing to worry about. We can treat each other as old friends. I'm telling myself that it's ridiculous to feel things so deeply after eight years. It's been almost a third of my life. So much has happened. So much has changed.

But all the logic in my brain can't change my feelings. Eight years might as well have been eight days. I still love him.

When I'm finished helping with the cycle, Mary's words jolt me from my thoughts. "Do you know those men, Anne?" She nods toward Jack and Neil, who are just driving off. Since she stayed with our grandparents during the summer Neil and I dated, she doesn't know much about our relationship.

"Yes, we were friends when we were younger. The red-haired one is thinking of buying the house . . . Why do you ask?"

"Oh, nothing. It's just that the dark-haired one was saying something about how much you'd changed and how he hardly recognized you." Mary's never been tactful. I'm usually prepared for it, but this time it stings.

I look down at the floor. "Hardly recognized me!" The words echo in my mind. I'm mortified. But it's true. I've changed, and he hasn't. I would have recognized him anywhere. I've been noticing this for the past half hour, and I can't deny it. The years that have worn me out like some faded old T-shirt—those same years have given him a more manly, open look. I saw the same Neil Wentworth.

"Hardly recognized me!" The more I think it, the less agitated I feel. I might even be thankful for Mary's eavesdropping. Sure, I'm disappointed, but better to be disappointed sooner than later. Yes, I still love him, but I can't have him. At least now I don't have to wait anxiously to know his feelings for me. Maybe this is my chance to really start over—to finally get over him and get on with my life.

3

oday I helped Neil shop for a car. The one that seemed to be the best deal was a Subaru with a manual transmission. Since Neil had never driven a stick shift, I test drove it for him. After I told him I liked it, he asked me if I'd teach him to drive it. We spent about an hour in the stake center parking lot with him at the wheel, and then he drove it back to the owners' home without any trouble. He got such a good deal on the car that he didn't even need a loan. When I told Dad about it, he said I must have been mistaken about the loan. He said everyone gets loans to buy cars, even used ones. I guess I should have told him it's a 1993.

A little over a month has passed since the garage sale. I've settled myself into a routine—work all day at the brokerage firm, come home, eat, exercise, socialize occasionally, and sleep. I've given up on that diet I started last month. Jack Wentworth now lives in my childhood home. And Dad and Liz have moved into a nice apartment in the same complex as mine. Their place is newer than mine (of course). Theirs has an open floor plan, featuring a great room that combines the kitchen, living room, and dining areas. Liz chose it because it's good for entertaining.

Dad says they're living in the apartment just until they pay off a few of the credit cards. But Liz has already bought a whole new set of furniture on credit. Every time I go over, Liz wants to show off one of her new decorating schemes. Dad, if he isn't at work, is usually reading a consumer magazine. "If I could just afford a new car," he might say, "I could save a hundred dollars a month on gasoline." Or, "The new laptops are so superior to the older ones. I think it'd definitely be worth the investment." Or, "Did you know that most washing machines only last seven years? Ours is at least ten years old. The newer models are much more efficient."

One day, I'm compelled to say something about it. "Dad, I'm not sure those magazines are helping you to save money. Maybe it's just me, but it seems like they're encouraging you to spend more."

My father looks up from the magazine and takes off his reading glasses. "You know, Anne, I think I was supposed to tell you something." He calls to Liz, who's in the other room. "What was it I was supposed to tell Anne?"

Liz walks in, wearing a jacket and pants that still have the tags on them. "Oh, Mary wants you to call."

Dad puts his glasses back on and turns back to his magazine. "That's it. Mary's not doing well with her pregnancy. The doctor's put her on bed rest. She's been trying to call you all week."

I lean against the kitchen island. "That's too bad."

Liz twirls around to display her new clothes. "She wanted me to come help her with the kids, but I told her I couldn't. I got a new job today."

I feel like jumping up and down, but I restrain myself. "That's great. Where is it?"

"At the store where we bought all our furniture. I love it there. They hired me right after the interview. They were impressed that I have a degree in fashion merchandising."

I'm smiling so big my gums are showing. "Good for you."

Dad laughs. "And we have Mary to thank for it. As soon as Liz found out that Mary was on bed rest, she went out and applied. Got the job the same day."

I'm less impressed with this bit of news. "I guess Mary's pretty desperate. She'll probably be asking me next."

Liz examines her latest manicure. "No, I think she's more likely to ask Charlie's sisters. They're both home from school for the summer. And they live right next door to her."

Dad puts up his magazine again. "I suppose there are some advantages to living next door to your in-laws."

I'm feeling guilty as I leave their apartment. I've deliberately kept my cell phone turned off for the entire week. This is because I noticed the week before that nearly every time someone called me, it was to ask me to do something for them. Mom called to ask if I could take Todd, my stepbrother, to the dentist. Mary asked me to bring her a bottle of sauerkraut—she had a craving and couldn't get to the store. Someone asked me to substitute in Sunday school. Liz wanted to borrow my membership card to the gym—she'd misplaced her own. No one called just to talk or to see how I was doing. I was starting to resent it. But now that Mary really needs me, I'm not there for her. I dial her number as soon as I get home.

Her voice is somewhere between a sigh and a whine. "Oh, Anne, I'm so glad you called. You'll never guess what's happened."

I tell her I already know and volunteer to come stay at her house every day after I get off of work to help her. I'll stay in Mary's guest room until the doctor takes her off of bed rest. Since Charlie's sisters will be there to help during the day, Mary now has nothing to worry about—at least not until she thinks for a while.

I pack my bags that night. Figuring I probably only need a week's worth of work clothes and casual clothes, I pack light. Everything fits into the battered old suitcase I brought home from my mission. Sure, it's not the most attractive piece of luggage I own, but I've grown accustomed to using it as a substitute dresser. The next morning, I wheel the monstrosity out to my car and heave it into the trunk.

I work as a stockbroker, which, depending on the day, can be a high-stress job. Stocks are plummeting today, which means my clients are panicking. Of all the brokers at the office, I'm the one with the most widows—women whose accounts used to be managed by their husbands, but now they have to manage them with my help. My boss says I have a calming personality, which is why I have more of these little old ladies than anyone else on the team. On most days, I love it. Senior citizens tend to be polite, complimentary, even laid-back. But in a bear market like this, when stocks take a nose-dive, these women have skyrocketing anxiety.

The first message I return is from Mrs. Slater, who's actually sobbing on the phone about how much she's lost. I reassure her that the market will eventually correct, all the while wondering why I've never taken a course in grief counseling. Then there's one from Mrs. Goldstein, who feels guilty that she's not managing her accounts as well as her husband would have liked. She's worried that she's offended his spirit. I tell her basically the same thing I told Mrs. Slater, then we chat a little about her new grandson. It goes on like this all day.

As I head out of the office, I'm not in a mood to be polite to anyone, especially not my relatives. What makes it worse is the sweltering July weather. It's humid and hot, over ninety degrees. On my way home, I stop to get Chinese take-out for Mary's family, and a large raspberry smoothie for myself. If I had the time, I would stop and take a walk—it's too hot to run. But I know Charlie's sisters, Hannah and Lily, will be waiting for me. While waiting in the bottleneck around Tyson's Corner, I'm listening to an MP3 of general conference.

The traffic is horrible. By the time I reach Mary's house, I've listened to three conference talks on patience, counted one hundred and thirteen of my blessings, drunk my raspberry smoothie, and given myself a scalp massage at a red light. I park my little Ford—yes, I know, I should never have bought an American car—in the driveway next to Mary's split-level then climb up the back stairs to the kitchen. Mary's kitchen is nice, though not at all new. The dark wood cabinets are beginning to show wear around the edges. The appliances, all dark brown from the eighties, are the kind that refuse to give up the ghost. They'll probably all be running fine twenty years from now. The walls are painted a dusty sort of light blue, and a flowery wallpaper border runs around the top of the wall next to the ceiling.

My shoes stick to the tan linoleum floor as if I have suction cups on my soles—I'll need to mop soon. Charlie's sister Hannah is at the counter, filling three glasses of water with ice. Charlie's sisters are both small ballerina types. Hannah wears her brown hair long and straight. "Oh, hi, Anne. What've you been up to?"

"Battling bureaucracy . . . that, and traffic. How's Mary?"

"She's asleep. We've been watching a movie with the kids to keep them busy."

I nod as I put the take-out on the table. I can hear the familiar sounds of the latest animated movie coming from the living room.

Hannah picks up the glasses and nods toward the living room. "Hey, there's someone we want you to meet."

I follow her into the living room where I see—once again—Neil Wentworth. This time his right arm is in a cast. His other arm is around Lily Musgrove. They're sitting together on Mary's blue second-hand sofa with the boys in front of them on the floor. Lily is resting her curly blonde head of hair on Neil's shoulder. Lily is a Scandinavian beauty with a perfect oval face and a little curve of a nose. I don't think she's ever had a pimple.

A look of surprise flashes across Neil's face. He brushes his hand over the back of his head, where the hair always sticks up.

Hannah hands him his water. "Neil, I want you to meet Mary's sister, Anne."

I smile without showing my teeth. Maybe it's a good thing I'm not in a polite mood. "Oh, we're already acquainted."

Neil stands up and offers me his left hand. "We meet again. I had no idea Mary was your sister." If he's embarrassed, he hides it well.

Lily flutters her thick, dark eyelashes in his direction. "Neil's been staying with his brother while he recovers from his accident. He was in a high-speed chase. Can you believe that?"

I raise an eyebrow. Is it my imagination or is Neil's face a little redder than normal? I notice now that he's wearing some sort of brace on his knee.

Hannah jockeys for a position beside Neil, not an easy task considering all the toys on the floor. "Neil is so good with the kids. You should see him play Candy Land with Joseph. They are so cute together."

Lily holds on to his good arm right around the biceps. "And he's fixed our pool so we don't have to use chlorine anymore. You should bring the kids over to swim tonight. It's so nice."

I thank them, glad for the excuse that I haven't brought my bathing suit. Though I feel a lot less awkward than the last time I saw Neil, I still don't want him to see me in a bathing suit. Plus, I can't begin to compete with Lily and Hannah's doll-like figures.

After they leave, I steal a quick look in the mirror. My hair is a little messy from the scalp massage. And I've got a raspberry seed between my two front teeth. Other than that, I think I look pretty good. At least I look better than I did at the garage sale.

I'm thinking how strange it is that Neil's dating Lily Musgrove. Not that I don't like her—Lily's a lively girl. She's just not at all what I thought Neil would like. Sure, she's smart and athletic, but there's a certain lack of depth about her. She isn't exactly the type to sit around watching historical documentaries or reading classic novels. And, I could be wrong, but I think she's only about twenty years old.

When I deliver a plate of take-out to Mary's room, I discover she isn't asleep after all. She's crying. "I can't believe Charlie's working late again." She sniffles and wipes her eyes with the back of her hand.

I wait a while, trying to decide what to say. Isn't it ironic that Mary, the one who's happily married, should be crying? I sit down beside her on the bed. "You know he works hard because he loves you."

"Do you really think so?"

I find a box of tissues on the floor under a pile of Charlie's shirts and give one to Mary. "Of course. Listen, I've got to feed the kids in the kitchen. Why don't you move into the living room? That way we can all talk."

"But the doctor said I can only get up to go to the bathroom."

I try not to sound exasperated. "Well, go to the bathroom on the way." I grab Mary's blankets and her plate to carry into the living room.

Mary swings her legs out of bed. "You never told me how you know that boy that was with Lily and Hannah."

I decide to change the subject. "He's hardly a boy. He's got to be at least twenty-nine."

"He seems nice, the poor thing. Lily and Hannah are both after him. How's he ever going to decide which one to pick?"

I'm not in the mood for this conversation. "I'm sure he'll survive."

I don't have time to wonder whether I'll see Neil again. I see him again that evening as I'm taking out the trash. He's leaving the Musgroves' house as I'm carrying three giant trash bags out of Mary's. He gives me a policeman-like wave with his good hand as he limps along in the direction of Jack's house. I think it's probably the same wave he'd give to someone on parole.

4

Tuesday, May 28, 2002

I just got back from a date with Neil. He took me to a free concert at the Jefferson Memorial, right on the banks of the Potomac. It was beautiful—breezy and cool—but not chilly—with the sun setting pink against a gray-blue sky. He held my hand!

After the concert, on our way back to the car, we saw a bunch of eels lying out on the grass. They were the strangest looking things—all black with heads like fish and short, fat, snake-like tails. Their gills were sucking in and out, so we knew they were alive. Neil called a biologist friend, who said it sounded like the eels were trying to escape some sort of pollution in the water. So, before I knew it, we were heading up an eel rescue operation. About five other people helped us gather up the eels in whatever we could find—coolers, buckets, and even one lady's purse. We dumped in some water then drove as fast as he could upriver, where we put them back in. Definitely a date to remember.

Did I mention that Mary lives next door to her in-laws? Normally, that wouldn't be a problem for me. But since I'm now living at Mary's house and Neil is dating Lily Musgrove, it's beginning to be a problem. I'm invited to dinner at least every other night—and so is he.

The Musgroves are comfortable people—Mary couldn't ask for better in-laws. Steve Musgrove, the father, runs a successful remodeling business. And together he and his wife, Janet, have created a home that is built for parties. We usually dine beside the kidney-shaped, turquoise pool in the backyard. There's a shady spot on the patio, under the old oaks, where the Musgroves cluster glass-topped tables. I try to focus my attention on Mary's kids when I eat there. I sit next to Joseph and put Daniel on the other side in a highchair. But my attention is inevitably drawn to Neil. It's like sitting on an airplane and trying not to watch the in-flight movie.

Neil, on the other hand, has no trouble keeping his eyes off me. Even when he talks about the time when he used to live in McLean— the time when we were in love—he never mentions me. And, though his eyes never drift in my direction, he's got to remember some of the same things I do. How can he talk about the Potomac River without remembering the time we went fishing there? Could he have forgotten that I met him every night after he finished his job at the country club? Can he talk about the stake center and forget how I taught him to drive a stick shift in the parking lot? I know he has to remember, but I doubt that he remembers with the same feelings of regret that I feel as I sit here silently listening.

Just as I'm wondering if it's possible to give myself amnesia, Hannah starts the conversation by asking the question I always expect and always dread. "So, Anne, have you been dating anyone?"

I'm tempted to lie, but I'm a good girl. "No." I try to act nonchalant.

Janet Musgrove, Hannah's mother, comes to my rescue. "I used to hate it when people asked me that." I want to jump up and hug her for saving me. She's a jumper-wearing, casserole-carrying Mormon mother, the type who's always looking out for me. Janet shakes her head, but her short brown hair doesn't move at all. Somehow she's found hair spray that's invincible to humidity. "But it's always that way. When you're single, people ask who you're dating. When you're dating, they ask when you're going to get married. When you're married, they ask when you'll have children. When you have a child, they ask if you're going to have another. It goes on and on."

Steve, her husband, grins and rubs a hand over the top of his balding head. "And what do they ask you now that your children are grown up?"

"Who my children are dating, of course. The cycle goes on and on."

Because Neil's right arm is broken, Lily and Hannah sit on either side of him, helping him. While Hannah cuts his barbecued chicken, Lily lifts the fork to his mouth as if she's feeding a child. It wasn't so long ago that I would have been sitting next to Neil. Eight years ago, nothing could have kept us apart. Eight years ago, he would have had his arm slung around the back of my chair and whispered to me. He used to call me "Annie." He's the only one who ever called me that.

When Lily is busy feeding herself instead of Neil, Hannah leans in toward him. "I'll bet police work is pretty different from what you see on TV."

Neil takes a sip from his glass before he replies. "Well, in real life, you don't get to meet as many attractive women. I had to get away from the work for a while to meet you two."

Lily giggles. "You can't be telling the truth. I'll bet you have pretty girls chasing you all the time."

Janet stands up to bring the Jell-O salad to my table. "I'll bet he meets a few when he's handing out speeding tickets."

Neil shakes his head. "I don't do much of that anymore. I work in narcotics. Believe me, there are some days when I wish I could write speeding tickets all day long."

Hannah gasps. "Narcotics—that sounds so dangerous."

Neil shrugs. "It can be."

"Do you ever get scared?" Hannah asks.

Neil laughs. "If I weren't scared of criminals, I'd be a pretty bad police officer."

"Do you wear a bullet-proof vest?"

"Every day."

"Do you wear your gun to church?"

"Most of the time. We're targets, you know. We have to be on guard even when we're off-duty."

"So, there are people who would like to kill you?"

"Sure. There are a few gang members who'd like to shoot me, and others who'd kill me just for being a cop. It wouldn't be a bad way to go, actually. I'd rather they shoot me than someone with a wife and kids."

There's a general gasp, and everyone takes turns remarking on how terrible it would be if he were killed. I don't dare to look in his direction as fear wells up inside of me. What was that he said? "I'd rather they shoot me than someone with a wife and kids." Is it my fault he feels that way? I wonder if that's why he said it. I scoop a big serving of Jell-O salad onto my plate, not even realizing that it's the kind with bananas.

I don't notice that I'm ignoring the kids until Neil says something about it to Lily and Hannah. "Since you two are so good at feeding people, maybe one of you should help with the children. There's only one person feeding two of them."

I'm startled back to reality. Joseph and Daniel are both begging for more food. I swallow. "Oh, I'm fine."

Lily drags a chair over to the table where I'm sitting with the boys. "I'll help. I think Daniel and Joseph take after me. They'll both do anything to get their way."

Hannah digs a fork and knife into Neil's second piece of chicken. "I don't know about that. I think you're much more stubborn than they are." She turns to Neil. "Once Lily decides something, that's it. No one can get her to do anything else. She never changes her mind."

Janet wipes her face with a napkin. "Lily has always been our most persistent child."

Neil leans back and looks at Lily. "Persistence is something that is definitely lacking in the world. I admire Lily for being persistent."

Okay, maybe he didn't direct that comment to me, but it felt like he did. I wish I could have a real conversation with him. "Okay, Neil," I would say, "I was a wimp. I regret breaking up with you. I should have been persistent and married you despite all my fears and my parents' disapproval and despite the fact that I was only nineteen years old. And, really, if you knew me now, you'd know I'm different than I used to be. I'll bet you could even call me persistent." It's so odd for us to never talk. We used to be inseparable.

I'm still thinking of what I'd like to say to him as I'm out running the next evening. I've hit a good pace. My breathing is even. I'm starting to feel calm and ordered. Maybe it's the endorphins flushing away some of my jealousy. Yes, I've admitted it: I'm jealous. Maybe

I wasn't as persistent as Lily. That's fine with me. I don't want to be that persistent. The way I see it there's a fine line between persistent and stubborn. Isn't it good to be flexible sometimes?

The further I run from Mary's house, the more familiar the houses become. I'm closer to my old home now. The trees, the flowers, even the cracks in the sidewalks bring back memories of my childhood. I'm passing the yard where I once played flashlight tag. I went sledding down the hill across the street. This is where my friend Alicia used to live. What happened to her anyway?

It's growing dark. I see a couple of fireflies flickering around me. I hear thunder and feel a few drops of rain. The cold, wet drops refresh me. The trees sway back and forth, rain dripping off their leaves. I breathe in the air that smells so clean and musty and muddy all at once.

Now it's darker, the rain heavier, as if the clouds opened up their trap doors. Drops pound down on my head. Water gushes down the side of the street. Great, muddy pools grow in the low places on the street and on the sidewalks. Cars drive slowly, making great waves across the flooded places. Their headlights reflect off the wet, black pavement, creating a confusion of reflection.

I hear the low growl of an engine coming up from behind. Glancing back, I squint into the glaring lights to distinguish a couple on a motorcycle. Both are wearing black leather and matching black helmets. When they come to a stop ahead of me and take off their helmets, I see it's Jack Wentworth and his wife. Jack has short red hair, glasses, and a goatee. I met the wife once before at church. She impressed me as a very practical type of woman. She has short brown hair, short fingernails, and never seems to say anything that doesn't need to be said.

"Hey, Anne," Jack calls out, "almost didn't recognize you with all this rain. Have you met my wife, Susan?"

Susan smiles. "We've met. Why don't you come over to see the house? It'll give you a chance to dry off. I'll make some hot cocoa."

Rain is dripping off my nose as I reply, "That would be great. I didn't realize it was going to rain so much."

Susan laughs. "Neither did we. Of course, it's lucky none of us paid attention to the forecast or we wouldn't have run into each other."

Jack tilts his head in the direction of the house. "I guess you know where it is. See you in a minute."

From the outside, the house is the same—the boxwoods line the driveway and all the flowers and plants seem just as I remember. The inside, however, is very different. The furniture has changed from dark and sophisticated to light and casual. A couple of beige recliners now sit where Dad's black leather sofa used to be, and there are a lot of plants sitting on tables and in corners. The kitchen, which was hardly ever used after I moved out, scents the house with a cinnamon sweetness. The curtains are open, letting light pour out onto dripping branches and patches of the green backyard.

I have to admit I'm a little nervous as I sit with Susan and Jack on bar stools in the kitchen. Here I am in my house, which isn't my house anymore, wondering if Neil and I are going to have another accidental meeting.

Susan looks at me. "It must seem strange to be in the house again with everything so different." What's that old cliché about someone reading you like a book?

I shift on my stool. "Oh no, I like what you've done with it."

Jack chuckles. "We're not much for fancy decorating. We like things simple and comfortable. The type of furniture that could survive children."

Susan forces a smile. "We've been trying to adopt."

Jack shakes his head. "It hasn't been easy. There are a lot of loopholes. So, right now, Susan has no one to spoil but Neil and me."

Susan laughs and gets up to check the water she's heating on the stove. "And, believe me, those two get into plenty of trouble."

I notice a stack of library books sitting on the kitchen table and wander over near Susan to examine them. It's always my favorite thing when I'm visiting people to look at their books. "Oh, are you reading *Robinson Crusoe*? I just read that last month. And I've always loved Chaim Potok."

Susan, who's dumping hot cocoa mix into mugs, glances over at the books. "I think those are Neil's. They aren't yours, are they, Jack?"

I don't dare look up. I'm holding the slick, hardcover copy of *Robinson Crusoe* in my hand. The bookmark, really a supermarket receipt, is somewhere near the end. I should have known. Neil always used receipts for bookmarks. I can feel Jack looking at me.

"Jack?" Susan repeats.

I look over at Jack, who's looking at me with his eyebrows raised. "No, Neil's been reading those." He speaks slowly, as if he's too distracted by his thoughts to say much more.

Susan sighs. "Poor Neil. I think he gets bored, being home alone all day long. It's driving him crazy to have this sick leave. Of course, if he didn't have it, he wouldn't have met those Musgrove girls. I hope he marries one of them. I think he gets lonely up in Baltimore all by himself." She carries the mugs of cocoa over to the kitchen island. They're heaped to the top with marshmallows.

I swallow and stare at a philodendron on the counter. I feel cold. I should have known not to sit next to a vent. The air conditioning is blowing right on me.

Jack leans on his elbows over his mug. "So, I hear you're a stockbroker now. That must be exciting. I'll admit, I never thought—"

There's a loud clap of thunder that sounds as if it's right over the house. The lights flicker, and then go out. The kitchen is all shadows.

Jack jumps up. "It's our first blackout. We'll have to break out the candles." He seems excited about it, like this whole situation is going to become a treasured memory.

Susan bites her bottom lip. "We'll have to find them before it gets too much darker. I think they're in a box somewhere."

The two of them head out to the garage, discussing where they might have put the box. I stay in the kitchen, feeling relieved that the air conditioner won't be working for a while. I sip my cocoa. It feels good to have something warm sliding down my throat. Rain drops pound against the window over the sink. Would anyone notice if I sneak over to the kitchen table to see the other books in Neil's stack? Since I can hear Jack and Susan shuffling through cardboard boxes in the garage, I decide to chance it. I have my hand on the stack of books when the sound of a cell phone startles me. It's playing "Flight of the Bumblebee."

"Can you get that for me, Anne?" Jack calls. "It might be the hospital."

I scramble around the semi-dark kitchen, feeling along countertops, and trying to follow the sound. I finally locate the phone in a pocket of Jack's leather jacket, which is draped over the back of a chair. The caller ID says, "Neil Wentworth."

I take a breath and shiver as I answer, "Hi, Neil," in what I hope is my most business-like voice.

Neil's voice is so casual and deep and gentle. "Oh, hi, Susan, I was calling to see if you lost your power over there?"

I take another breath, but I can't really fill up my lungs. "Actually, Neil, it's Anne Elliot. I was just, umm—visiting over here. Jack wanted me to get the phone. He's looking for candles. And, yes, the power's out."

There's a pause on the other side. "Did you want to talk to Jack?" I ask. I'm still shivering. Another pause.

"No, that's all right. Tell Jack we'll bring some candles over."

Five minutes later, Neil bursts in through the front door with a flashlight. Hannah and Lily follow him, carrying scented candles in jars. Susan rushes from the garage to greet them. "Thank you so much. Now if I can just find the matches."

Lily looks at Hannah. "Oh, I guess we should have brought matches." Hannah holds out the candles to Susan. "These smell really good. They're cantaloupe scented."

As Neil limps off to find some matches in his room, the rest of us pass the candles around to smell. Jack is still in the garage, hunting through boxes. A minute later, Neil comes back with a box of matches and a navy blue fleece blanket. "These are for you," he says, handing the matches to Susan. "And this," he says, handing me the blanket, "is for the hypothermia victim."

Everyone laughs as I stretch out a shaky hand to take the blanket from him. I know everyone thinks I'm shaking because of the cold, but that's not the only reason. The truth is, he still makes me nervous. I don't know if I'll ever get over it. Lily, in her best nurse impression, hurries to wrap the blanket around me. It smells like fabric softener.

I smile. "Thank you."

He either doesn't hear or he chooses to ignore it. He's looking at Hannah and Lily, who are already discussing how quickly they can get me home to change into dry clothes.

It's an hour later now and I'm sitting on my air mattress in Mary's unfinished basement. I feel a little like Robinson Crusoe, holed up in his cave. Alone. Does Neil ever feel alone? Is Susan right about him being lonely? I look at his blanket, draped over the folding chair beside me. Of course, I'm going to have to return it, but, for tonight, it could be a sort of treasure. I take it off the chair and wrap myself in it, allowing myself the fantasy that he still cares. Even folded in half, the blanket engulfs my body in soft warmth. I try to forget that Neil's a policeman, that he's trained to rescue people, to look for signs of suffering. For just tonight, I imagine that he loves me again.

5

I took Neil to Mom's last night for a cookout. I thought everything went well, but leave it to Mom to find a problem. She called this morning to tell me Neil doesn't have enough ambition for me. It's because he wants to be a police officer. (I'll admit, that does worry me, but mostly because it's so dangerous.) I tried to explain to her that Neil's planning to go to college this fall, and that he's intelligent, and he works hard. But it was like she didn't even hear me.

She sure has higher standards for my boyfriend than for her own. Mr. Antiques Roadshow spent almost the entire evening talking about costume jewelry. Neil is so patient. He reminds me of that scripture in Galatians 5:22: "The fruit of the spirit is love, joy, peace, longsuffering, gentleness, goodness, faith." I want to be like that.

The smell of fresh-cut grass hangs in the air as Mom and I set out across the backyard toward Mary's overgrown vegetable garden. It's a cool, breezy Saturday—a rare event in August. Even rarer is the opportunity to spend any time at all with Mom. She's a real estate agent, so she works nights and weekends. Plus, she got remarried last year. If I do happen to see her, she's most likely to be dressed in a power suit and heading off to an appointment. Today, though, she's wearing shorts and a T-shirt.

I've always wished I inherited more of Mom's good looks. I got the big, brown eyes, but not the graceful nose or the thick hair or the radiant skin. Liz is the one who gets to hear how much she looks like our mother. Though, in most ways, Liz and Mom couldn't be more different. I have much more in common with Mom than either Liz or Mary. Mom and I are both deep thinkers. We love to read and investigate things.

We're also the green thumbs of the family. That's how we've ended up in Mary's vegetable garden. Poor Mary, in her effort to conform to Musgrove family ways, has gotten in over her head. The grasses and weeds are taller than her tomato plants.

Mom stands with her hands on her hips, surveying the mess of weeds. "So, tell me, what have you been up to? Every time I try to call, I get your answering machine. Sometimes I feel like I've raised a robot."

I laugh. "Sorry, Mom. It's just that—"

"I know, you've been helping Mary and you've been busy at work."

I hack at some weeds with a hoe. "Yes."

Mom reaches for the hoe. "Put some gloves on, Anne, you're going to ruin your hands. You need to take better care of yourself." She holds the hoe while I put on my gloves. "This is really a mess, isn't it?"

I start hoeing again. I'm hoping my mother won't ask any more questions. "I don't think this hoe is working." I drop the hoe and get down on my hands and knees to pull the weeds. "These are huge."

We work in silence for a while. "Are they keeping you busy at church?" asks Mom in what I know is a final act of desperation. She's not at all interested in what I do at church.

Actually, I'm relieved the question has nothing to do with my social life. I explain that I have a new calling at the family history center. And, without mentioning that most of the people who go there are senior citizens, I tell her I'm meeting lots of interesting people. The truth is, everyone there loves me because I can figure out computer problems.

I'm about to mention the family research I've started when I hear Lily's voice on the other side of the fence. Mom, who is a terrific eavesdropper, holds a finger up to her lips. I cast her a disapproving look.

Right away, it's obvious to me that the other participant in the conversation is none other than Neil Wentworth. I doubt Mom will recognize his voice. Still, I feel a wave of nervousness rising inside me.

"Mary doesn't have any control over those children," Lily is saying. "She lets them get away with so much. Then she's constantly complaining about them as if all their problems come from our side of the family. And she's got this crazy double standard. When they're at her house and she's watching them, they can do anything they want. But when they're at our house, they suddenly can't have sweets and they can't watch television, not even educational television. Then she's always getting sick, so we have to watch the kids. We wish Charlie'd married Anne instead. We like Anne so much. He dated Anne too, you know, before he dated Mary. He really liked her." At this, Mom covers her mouth to keep from exploding with laughter.

"When did all this happen?" Neil asks.

"Oh, I don't know, a couple of years before he got married. It was after Anne's mission."

"And Anne broke it off?"

"Yes, I guess he just wasn't her type. Poor Charlie! He really is a good husband."

I don't get to hear the rest of the conversation because Mom, unable to contain her laughter anymore, drags me across the yard and in through Mary's back door.

That evening, when I arrive for dinner at the Musgrove's house, Lily insists that I sit with the adults. The table is completely full, and I have to squeeze a chair in somewhere. Charlie has persuaded Mary to come—he rolled her over in an office chair. And Hannah's long-time boyfriend, Barry, is home from his summer job as an exterminator in Texas. I always think of Barry as a football player. He hasn't played since high school, but he still looks the part of a fullback.

Since Janet Musgrove has a sit-wherever-you-like attitude about entertaining, I'm left to find my own place. I notice that Hannah is sitting next to Neil instead of Barry, so I decide—somewhat reluctantly—to sit by Barry, who is, just as I guessed, in a sullen mood.

Hannah opens up the conversation by discussing Broadway musicals. While she and Neil compare which ones they've seen, I try to think of a topic that will interest Barry. "How did you enjoy Texas?" I ask.

He takes a bite of his chicken, chews, then swallows. "Fine."

"I've heard they have great barbecue down there."

He nods and glares at Hannah, who is telling Neil how much she'd like to see the musical that's currently in town.

"It must be really hot down there at this time of year."

It takes a few seconds before Barry responds. "Oh yeah, brings out the bugs big time. You oughta see some of the cockroaches down there."

I'm stumped. I can't very well keep talking about cockroaches at the dinner table. Steve Musgrove tries to come to my rescue. "You know, Barry, with all the money you're making in this exterminating business, you ought to think about investing. And Anne's just the person to talk to about investments. She's a stockbroker, you know."

Barry takes another bite of chicken and nods. Neil and Hannah stop talking about Broadway musicals. There is dead silence. Finally, Lily speaks from the other table. "Oh, Dad, why would Barry want to invest his money? He's still going to school."

Even though I'm staring down at my plate, I sense that Neil is looking at me. Maybe he's noticing how much I've changed, trying to trace in my features the ruins of a face he once found attractive. Or maybe he's surprised to hear that I'm a stockbroker. It isn't something I ever really planned to do. I speak loud enough for Lily to hear. "A few years ago, I would have told you to invest in a money market fund, but right now the interest rates are higher in savings accounts." I glance over at Barry, who doesn't appear to understand anything I've just said. I wish I'd read the sports page.

Mary groans. "I hate talking about money."

Charlie snorts. "You hate talking about it, but you love spending it."

Everyone laughs. Then Lily breaks in, "Anne, I hope you have some vacation time because we want you to take a few days off. Neil's going to take us all down to North Carolina before he goes back to work, and we want you to come too."

I look down at my plate. "Oh." I don't know what else to say. Sure, I want to go to the beach, but do I want to go with Neil and his two girlfriends? Or, more importantly, does Neil want me to go? I'm pretty sure I know the answer.

Lily twirls a curl around her index finger. "We have it all worked out. We're going to get a hotel room for us girls. Neil's going to stay with his friends down there. We'll drive down on a Friday. See the sights on Saturday. We can go to church down there. Then we'll drive back on Sunday afternoon. You can go back to work on Monday. It's the week after next. We have to go then because Neil has to go back to work after that. Do you think you can get some time off?"

I stab at a piece of lettuce with my fork. "I don't know. I'll have to see."

Later that evening, I take Mary's boys swimming in the Musgroves' pool before bedtime. The Musgroves are all out shopping, so we have the pool to ourselves. I'm in the shallow end holding Daniel and watching Joseph jump off the diving board when I hear the gate opening. I turn to see Neil entering the pool area.

The surprise of finding himself alone with me robs him of his usual composure. He starts to turn back. "Oh, I'm sorry, I thought Lily and Hannah were here. They told me they'd be here."

If I weren't so embarrassed, this would be funny. I call out to him. "They'll be here any minute." I'm wondering how much worse things can get—first he sees me in sweats at the yard sale; then in my wet running clothes; now he's caught me in Mary's bathing suit. "I think they just went down to the grocery store. You're welcome to stay. We were about to leave anyway."

Neil sits down on a lounge chair and stares at a potted plant. "It's a beautiful day today." He then leans back in the chair and remains silent, apparently contemplating some distant point in the sky.

I tell Joseph we'll have to be going home, but he begs to stay longer. Daniel wants to play ring-around-the-rosy in the water before we leave, so I sing the nursery rhyme and dunk myself four more times. I probably have mascara running down my face.

I'm relieved to hear the gate opening again, hoping to see Lily and Hannah. But it's Barry. This only adds to the awkwardness of the situation since Barry now regards Neil as his rival. I wave. "Hi, Barry. Hannah will be around any minute now. They've just gone out on an errand."

Barry says something inaudible. When Neil tries to talk to him, he sneers and walks to the other side of the pool. Neil, still unaware of Hannah and Barry's relationship, looks puzzled.

The towels, unfortunately, are located quite a distance from the shallow end. I have to walk right in front of Neil to get them. Of course, he doesn't want to look at me anyway, so I shouldn't be embarrassed.

Daniel won't leave the water even after the game, so I have to carry him kicking and crying to the chair where I left the towels. In the moment it takes me to wrap a towel around myself, Daniel escapes and runs for the deep end. Once I grab his slippery little body, I call for Joseph to come get dried off and take a towel over to him. He climbs out, shivering. I wrap the towel around Joseph while I'm still trying to hold onto Daniel. "Put on your flip-flops, Joseph. Your mom doesn't want you to go barefoot."

Joseph jumps up and down, going into temper tantrum mode. Then he whines, "I don't want to go bear foot. I want to go tiger foot. Why don't you carry me?"

"I can't carry you, Joseph. I'm carrying Daniel." I wouldn't care about the shoes, except that Mary always worries about her kids stepping on broken glass. I kneel down to put the shoes on his feet, but instead of cooperating, he throws himself across my back and grabs my neck. Since I'm still holding Daniel, this leaves me unable to do anything. I can't shake him off. And, worse yet, the towel is slipping off of me, leaving my bathing-suited behind for the two men to see. "Please get off of me, Joseph," I plead.

"Joseph," Barry says in a very stern voice. "That's no way to treat your aunt. Come over here and I'll carry you home."

Still, Joseph refuses to budge. His towel is hanging over my face and I can't think of any way to get out of his grip without injuring Daniel.

Then, I find that someone is taking him off of me. His hands are released from around my neck and he's gently lifted up. I'm sure it's Barry, but when I stand up and look, Neil is standing beside me, holding Joseph. Barry is looking at us from across the pool.

Neil rescued me, even with his broken arm. I'm astounded. I can't speak. I can't even thank him. I try to sort out my feelings as I wrap the towel around myself again.

Neil carries the little boy over to the lounge chair and sits down with him. "Now, Joseph," I hear him saying, "let's get your flip-flops on." He goes on talking to Joseph about the cartoon character on the shoes. He doesn't look at me. It's obvious he doesn't want to hear my thanks.

When I walk over to retrieve Joseph, Neil looks at me. "He's a handful, isn't he? It's a good thing he's cute. I'll help you get him home." He leads the way out of the pool area and holds the gate open for me as I carry Daniel through.

He follows me across Mary's backyard, all the while talking to Joseph. My hands are shaking as I open Mary's back door. Neil sets Joseph down inside the kitchen then turns to leave. I put my shaking hand on his shoulder. "Thank you."

Neil looks at me briefly before he turns to leave. "No problem."

After I put Joseph and Daniel in the bathtub, I stare into the bathroom mirror. My dark hair is wet and flat against my head. The mascara is still intact. Mary's bathing suit is sagging a bit around the waist, but at least it's modest. I don't look as terrible as I thought I did. But I feel as if I hardly know the person in the mirror. Who have I become? And what am I feeling? There is such a rush of different emotions within me. I'm scared, excited, proud, and embarrassed all at once. I don't know which feeling to choose. What must he think of me?

6

Sunday, June 9, 2002

I got in a terrible argument with Mary on the phone today. She's been staying with grandma for the summer up in New York and has met a boy she likes up there. All I know about him really is that he works at the grocery store. She says he takes her out every night and that Grandma is always asleep when they get back home.

I told her she's not supposed to be going steady already. She just barely turned sixteen. She got really mad and said I was being a snob because he wasn't a member of the church. I tried to explain about group dating and standards, but by then she was so mad, she wasn't listening anyway. Dad and Grandma don't seem worried at all. They think it's cute she has a boyfriend.

Last night, Neil and I went to the singles' ward dance with Liz. I can't believe how old everyone is at those things.

As if I don't see enough of Neil Wentworth, I get to hear about him whenever I'm around Mary and Charlie. They are constantly gossiping about him. Charlie is sure that he'll propose to Lily within the next week. Mary, on the other hand, believes he's slowly falling in love with Hannah. I never dare to offer my opinion on the subject—though I can't agree with Mary that Neil likes Hannah better than Lily. I know Lily is his favorite; however, if I can trust my memory, I don't think he's really in love with her either. Nor do I think Lily, or

Hannah, is in love with Neil. "Infatuation" would be a better word for it. Still, it's likely that one of them will fall in love. It's only a matter of time.

"What do you think he makes?" Mary asks me one day at breakfast.

I look up from the paper I'm reading. "What do I think who makes?"

"Neil, of course."

Thinking Mary's referring to some sort of hobby, I tell her I have no idea what Neil does in his spare time. I guess if I was being totally honest, I might mention the stack of books I saw in Jack's kitchen, but I'd rather avoid the subject.

"I meant, how much money does he make as a police officer?"

I sigh. "I imagine he does pretty well. He's a captain, you know."

"Charlie says he has his own house in Baltimore. Can you imagine having your own house and not even being married? I think Hannah is much better off with Neil than with Barry. I think Barry's about to give up. He's quit coming around so much. I've never really liked Barry that much."

Charlie, who's watching a game on TV, decides to join the conversation. "How could you not like Barry? He's never done anything to make you dislike him. He's quiet, but there's nothing wrong with that. He's a good guy. And he shows up for all the service projects at church. If Hannah was smart, she'd want to marry him just for that."

I get up and throw the paper in the recycling. "I think Barry's doing the right thing. Hannah shouldn't be treating him the way she is. He deserves better than that."

Charlie slaps the table with his hand. "Hannah definitely needs to learn her lesson. I hope she learns it quickly."

The next day, I get a call at the office from Lily. There's been a change of plans. They're having a picnic at a park instead of the usual dinner at home. And, because Mary's boys are coming, they want me to meet them there. I'm happy to do something different from the usual, so I agree to the plan without thinking about it too much.

I find out later, when I arrive at the park, that I should have been suspicious. Lily, Neil, and Hannah are standing on the curb waiting for me. Hannah is carrying a large shoebox. Lily has a grin on her face, and Neil is hanging in back of them with his free hand in his pocket. That's what he does when he's nervous—he puts his hands in his pockets. I drive up beside them and roll down my window.

Lily bends over to talk to me, placing her hands on the edge of my window. "There's been a change of plans, Anne. Mom and Dad took the kids to the movies. They wanted us all to go out and have some fun."

Hannah giggles. "Guess where we're going. I'll give you a hint." She holds out the shoebox so I can look inside. It's filled with men's deodorant.

"The homeless shelter?" I guess.

The two girls laugh while Neil shakes his head. Lily puts a hand on her hip and shakes a finger at me with her other hand. "We're going to the single's ward dinner dance, silly. Don't you remember that you said you wouldn't go to another single's ward dance unless you were sure all the men were wearing deodorant?"

I do remember saying that, and now I'm wondering if I can come up with another excuse. No doubt this is Lily's idea of a service project for me. If her hands weren't on my window, I'd be driving off right now. "I'd rather not."

Lily shakes her head. "Come on, Anne. You're our only transportation. It'll be fun." Am I really so boring that I need to go to a single's ward dance for entertainment?

I unlock the car doors and the two girls climb into the back seat. Neil is following them, but Lily insists that he sit in the front. "There's no leg room back here, Neil. I think you'd be happier in the front. It's only a ten-minute drive. And I'll give you a neck massage."

Neil bends down to look at me through the open window. I clear my throat. "It is cramped in the back," I apologize. "Unfortunately, I have half of my apartment in here." I grab my purse, my scriptures, and my running shoes off of the passenger seat to put in the trunk. "Just let me put this stuff in the trunk."

Neil meets me at the back of the car with a box of files that were on the floor. He glances down at them as I open up the trunk. "So you're into family history?"

I take the box from him and set it in my trunk. "I know, it's kind of a senior citizen hobby, but I like it. I'm the family history consultant in my ward." It's the most personal information I've given him in seven years.

His hand is back in his pocket. "That's nice. I'd like to learn more about my family history."

"Have you decided to come to the beach, Anne?" Lily asks on our way to the church. She is leaning forward, massaging Neil's neck.

I don't know what to say. Besides that, I'm trying to merge into another lane during rush hour traffic. "I don't know." It is hard to think of anything when Neil is sitting beside me. I can smell his cologne—it's the same sandalwood scent he wore when we were dating. It reminds me of the night we went to the concert at the Jefferson Memorial. We sat very close together on the cold marble steps. I remember the warmth of his hand as he held mine and how he whispered into my ear between the songs.

Lily slaps my shoulder. "Don't tell me you don't want to because Mary already told me how much you love going to the beach. And don't tell me you have to help Mary. Mom and Charlie will be around if she needs anything. Besides that, Charlie said he thinks the doctor's going to take her off bed rest by then. You have to decide soon. We only have room for one more."

I can't think of any reason not to go. I have plenty of vacation time. Neil and I are friends now—I think. He's seen me in a bathing suit. And I've seen him with Lily so many times that I'm almost used to it. At least, I want to be used to it. "Will you let me drive?" I've seen Lily and Hannah speeding along in the neighborhood enough times to know I don't want one of them driving.

Neil laughs. "You can drive . . . as long as we take my car." I don't know what to think of this answer. Is this his way of saying he doesn't want me to go? Lily and Hannah are giggling again in the back. Neil shifts in his seat. "Not that I don't like your car. It's a very nice car. I just think we'd be more comfortable in something larger."

I wrinkle my nose. "How much larger is your car?"

"Not much. It's a small SUV. No one's driven it since my accident. It needs some time on the road."

Somehow, I can't imagine Neil driving an SUV—even a small one—but, then again, I probably couldn't have imagined myself working as a stockbroker a few years ago. I guess this makes us about even.

"So, Anne, this means you're going?" Hannah asks.

I pull into the church parking lot, which is packed with cars. "Sure." Why not take a risk? What's the worst that can happen? If I hate hanging around with them, I'll take off by myself. "It sounds like fun." Still, I'm not convinced I've made the right decision.

The cultural hall is decorated as if for a wedding reception. There are little goldfish in glass bowls on each table surrounded by gold-wrapped candies. Someone has strung a rope between the two basketball hoops and draped cascades of white fabric from wall to wall across the chapel. The lights are low. Subtle, classical music is playing. Hannah puts the box of deodorant down on a little table at the entrance and looks around. "Maybe we're in the wrong place." Then she sees Barry across the room, sipping peach-colored punch at a table with a bunch of girls. "No, this has to be it. There's Barry."

Neil rubs his stomach. "I hope they feed us more here than at a reception."

I laugh. Lily puts her hands on her hips. "Is that all you men think about?" She's already acting like his wife.

As Hannah walks across the room to join Barry, Lily whispers, "I hope those two make up. Hannah's been such a grump this week."

A grin spreads over Neil's face. "You mean, Hannah and Barry?"

Lily nods.

He chuckles "I didn't know they were dating. I guess that explains a lot."

I take a few steps away from Lily and Neil. The place is packed with people I don't know. All of them seem very young. I think most of them are girls that have just graduated from high school. Who am I going to talk to? They all probably think I'm a hopeless old maid. I can imagine what they might say about me. "That woman has got to be at least twenty-nine. Pretty soon, she won't even be allowed at these dances." Grateful that I at least wore my red dress, I make my way across the cultural hall to the women's restroom.

In the restroom, I stand beside two other women in front of the mirror. One is curling her eyelashes. The other is using a flat iron on her hair. Looking at my reflection, I decide I'd better reapply everything. It's lucky that I've started carrying makeup in my purse again. I haven't done that since high school.

The woman curling her eyelashes removes the curler and blinks. "Well, if my fiancé broke off our engagement, I certainly wouldn't go ahead and decorate for the reception."

The second woman clicks the flat iron onto a section of her long, brown hair and eases it down to the end. "I wouldn't either."

I can't resist asking. "Do you mean that all these decorations were really for someone's reception?"

The one with the eyelash curler whips out her mascara. "Yep. Her fiancé called it off last week. She'd already bought all the decorations and planned it out, except for the goldfish—poor things. It's not their fault they're cheaper than flowers. She bought them this morning. I wonder what she's going to do with all of them when this is over." She takes out a tube of orange lip gloss and smears away at her lips. "What kind of person calls off an engagement anyway? I mean, aren't you supposed to be really committed before you get engaged?"

I can't help myself. I jump in to defend the man, even though I don't know him. "It's better to break off an engagement than to get married when you don't feel right about it." Maybe I'm a little too forceful in giving my opinion because the two women are dead silent afterward.

I decide that this is not the type of gossip I want to share with Lily and Neil. In fact, I'm determined to be as far away as possible when they discuss it. Why are people in the singles' ward always talking about marriage? There are so many other things to think about.

I feel like I'm back in junior high school again, nervous and competing for my place in the social order. I really don't want to be here, but I'm not going to sit cowering in a corner, watching Neil and Lily flirt. I'm going to prove that I haven't gotten old and dull. I'll show them I'm capable of having fun. "Would you mind if I borrowed your flat iron when you're done?" I ask the one with the long hair.

"Not at all," she says. "I was about to unplug it."

I've been watching Liz "work a room" for years. Now it's my chance to apply what I've learned. All I have to do is grab a cup of punch, stand all by myself, and catch the eye of some guy who is trying to mingle. It is manipulative and shallow, but it works. After only five minutes of this strategy, I've attracted an ordinary-looking guy named Chris, and I'm sitting down with him, eating croissant sandwiches.

I congratulate myself, thinking that from across the room, I probably seem to be successfully navigating the sea of single men. Since my only goal is to appear as if I'm having a good time, things are going perfectly. I smile, ask questions, and listen. By the end of dinner, I've learned quite a bit about the care of goldfish, most of which I don't really want to know.

After we've each gotten a slice of wedding cake and I hear a little about Chris's family history—he's somehow related to Peter the Great, not that I really care—my plan starts to go awry. He asks me to dance. This is when I find out that Chris, though he looks ordinary, has a hobby other than goldfish. He is a dancer.

On the first song, which is slow, this is not such a problem. Probably very few people notice how he subtly leads me through the foxtrot. It's more of a problem on the next song, which is faster. He starts out with a few pelvic thrusts, then spins around and wiggles his body like a break-dancer. Aren't pelvic thrusts against the rules? Does he expect everyone to make a circle around him? I try to move a little further away from him, but he grabs my hand and twists me around in some sort of disco move. As soon as he lets go, I take a large step backward. It is hard not to laugh a little. He's jumping, lunging, shuffling, and kicking. All I'm doing is stepping backward. Maybe it's rude, but I can't stop laughing. I turn around a little to hide my smile. It doesn't matter. He isn't looking at me anyway. He's too into his moves. I wonder if he choreographed his routine before the dance. When will this song be over? It goes on and on as I two-step back and forth, seemingly without a partner. Once it ends, I make my escape.

Lily and Neil meet me at the edge of the dance floor. They're holding hands. Lily frowns. Neil, though his lips are quite serious, has a little glimmer of amusement in his eyes. I smile and shrug my shoulders.

Lily puts a hand to her forehead and tilts her head back. "Oh, Anne, we've been trying to warn you about that guy for the past half hour. Why didn't you ever look at us?"

I do not want this to turn into a pity party. I giggle. "Well, now I know how to fox-trot."

Lily does not laugh. "I hope you didn't give him your number."

I shake my head and deadpan, "I don't think he liked the way I danced."

I can hear Neil laughing as Lily points her finger at me again. "You know, Anne, now that you've danced with one of them, the rest of them are going to start asking you. Poor Anne, if you'd only come to the singles activities more often, you'd know who to avoid."

Neil glances in my direction, and then looks back at Lily. "Go easy on the poor guys. It'll give them a thrill to dance with Anne."

I can feel the redness coming back into my face. I turn my head and pretend to look at the dancers. The lights are dim, so he probably can't tell I'm blushing. Why can't I be as casual about him as he is about me?

Lily puts her hands on her hips. "Maybe I could introduce you to someone. There's a really nice guy over—"

"It's just a dance, Lily," I interrupt. "It's not like they're asking me to marry them." There it is. I brought up the very topic I promised myself to avoid. Am I ever going to stop blushing?

The three of us stand here without anything to say, listening to the throbbing music. I can smell sandalwood again. I wish I could think of some reason to dislike him. But everything about him is right—even the way he dresses. His button-down shirt is exactly the right shade of blue. I want to run my hands across his shoulders. He really does have nice shoulders.

Lily hops up and claps her hands. "I know. You can borrow Neil." As if he's her possession.

I look at Lily. "What?"

"If you dance with Neil, it'll throw all the weirdos off your track."

I try to laugh, but it only makes me sound nervous. "Really, Lily, it's okay. I'm sure Neil would rather dance with you." But Lily pushes us both out onto the dance floor. Why does he always have to rescue me? Can't I maintain the least amount of dignity? First, it was the garage sale, then the hypothermia thing, then it was the swimming pool, and now this. He looks so confident, so capable, while I look completely inept.

We stand at the edge of the dance floor for a few seconds, startled, until Neil reaches for my right hand and asks, "Would you like to dance?" It's a slow song, "Kiss Me" by Sixpence None the Richer. I used to listen to it a lot while I was dating Neil, but he probably doesn't remember that. I rest my left hand on his shoulder above the cast. We're dancing the old-fashioned way, just the way I like it.

I force myself to look up at his face. He's winking at Lily, who is blowing kisses at him. Without thinking, I roll my eyes. His grip on my hand tightens. "What do you mean by that?"

Embarrassed to be caught, I sigh. "Nothing. I guess I just feel stupid."

He clenches his teeth and squeezes my hand harder than he probably realizes. "Well, don't."

He sounds angry, and, instead of looking at me, he gazes over the top of my head at the other dancers. I'm surprised by his reaction—he's not usually so impatient—but I think I know what it means. He is still angry at me. I wish I could apologize—tell him how much I regret how I treated him all those years ago. But what can I say? He's Lily's boyfriend now. If I bring up the past, it might cause more problems. Humor is the only way to go. "Lily is very nice to let me borrow you."

He shakes his head. "Listen, Anne, about this whole thing—I told her not to trick you. But you know Lily. She's very persistent."

"Yeah, I'm starting to see that." Manipulative would be a better word.

"If I were you, I would have driven off and left us standing there at the park. You need to stand up for yourself." He is still squeezing my hand.

I squeeze back. "You're squeezing my hand really hard."

He loosens his grip. "Sorry." He looks away.

"It's okay. You know, being a doormat isn't all bad. Like right now, I'm dancing with the best-looking guy in the room."

I can tell I shocked him with that one. He's stopped moving. I can't believe I said it either. When I finally get up the courage to look back up at his face, he's staring down at me with his mouth open. I smile and shrug my shoulders. He doesn't smile back, but he starts to dance again. He's looking away across the room, probably at Lily.

Definitely time to change the subject. I force myself to look at him again. "How's your knee?"

"It's getting better."

By this time the music's winding down. I'm afraid to say anything else—who knows what will come out of my mouth if I do? I loosen my grip. "Thanks for the dance."

He looks down at me, then away again. "It's not over yet." We dance for a few more seconds. He doesn't let go of my hand when the music stops but leads me back to where Lily is standing. "I hope I didn't hurt your hand too much."

"You didn't."

I'm still evaluating our conversation as I'm dancing with the next guy. I suppose it wasn't so bad for our first tête-à-tête, as they call it in the classics. Surprisingly, I don't regret being a little flirtatious. After all, he's been hanging around with Lily and Hannah.

As it turns out, Lily's plan worked very well. After I dance with Neil, I get about five or six dances in before it's time to go home. Isn't it strange that men would rather pick women who are already dancing, not the ones who are waiting on the side to get picked? It makes me think of one of those nature films where two bucks are fighting over a doe. Shouldn't attraction be motivated by something other than jealousy?

7

Saturday, June 15, 2002

*W*e ate dinner with Neil's brother, Jack, today. Jack's in medical school, but he doesn't really act like it. He is such a tease, always joking that Neil's going to get married before he is. Neil told me later that since he started medical school, Jack has no time to date, much less get married.

I think Neil could tell all the teasing made me nervous. I know it's the guy that's supposed to get nervous about marriage talk, but I have a right to be worried too. I mean, look at my parents. It's hard to believe I'm old enough to get married. I know, technically, I'm an adult. I'll be twenty in a few months. I always thought I'd feel older when I got to be this age.

We rented a movie to watch. Jack picked it out because he really wanted to see it, but he fell asleep almost as soon as it started.

Neil, who's just gotten his cast removed, drives up to the Musgroves' in what I decide is a very large sport utility vehicle. Wondering why I agreed to drive it before I'd even seen it, I decide that it is definitely not a small SUV. Hannah and Lily are already standing in the driveway with their suitcases—six of them. I'm dragging my duffel bag out of Mary's house. As Neil parks and gets out, Lily jumps up and down, shouting. "I love your car!"

Neil brushes a hand through his hair and walks around to open the back door. Then, acting as if his arm has never been broken, he

46

carries Hannah and Lily's suitcases, two at a time to the back of his car and places them inside—there's plenty of room for all six. I heave my duffel bag on top of the others. I want to say that I don't think this car qualifies as a "small SUV," but decide it might sound offensive.

Neil opens the back door for Lily, the passenger door for Hannah, and, finally, the driver's door for me. "You said you wanted to drive, Anne. I have a Sherlock Holmes I want to finish. I'm just getting to the good part. But I'll take over if you get tired."

I hop in and adjust the seat, which appears to be leather. There is definitely a new car smell inside. I glance at the controls. The odometer reads "1430 miles."

Hannah runs her hand along the leather upholstery. "This is really nice."

Neil slides into the back beside Lily and puts his arm around her. "I saved up for a long time for it, so we might as well enjoy."

I admit, I'm nervous to even back this huge beast out of the driveway, but I do it anyway. As we drive toward the highway, I get used to the width—it's only about two feet wider than my car, but its height makes it easier to navigate. Once on the highway, I enter a Zen-like state, focusing on driving and only barely following all the conversations going on between the other passengers. It's peaceful in a way, kind of like running.

Soon we've left behind the bumper-to-bumper traffic of northern Virginia and are cruising along a three-lane highway with woods on either side. In the backseat, Neil is reading his book while Lily rests her head on his shoulder, pretending to be asleep. Hannah has been talking to me for the past half hour about Barry. How very considerate he is. What a hard worker he is. How much her parents like him. All the fun times they've had together. How much she likes his family. "Really, Anne, I'm in love with him. And I know he loves me. He's told me so. And he keeps talking about getting married, but he hasn't asked me yet. I don't know if we have enough money to get married. And, he still has three more years of school. If it wasn't for that, I don't think I'd hesitate to say 'yes.'"

Here it is again, I think, I'm going to have to say something about marriage. Worse yet, I'm going to have to give advice about marriage.

"I think it would be a mistake to make such an important decision just based on money." I try not to speak too loudly or too quickly. "I'm probably not the best person to give advice, but I think if you make decisions because you're afraid of something, then you're going to have a lot of regrets. It's not that you shouldn't worry about money. But I think you and Barry are capable of living on a tight budget. Base your decisions on more important things, like faith and love." When I glance up at the rear-view mirror, I meet Neil's eyes.

"I think you're right, Anne," Lily calls from the backseat. "No wonder everyone thinks you're so smart. I'm glad you're coming on this trip with us. Honestly, I don't know if Mom and Dad would've let us go if you weren't coming. I think they think of you as kind of like a chaperone or something."

Neil responds in a voice loud enough for me to hear. "You could hardly consider Anne a chaperone. She's only a few years older than you. And, right now, she's going ten miles over the speed limit."

I can only be flattered by his teasing, knowing it means he's warming up to me, maybe even starting to forgive me. Still, I keep a better watch on the speedometer. And, when Neil finishes his book and trades places with me, I'm only too happy to sit on the back seat with my legs curled up beside me.

We're now driving along a smaller highway that takes us through farms of tobacco, corn, and sorghum. There are little white houses not too far off the road, and sometimes we see people sitting out on their front porches. Every once in a while, there are roadside fruit stands with melons, corn, peaches, and tomatoes. Occasionally, we pass an antique shop.

I distract myself from another marriage conversation between Lily and Hannah by reading out of Neil's *Hound of the Baskervilles* for an hour or so. Towards the end of it, we pass through the Dismal Swamp, and I can't help wondering if the swamp is something like the moors that Sir Arthur Conan Doyle describes. I love the way the Spanish moss hangs from the trees like Halloween decorations.

Lily and Hannah go on and on about the type of house they'd like to live in once they get married. Lily wants her own personal office, as well as a sewing room—she's planning to learn to sew—and also a conservatory for her piano. Hannah wants a large apartment in the middle of a city. She wants everything in it to be white.

I remember a picture Neil once drew for me. It's at the bottom of my dresser drawer. With a pencil, he sketched out a cottage with a tree in front for children to climb. There are stick figures of children all over the yard. One is rolling down a hill. One is fishing in a pond. Two are playing basketball. Another is reading a book.

I guess men don't really have to worry so much about their biological clocks. Neil could still have that same dream home with Lily if he wanted to. With me, though, it's a different story. I have maybe ten or fifteen years left to have children. I'd never admit this to anyone, but sometimes I count in my mind how many children I might be able to have if I get married within the next year or two. If I could have a child every two years until I turn forty, I still have time to have about five children. And even that depends on finding a husband. I giggle to myself at the thought, realizing I'm almost as silly as Lily and Hannah with their dream houses. It's not as if you can actually plan out your life.

The scenery changes again. We're on a larger highway once more, and I catch a few glimpses of the Sound in between views of shopping centers and fast food restaurants. There are some seagulls, and when we finally cross the bridge to the Outer Banks, Neil points out osprey nests on top of posts. The houses on the Outer Banks all stand on stilts in case of hurricanes. Lily notices wooden observation decks on some of the roofs. "Oh, I wish we could have gotten a place with an observation deck. I would have loved to have a view."

We pass huge sand dunes and a plethora of little shops designed to attract tourists with colorful kites, artwork, jewelry, surfing supplies, and souvenirs. Hannah is already planning her shopping route. When I admit I'm eager for the sound of the waves, Neil rolls down the windows. We can already hear the roar of the ocean and feel the salty sea air. Looking down the narrow lanes we pass, I look at the sea oats waving in clumps on dunes that border the beach.

As soon as we've checked into the hotel, we sink our bare feet into the sand dunes that lead to the beach and lunge forward the way anyone must when they walk in deep sand. With each step, the sand under our feet grows harder and wetter until we stand just beyond the waves. I let the waves lap at my toes. The beach has a way of taking down all my defenses. I'm a child again. I love to watch the white foam ride along the edges of the water and feel the wind blow into my face. The breakers are exactly the way they should be—strong enough to carry someone along, but not powerful enough to knock over an adult. Sometimes the tide brings up jellyfish that look like shiny glass paperweights. And almost every wave brings up a few tiny mole crabs that burrow down into the sand before the water disappears.

We can't stay long at the beach. Neil has already arranged to meet up with his friends at a restaurant. So we hop in the car once more and drive a few miles down the main road. While we drive, Neil interrupts Lily and Hannah to explain about his friends. "We're going to meet Dave and Valerie Harville. Dave and I worked together in Baltimore before he took a job down here. You'll also notice a young man with my friends. His name is Jay Bentley. He was once engaged to Dave's sister. But before they got married, she died in an accident with a drunk driver. That was about eight months ago."

We don't have time to ask any questions before we arrive at the restaurant. Inside, we meet Dave, who looks like a police officer, with his short blond hair, tanned face, and thick mustache. His wife, Valerie, a curly-haired woman with a big smile, stands beside him, surrounded by three small, redheaded children. Dave and Valerie hug each one of us even though we've only just met. And Valerie is careful to compliment each of us women on our hair or clothing.

I'm enchanted by the couple's southern hospitality, so unlike the give-and-take kind of acquaintances I usually experience. There is so little formality and so much genuine feeling. I wonder if all police officers form such close attachments with their fellow officers. And I try to suppress the thought that these people might have been my friends too if I'd married Neil.

I notice a thin, dark-haired man who sits shyly in the background, hardly waiting to be acknowledged by anyone. His pale skin and long sleeved white shirt proclaim him out of place in this beach town. I guess that this must be Jay Bentley, the one Neil described to us earlier.

When we sit down to dinner, it works out that Jay and I sit together at the far end of the table next to the children and away from the other adults. Since I'm so used to taking care of Mary's kids, it seems only natural to sit by the kids. I grab a crayon and help the little three-year-old girl color her children's menu.

As we color, I challenge myself to talk to Jay, despite his melancholy attitude. Though I'm sure I won't be able to cheer him up, I think maybe I can at least make him more comfortable. I can think of a lot of things I probably shouldn't talk about—his job, his social life, his family, what he likes to do. When I finally think of a topic, I have to leave all my inhibitions aside: I lean forward across the table toward him. "So, how did you get to know Neil?" I only feel comfortable asking the question because I'm sure that the other adults won't hear us.

He looks down at the salt and pepper shakers, and then moves them around as if they are chess pieces. "Oh, that's a good story . . . I locked my keys in my car one day down at the university. I'd just barely moved to Baltimore. I didn't know anyone yet, and the car was still running. I called the bishop's house. His wife said she'd find someone to help me. And about ten minutes later, I saw a police car driving up. Boy, did that scare me. I thought someone reported me for trying to steal my car. But it was Neil. He was off duty. He opened the car in less than a minute. I wasn't even late for class."

The last thing I want to talk about is how wonderful Neil is. I didn't come here to fall more in love with him. So I jump at the chance to change the subject. "What did you study at school?"

"Anthropology . . . I was in grad school—finished a few months ago. My specialty was the native people of the Andes Mountains. I did my dissertation on the cultivation of Andean potatoes. I can tell you whatsoever you want to know."

"Oh." I stumble around in my mind for a response. Did he just used the word "whatsoever" in a sentence? "I didn't realize they had potatoes in the Andes. I guess I just associate them with—"

"Ireland, Idaho—that's what everyone says. There are actually hundreds of different kinds of Andean potato. Am I boring you? Most people get pretty bored with Andean potatoes."

I shake my head and smile. "No, you're not boring me at all."

After all, I'd rather talk about Andean potatoes than another one of Neil's service projects. "What interested you in the Andes?"

"I served my mission in South America—Brazil actually. The Andes don't go through Brazil, but it got me interested."

Realizing I'm on the edge of a conversational victory, I widen my smile. "Then you and I can speak Portuguese together. I served in Cape Verde."

With that, the conversation takes off in a mix of Portuguese and English. Even though both of us strain to remember any words, we find enough to say about Brazil and Cape Verde to take up the next half hour. We share stories about the wonderful, humble people, reminisce about the food, and try to describe the beautiful landscapes. By the time the server takes away our plates, Jay is telling me that he wishes I could have known his fiancée, Wendy. He's sure I would have liked her.

8

I feel like I've known Neil for such a long time, even though it's only been about a month. The more I get to know him and his friends, the more I admire him. Yesterday, he took me over to visit his grandmother in Bethesda. (A guy who's nice to his grandma—if that isn't a good sign, I don't know what is.) She's a spunky old lady, the kind that people like to interview about aging well. We helped her with her grocery shopping, then did a few projects around the house. She told me that if she had her life to live over, she'd have joined a bowling league when she was my age. She couldn't believe I've never been bowling, so, of course, she had to take us over to her bowling alley—a place that looks like it hasn't changed in fifty years. I actually got a strike.

Neil picked me a mason jar full of flowers out of her backyard.

The next morning, Hannah and I decide to walk out on the beach before breakfast, hoping to collect shells. The sky is gray with wisps of white clouds, and the wind blows steadily. The waves crash onto the shore, overlapping each others' white, frothy borders. We meander across the wet sand, looking for shells that might have come up with the waves during the night. It's a good day for imperfect, white ones—mostly scallops and limpets, along with a few snail shells that are now clicking around in my pocket.

Looking far out on the sea, I see what look like dolphins' backs emerge and then disappear. We stand and watch for another glimpse. The dolphins surface only occasionally, showing the curve of their backs and dorsal fins. I could stand here and watch for hours, listening to the rhythm of the waves and the call of the seagulls, letting the wind make a mess of my hair. I'm amazed at how a place so close to civilization can still be so close to the way God made it.

Hannah interrupts my reverie by pointing out the approaching figures of Lily and Neil. Then she looks at me sideways. "Before they get here, I should tell you I think that James guy like you. He's kind of a nerd, but I can really see you two getting together."

"It's Jay, not James," I remind her. "And I don't think he's interested in me. He still misses his fiancée."

Hannah draws a heart with the initials A.E. and J.B. inside. The waves barely erase it before Lily and Neil meet up with us.

Neil carries four pairs of flip-flops, including mine, and announces that he is treating us to breakfast at a little place not too much farther down the beach. He explains that a member of Dave's ward owns the place, and all the members are trying their best to patronize it. "I think it'd be good for us to show our support. It's not easy to have a successful restaurant here without a bar." We all agree and set off across the beach with Neil and Lily in the lead.

When we get to the wooden stairs leading off the beach, there's a man at the top of the stairs, who allows us to go up first. As we pass him at the top, I notice that he's staring at my face. Is he attracted to me? I can't imagine what might make me seem attractive right now. I didn't spend any extra time getting ready this morning. Still, why else would this man, who's quite handsome himself, look at me that way? As we pass him, Neil looks around at me in a way that shows he's noticed. It's only a glance, but it seems to say, "That man thinks you're beautiful—and even I see someone like the Anne I used to know."

The restaurant is a couple of blocks off the beach. The outside is designed to look like an old, wooden ship. Inside, it seems more like a cottage. Each table is covered with a lacy tablecloth, the wallpaper is flowery, and shelves on the walls show off fancy teapots and cups. Lily turns and whispers to us. "If this place is owned by members of the Church, why do they have teapots all over?"

Hannah whispers back. "Maybe they drink herbal tea."

Dave Harville is already there saving us a table. As we approach, he stands and helps us take our seats. When we're all seated, he pulls a chair up beside me. I'm already looking over the menu. He leans toward me. "I recommend the pecan waffles." I look down to where he points them out on the list of customer favorites. I fold the menu back up and place it in the middle of the table. "That sounds fabulous. I always have such a hard time making up my mind. Thanks for saving me the trouble."

"No problem," Dave replies. Then in a quieter voice, he adds, "Actually, I should be thanking you. You did me a favor by talking to Jay last night. That's the most I've heard him say since my sister . . . I guess you heard about the accident."

I nod just as the server interrupts to take our orders.

After the server leaves, I turn to Dave once more. "I'm very sorry about your sister."

Dave shakes his head. "Yes, it's been hard. And Jay's had the hardest time of us all. I guess that's only right, but we worry about him. I wish we could have good company for him more often. He seems so depressed, always hanging around the house with us. Medication doesn't do much for him."

"He probably still needs time. It hasn't been that long since she passed away, has it?"

Dave sighs. "No, it was only last fall—right after Halloween. Valerie and I were up in Baltimore, visiting family. We got the news first. We were all in shock. She was so young and about to be married. I don't know what we would have done without our good friend here." He nods toward Neil. "He was the one that told Jay. I don't know how he did it, but he did it. Then he stayed with him through it all: the viewing, the funeral, and even afterward. He never left his side for a week."

I glance across the table at Neil, who's chatting with Lily and Hannah. I draw in a breath before speaking. "That kind of compassion is so rare. We are all lucky to have him for our friend." It's the most I can say without revealing deeper feelings. I mean it. I'm even starting to wonder if Neil is more charitable and caring than when I knew him before. He's certainly treated me with more respect than I deserve.

Dave takes a deep breath and pats my hand the way a father would. "Yes, we are very blessed."

Across the table, Lily holds both of Neil's arms, trying to compare the size of his left biceps with his right. "I don't think it shrank at all while your arm was in the cast. Maybe if you flexed them—"

Neil shoots an embarrassed look across the table, then looks back at Lily. "I'm not going to do it here. I shouldn't have mentioned it. If it weren't for my job, it wouldn't matter at all."

Hannah looks out the window. "Hey, there's the guy we saw earlier. He's getting into a Jaguar." All heads turn to gaze out the window, where we see the very same man we passed on the stairs.

Lily turns around in her seat, completely enchanted. "Great car."

Dave rises from his seat to look over their heads. "Oh, that's Will Grandin. Nice guy. He owns some property down here. Comes to our ward when he's in town."

Hannah fluffs up her hair. "He's kind of cute. I know I'm not supposed to be looking, but he has great hair—I don't usually fall for blond guys though."

Lily nods. "He has good taste in clothes. I love his sandals."

I can't resist saying, "I like the way both his biceps are exactly the same size." We all laugh. "Did you say his name is Will Grandin? I think I've heard that name before."

"You probably have," Dave replies. "He's from up in Maryland—Potomac, I think. He's got some sort of hotshot job. Obviously makes a lot of money."

Neil smiles and looks at me. "I'll bet you've heard Liz talk about him. He seems like her type."

We watch the Jaguar drive off, then I look back at Neil. "You're right. That's probably how I know the name."

Lily leans over to Neil, trying to re-establish eye contact, "How do you know Liz? Don't tell me you dated her." She reaches out for his hand.

Neil's lip curls at one side. "No, I never dated Liz."

Hannah pokes his arm and accuses him, "You never did tell us if you dated anyone while you lived in McLean before."

Neil shakes his head, then looks at me again. "You should ask Anne. She knew me pretty well back then."

I can feel my heart beating faster. He's finally said something to show he remembers. It's almost worth being made to answer Hannah's question. As I'm thinking how to respond, the door opens and Jay walks into the restaurant.

Neil stands up. "Well, I think now's the time to change the subject." He grabs a chair for Jay and pulls it up to the table beside me.

For the rest of the day, Jay is my constant companion. I think he thinks of himself as my tour guide, pointing out interesting aspects of the sites we visit. He knows the names of birds and flowers. He knows where to get the best deals at the outlet stores. He shows me his favorite exhibits at the Wright Brothers' museum. Then, when I ask about lighthouses, he guides us to a couple we want to see.

In between the sightseeing, Jay opens up to me. We're sitting in Neil's backseat when he asks me why his fiancée Wendy had to die so suddenly. Why, when he was righteous, did he have to endure so great a trial? I don't know exactly what to say, but I fumble around, trying to explain some scriptures I've found comforting. Neil gets me his scriptures out of the glove compartment—once again I kick myself for ever dumping him. That was one of the first things that impressed me about him, the way he kept scriptures in the glove compartment. I open up to 1 Nephi 11:17 and read: "I know that he loveth his children; nevertheless, I do not know the meaning of all things."

Jay writes the quote down on a piece of scrap paper and puts it in his wallet. He takes the scriptures from me and finds Doctrine and Covenants 122. He reads, "Know thou, my son, that all these things shall give thee experience, and shall be for thy good."

I reach out and touch the top of his hand. "Do you think that all the trials you've had this year are teaching you anything?"

He closes the scriptures on his lap. "Definitely. I'll definitely be better at sympathizing with people who are going through hard times."

I take the scriptures to find another verse. "Here's one in Moroni 9:25, where Mormon writes to Moroni about all the terrible destruction. He tells his son not to dwell on the sad things, but he says, 'may Christ lift thee up.'"

He rubs his hand on his chin. "I think I know all the standard answers to the question of how to find happiness. I've tried anti-depressants, therapists, scriptures, prayer, service, exercise, temple attendance. Nothing seems to work. I can't be happy."

I sigh. "I'm not really qualified to teach you how to be happy. I mean, I don't think I have any qualifications to counsel you. And I've never suffered such a huge loss. But I've struggled a little with the same kind of thing, where it feels like I'll never be happy again. Give yourself time. When something bad happens, it's okay to be sad. But keep trying all those things you talked about. Maybe they'll start to work if you keep at it."

After all the sightseeing and counseling, when we finally return to the beach by our hotel, red flags are posted along the dunes. Jay runs over to read the sign on the flags. "It's about jellyfish. It says it's not safe to swim today. They're always worse when the weather's warm."

Lily sighs. "I really wanted to go swimming. Why didn't they tell us this at the hotel before we put our suits on?"

Neil puts his arm around her. "If you want to swim, the hotel has a pool."

Lily huffs, shrugs off Neil's arm, and walks down to the beach by herself. Hannah runs along behind her. Neil lets out his breath slowly and turns to Jay. "Did I say the wrong thing?"

Jay nods. "I brought some buckets in the car. Maybe they'd like to build a sand castle."

Lily is determined to swim, and no one, not even Neil, can convince her to abandon her plan. She leaves the rest of us to build the castle while she wades out past the waves.

Jay and Hannah busy themselves with the actual planning of the castle—where to put the towers and the walls. They bring buckets of wet sand to form the castle walls and towers. There is nothing left for Neil and me to do but dig the moat and add windows. We're kneeling almost side by side in silence. Finally, when Jay and Hannah are both out of hearing range, Neil whispers to me. "I should apologize for putting you on the spot earlier—you know, about my dating history. I shouldn't have done that." His eyes are such a clear blue, and he is looking right at me.

I can't help smiling. "Don't worry about it. You were probably surprised that I hadn't already told them."

Hannah and Jay return with their buckets and place two new towers at the corner of the castle. When they leave again, Neil continues the conversation. "Anyway, there's no need for you to get involved. It's my business. I'll take care of it."

Right as he says this, a big wave comes, pushing me up against Neil and soaking us both up to our waists. I laugh. He flicks a few drops of water off the tips of his fingers at me. I splash a handful at him and get him right in the face. He grins. Once the wave goes back out, we survey the damage. I push the hair out of my face and smile. "I guess we'll have to start over."

He looks at me a long time. "Yeah."

We move a few feet farther up on the shore. Again, we work in silence. I realize, after a few minutes, that I've carved out the same three windows over and over again. And maybe it's my imagination, but I think Neil's moat seems a little lopsided. Could he be as distracted as I am? I wish I could think of something to say. Neil finally breaks the silence. "Have you got any stock tips for me?" Now there's a desperate question.

"Well, the market's on its way up right now. Lots of people have sold out because of fear, but most stocks are bouncing back. The last two years have been rough and it's going to take time for the market to recover. If you want to buy, there are a handful I'm considering right now. I'd have to look it all up before I could give you details. Things change really quickly in the market." Neil nods. I'd forgotten how blue his eyes are. I look down at the sand castle and poke out another window. "You're probably wondering how I ever ended up with my job."

He smiles. His teeth are so straight. "You read my mind. I always assumed you'd end up working in a museum or helping the homeless—something like that."

I can't believe he actually wants to talk to me. "I know. I used to be so idealistic. But the economy was so bad when I graduated. The only place that would hire me was an investment firm. I thought I'd work there for a few weeks until I found something better, but I loved it."

"And, in your spare time, you're still Mary's personal Mother Teresa," he jokes.

"I used to think it was bad to think about money, but you have to think about it. It's important. It represents work and effort. I like helping people to plan out their finances. I feel like I'm making all their hard work count."

Hannah, who has finished bringing up wet sand in buckets, lies down beside us and, ignoring our conversation, changes the subject. "Maybe you could give me some advice, Neil. I've been thinking so much about Barry on this trip. Why do you think he hasn't asked me to marry him yet? We've been dating for a couple of years now."

Neil looks down at the moat and starts digging again. "I don't think I'm qualified to answer that question."

Jay dumps out his bucket of sand and jumps into the conversation. "Most men have two fears when it comes to marriage—one is commitment; the other is rejection."

Hannah draws a little heart in the sand. "That makes sense."

I decide that now's the opportunity to give my point of view—not only so that Hannah will understand, but also so Neil will understand. "I think you're right, Jay, but you may be oversimplifying in Barry's case. He probably has a lot of other fears and emotions. For one thing, you have to consider his family. I don't think he's ever been around his father. He might worry that he could never be the kind of husband Hannah deserves. And he probably worries about divorce and finances too. I think when your parents are divorced, you worry about that more than you should."

Maybe Neil gets my hidden meaning, maybe not. In any case, he's the next to speak. "I think that the best person to answer your question is Barry." He is looking at me while he says this. "You can't know what the other person is thinking unless—" He turns his head toward the water, and that's when I hear screaming. "It's Lily!" he yells, standing up and running toward the waves. "She got stung."

9

*L*iz called today to tell me Mom has breast cancer. I'm really scared and I don't know what to think. What's worse is they've been hiding it from me for a week now, even though she's been in and out of the hospital this whole time. Liz has known all along.

I visited Mom at the hospital. She's doing okay, considering she's had a mastectomy. I can't believe she told Liz and not me. Why couldn't she tell both of us? It makes the whole cancer thing even more upsetting because, on top of being worried about Mom, I wonder why she didn't tell me.

It's going to take her a long time to recover from the surgery. Luckily, it looks like her cancer hasn't spread. The way she explains all of it is so confusing—her cancer is stage 1, but then it's also a certain type of cancer that's fed by estrogen. She has to have chemotherapy, so she's going to lose her hair. It's hard to think of her without hair.

Her boyfriend wasn't around, and I thought I'd better not ask about him. Maybe she didn't tell him either.

We all run to the waves and watch as Neil swims toward Lily, who's struggling to stay above the water. Neil turns and yells back to us. "Don't come in. I can get her myself." He reaches her within seconds, grabs her under the arms, and starts to tow her into shore. It is slow progress for him to swim against the undertow. Lily really went too far out.

I wade out until I'm knee-deep in the water. I shout as loud as I can. "Is she okay? Do we need to call for help?"

"Call 911, Anne," he yells back. "It got her neck."

I run to find my phone. But once I get it out of my bag and open it up, I find the battery is dead. Another reason to regret my cell phone neglect. I find Neil's, where he threw it down before going into the water. Jay and Hannah seem paralyzed on the shore, watching Neil struggle against the undertow. I push the buttons on the phone. My fingers are shaking so much I have to try two times before I get it right. Soon I'm speaking to a dispatcher.

By this time, Neil has arrived on shore and is breathlessly calling to me. "Tell them, it's . . . anaphylactic . . . shock. She saw a blue jelly . . . probably a man-of-war." Lily's breath is coming in long, tearing rasps. Her eyes roll back into her head.

Neil's voice raises. "Anne, she's lost consciousness . . . Ask them about . . . the tentacles." He points to Lily's neck and legs, where there are thick, clear strands clinging to red skin.

It is so confusing, trying to talk to the dispatcher and Neil. Then watching Lily as she struggles more and more to breathe. A crowd of tourists from the hotel gathers around us, offering suggestions that may or may not be helpful. I have to yell at them to be quiet, so I can hear the dispatcher. I kneel down beside Lily and put my hand on Neil's shoulder. I tell him what the dispatcher tells me. "She says to pour salt water on the tentacles. Don't take them out."

Neil calls for Jay to bring some salt water.

I address the onlookers. "Does anyone have an epinephrine syringe?"

"I'll try to find one," a teenage girl volunteers.

I see Hannah standing at the edge of the crowd. She is much too pale. When Jay comes back with the salt water, I give him more instructions. "Jay, get Hannah. Make her lie down."

Neil pours salt water on the tentacles and checks Lily's vitals while I give the dispatcher Lily's full name and weight—or at least an estimate of her weight. Basically I subtract thirty pounds from my weight. Then I remember something. "Neil," I whisper, "she would want a blessing. I know she would."

Neil checks Lily's breathing. "Get Jay."

I push my way past the ever-growing crowd to where Jay is kneeling beside Hannah. Jay looks up as I come toward them. "How is she?"

I ignore the dispatcher, who's asking about allergies to medications. "She needs a blessing. I'll stay with Hannah."

After Jay leaves, I can hear the sirens approaching. I bow my head, close my eyes, and pray that somehow Lily can be healed. When I look up again, a man and a woman in uniforms are running onto the beach. One carries a medical bag. The other carries a stretcher. They break up the crowd and crouch down on either side of Lily. I thank the dispatcher and turn off the phone. Neil walks over to me and puts his hand on my shoulder. "I finished the blessing right before they got here. Will you go with her in the ambulance? I think it'd be best if you went."

"Of course."

"I'll meet you at the hospital with Hannah. I think Jay can get us there." He runs back over to where the paramedics are working on Lily. The crowd still lingers along the beach, watching. Neil stands by the paramedics as they lift the stretcher with Lily on it.

I give Hannah a hug, promise I'll take good care of Lily, grab my bag, then run over to where they're carrying Lily off the beach.

In the ambulance, I sit near Lily's feet and try to talk to her while the paramedics rip open her bathing suit and attach heart monitors to her chest. I can see now why Neil didn't want to go with her. Lily wouldn't want him to see all that I'm seeing. She's still unconscious. "It's okay, Lily," I tell her in what I hope is a calming voice. "You're going to be all right. They're just checking your heart. They're going to give you some oxygen now." Lily's face is so swollen. Is she going to die? Do people die from jellyfish stings? "You're going to be okay. We'll be at the hospital soon. Hannah and Neil will meet us there."

The paramedics are putting in another IV. What does that mean? A lot of good my humanities major is doing me now. I have no idea what is going on. I wish I'd gone into medicine. "We'll be at the hospital soon. You're doing great. Just hang in there. The doctors will take care of you."

At least Lily's heart is still beating. I can tell that much from the heart monitor. But is her heart beating too fast? I can't tell. "We'll call Hannah when we get to the hospital." I still hold Neil's phone in my fist. "You're going to be okay. Everyone's taking good care of you." They are putting a paper-like sheet on her now—but not over her face. Maybe we're close to the hospital. Or maybe Lily is cold.

The ambulance ride seems to take longer than it should have. But it is still not as long as the endless wait in the emergency room. Lily and I are in a little room by ourselves. I sit near the bed. Doctors rush in and out, prescribing drugs and ordering tests. One of them calls Lily's reaction "severe." It sounds bad, but it doesn't sound like she'll die. Her breathing sounds better. Where are Neil and Hannah? I dial Hannah's number over and over again. She must not have her phone with her.

I look for the Musgroves' number on Neil's phone. Should I call them? Maybe it would be better if I knew more first. Or maybe Hannah should call, or Neil. I decide to call them myself when I hear a knock at the door and see Neil's face peek in.

Hannah pushes past him. "Is she okay?"

I step aside to make room for them to enter. "Yes. She's still unconscious, but the doctors say she'll recover. She's breathing on her own."

Hannah throws her arms around me. "I'm so relieved. It's been awful, being in the car and not knowing."

"That must have been—sorry I took Neil's phone. I forgot to tell you. I tried to call you, but—" I gesture toward the chair. "Why don't you sit down."

Neil is standing against the opposite wall, staring at Lily with a look of grief on his face. It's a look I'm sure I'll never forget.

Hannah is holding Lily's hand. "Oh, Lily, please try to get better. We all love you so much. I couldn't stand it if—" She breaks down in sobs. I walk across the room, kneel beside Hannah, and put my arms around her. After awhile, she continues. "You should have seen Neil. He knew just what to do. He was so brave to go out and get you. He's so worried about you. He loves you so much. You should have seen him in the car. He kept telling Jay to drive faster. He's so in love with you. You have to get better for him."

I steal a glance at Neil, who is still leaning against the wall look-ing shocked. I remember I still have his phone and cross the room once more. I hold his phone out to him. "Sorry I took your phone. Mine wasn't working."

He answers quickly, almost with anger. "I'm the one who should be sorry. I should have prevented this whole mess."

It's no use arguing with him. It'll only make him angrier. "I was thinking. One of us should call the Musgroves."

He takes the phone from me. "I was thinking the same thing." His voice is calmer now. "I'll go out in the hall and call them. Come get me if you need anything."

I thank him and return to my post beside Lily's bed. Soon, a doctor comes in to explain Lily's condition. I listen carefully. They expect Lily to make a full recovery, but she'll probably be in the hospital for a few days, maybe even a few weeks. She'll need to be on an IV until the swelling goes down. She'll be in a lot of pain and nauseated. Considering our worst fears, this is good news. She isn't going to die. She isn't going to be brain dead. It sounds like she'll be back to normal in a few weeks.

I go out in the hall to tell Neil what the doctor said. He is standing outside the door with his back to me, talking on his phone. "Yes," he says, "I'm going to ask Anne to spend the night with her. I think she'd be the best one. I don't think you could find anyone as capable as Anne to take care of her."

I stop, trying to recover from the surprise of hearing this compliment. When he starts talking again, I step out in front of him. He looks right into my eyes. "Oh, here's Anne now. I'll ask her." He holds the phone to his chest and speaks gently, with a sort of respect that reminds me of the past. "Will you stay with her tonight, Anne? Someone needs to take care of her, and we think you would be the best."

I can feel myself blushing. Neil recollects himself and takes a step backward. I have to swallow before I answer him. My mouth is so dry. "I was already planning on it. But let me tell them what the doctor just said. It's good news."

Neil hands me the phone, and I give better news to Lily's mother, who's still in shock from hearing the worst. Neil, listening nearby, sinks down in a chair and leans over to hide his face in his folded arms. I suspect he's praying. He stays that way for the next few minutes while

I talk to Janet about what should be done. Of course the Musgroves will need to come down to North Carolina. She wants to come right away. But I convince her to take her time. She might have to stay for a week, if not longer. I promise her I'll call them with any concern or any change. Meanwhile, I'll do everything possible to help Lily recover.

Lily doesn't wake up until around midnight—after the others have left. She's confused and unable to talk. I spend a frantic night trying to keep her comfortable. She needs ice packs on her sores, but she is already so cold. The pain medication isn't strong enough. She's nauseated. She struggles to breathe. Her throat hurts. She doesn't like the oxygen tube in her nose. She can't move her legs. The IV is hurting her.

I try my best to help her. I feel like I'm constantly calling the nurse to ask a question or request more medications. One of them lets us borrow a stereo so Lily can listen to quiet music. While it's playing, I massage her hands. Then I try to cheer her up by talking about her parents, Hannah, Neil, or anything at all to distract her.

Lily finally falls back to sleep as the sun comes up over the horizon. I curl up in the vinyl chair beside the bed. My body is exhausted, but my mind is still racing, going over the events of the last day. Now that I'm sure Lily will get better, I turn my mind to Neil. There was something in the way he looked at me yesterday. I caught his eye more than once. Then there was the little conversation at the beach. I imagine I'm in his arms again, my face pressed against his chest. His hand gently strokes my hair.

As I'm drifting off to sleep, I hear a faint knock at the door. It's Jay. He's brought my duffel bag from the hotel along with a paper bag of something for my breakfast. He wants to stay with Lily while I take a break. I don't think I've ever needed a break as badly as I do now.

My clothes are salty, sandy, and itchy from the beach. I don't realize it though until I've changed into something clean and soft. The nurse even gives me some soap so I can take a shower. Once I'm done, I give Jay a few words of advice, explaining what he'll need to know if Lily wakes up. Then I wander through the labyrinthine halls of the hospital, looking for an exit. At last, I open a door and find myself looking out at a perfect blue sky.

Sitting on a bench under a honey locust tree, I open the paper bag Jay gave me. Inside, I discover a cup of fresh-squeezed orange juice, two muffins, and a container of cubed melon. I'm impressed that Jay already knows me well enough to pick a breakfast I like. The muffins are blueberry, my favorite. Even better, they're made with whole-wheat flour, just the way I like them. How could Jay have known?

I eat every bite of the breakfast, then deciding it would be best if I pay Jay for the meal—after all, he doesn't have a job—I pick up the little paper bag to look for a receipt. That's when I notice that Neil's name is written on the bag, as if he was the one who ordered it, paid for it, and waited for it.

I find the receipt crumpled up inside and stare at it as if it's a crystal ball, where I can read my future. The date and time are from 11:43 the night before. He must've planned ahead to avoid buying on Sunday. (I forgot it was Sunday.) Everything is listed: the muffins, the juice, and the fruit. Nothing else is on the receipt. It was all for me.

Jay stays with me throughout the morning, helping to care for Lily. Neil and Hannah are here too, but every time Hannah comes into the room, she breaks down crying, which only disturbs Lily more. Neil ends up walking the halls with Hannah, just trying to keep her busy.

Around noon, Dave Harville tiptoes into the room and motions for me to follow him into the hall. Outside the door stands the man we passed on the stairs, the man with the Jaguar. He is wearing a perfectly tailored suit. Everything else about him—the tanned face, the wispy blond hair, the casual smile—seems to belong at the Outer Banks.

Dave gestures toward Will. "Anne, I'd like to introduce you to Will Grandin."

Will smiles and reaches out his hand to me. "Pleased to meet you. I think I saw you and your friends on the beach the other day."

I shake his hand. "Yes, I remember." It seems like it was so long ago.

Will speaks smoothly and with an air of confidence. "I was sorry to hear about your friend's accident."

I try to focus on what he's just said. My lack of sleep doesn't help, neither does the sight of Neil and Hannah coming down the hall. "Yes," I mutter, wishing I could say something more sophisticated. "She's had a hard time."

"The jellies are really bad this year." He pauses. "Dave told us at church that you needed a ride home tonight. I'd like to help. I live up in the DC area too, and I'm going home this afternoon."

I look up into his light brown eyes. "That's so nice of you." As Hannah and Neil approach, I motion for them to come meet Will. "Will, this is Hannah—her sister's the one that got stung. And this is Neil."

Will shakes hands with Hannah, then looks at Neil and holds out his hand. "You must be the fiancé."

Neil shakes Will's hand, then puts his hands in his pockets. He looks at me, then back at Will. "Nope."

"Neil is Lily's boyfriend," I explain. "They're not engaged."

"Yet," Hannah adds, giggling then sniffling. Neil folds his arms and turns to look at the wall.

"Will's offered to drive me home tonight," I tell Hannah. "I wish I could stay, but they need me at work. And your parents should be here soon."

Hannah puts a hand beside her mouth and pretends to tell Will a secret, though everyone can hear what she says. "Anne has a really important position at her work."

Will looks back at me. "Where do you work?"

"Prosperity Investments, but I don't have a really important position. Hannah's just—"

"Do you work at their McLean office?"

"Yes."

A smile spreads across Will's face. "I know exactly where that is."

Neil stops looking at the wall and focuses on Will. "Look, it's really nice of you to offer Anne a ride, but we've had kind of a change of plans. It turns out I'm not able to get off of work tomorrow either, so I can take Anne home after all." He pauses, glancing at Hannah. "I'll have to try to come back at the end of the week." He turns again, walks away from the group, and takes out his cell phone.

I hear Neil's words with a sort of nervous excitement. I am going to spend seven hours driving in a car alone with him. While the conversation goes on between Will and Hannah, I try to stay composed. I don't know whether to look forward to it or fear it. What are we going to talk about? How can I keep him from reading my feelings?

Monday, July 1, 2002

I used to think I was a charitable person, but after this week I'm not so sure. I've been cooking for Mom. She'll ask me to make something she feels like eating, then, by the time I make it, she's changed her mind and wants something else. She's obsessed with dieting even though she just had surgery. She has this little notebook to write down her calories, and she wants me to weigh all her food. She thinks she got cancer because she was a few pounds overweight. I know she's sick, and I should be patient, but it is so hard to put up with her. Yesterday, I made her three different meals, all with fresh ingredients like she wanted—grilled chicken breast, linguine with clam sauce, and lasagna—she wouldn't eat any of them. I was in her kitchen for three hours. It's times like these when I wish she'd let me call in the Relief Society.

People talk so much about families in church. They say we need to put family first. But if I had put family first, I wouldn't have joined the Church at all—and then where would I be? I'd really be missing out. Aren't we supposed to put our Heavenly Father first, then our families? And another thing, I sometimes wonder why I got the family I got. Was I somehow less noble? Not that I don't love them. It's mostly that I wish we were sealed in the temple. That would be a real comfort right now. I mean, what am I going to do if Mom dies from her cancer?

When I pray about it, I know that I'm supposed to be in my family. It's just that sometimes the things that should be making me a better, stronger person pull me down instead.

I hear them before I see them. There's the clatter of little footsteps echoing down the hallway. Charlie's hushed warnings: "Be quiet. We're in a hospital." Then I hear Mary asking the nurse where Lily's room is.

I walk out into the hall to greet them. Once they see me, Charlie and Mary rush past into Lily's room, leaving Daniel out in the hall by himself. Steve and Janet are turning the corner into the hallway. Steve has Joseph on his shoulders. I wave. I didn't expect them to bring the whole family. But the Musgroves do most things as a family, even if it is less convenient.

Joseph and Daniel run up and down the hallway, eliciting smiles and occasional rebukes from hospital workers. After a while, Hannah comes rushing up the hallway and into the room, eager to meet her parents. Neil and I are left standing in the hallway, watching the two boys. "Finally," Neil confides, "I thought they'd get here earlier. It's past six o'clock. Are you all set? I have an early shift tomorrow." He walks over and peeks into the room.

"I'm ready whenever you want to leave."

We enter Lily's room, dragging Joseph and Daniel along with us. After a few minutes, Neil announces our intention to leave as soon as possible. Mary gives the loudest objection. "Anne, you can't leave. What am I going to do with Joseph and Daniel? If I'm taking care of Lily, who'll take care of them? I wouldn't have come at all if I knew you would be leaving so soon."

Used to these kinds of accusations from Mary, I explain that I have to get back to work in the morning.

Mary puts her hands on her hips. "Well, can you at least take the kids back with you? I don't see how we'll be able to handle them here at the hospital."

I grab the IV pole right before Joseph tips it over. "I have to work tomorrow."

Mary rakes her teeth over her bottom lip. "If you can drive them back home, I'm sure there'll be someone who can watch them while you're at work. Maybe Liz could watch them, or Dad." Daniel runs out the door. I follow him. Mary and Charlie are close behind.

"Really, Mary," I whisper. "I don't see how that would work. I wish I'd known you wanted me to watch them. I could have told you my plans. Can't you and Charlie take turns watching them?"

Charlie puts an arm around Mary. "Maybe we can find someone to watch them here."

Mary, now very angry, turns to her husband. "I am not leaving my children with strangers."

I am too tired to care very much about Mary's theatrics. Neil comes out into the hall, carrying my duffel bag. He slings it over his shoulder and looks at me. "Are you ready?"

I hook a stray piece of hair behind my ear. "Yes."

Mary grabs onto Neil, who's been saying good-bye to Lily and hasn't paid attention to our conversation. Her voice is much too loud as she begs, "You wouldn't mind driving my kids home, would you, Neil? They're really good in the car."

Neil looks at Mary with exasperation. "I'd like to help, Mary. But I've got to make it home in time for my shift." He picks up the duffel bag and starts down the hall at a quick pace.

I have to run to catch up to him. "Sorry about that."

He stares ahead down the hall. "Anne, you really are not doing anyone a favor by putting yourself last. Not that I don't appreciate what you've done for Lily—you've been great. But you really need to learn to balance it out. You think you're helping people by sacrificing your own comfort." He is walking so fast down the hall that I have to run to keep up with him. "It's not always good for people." He halts at the elevator and pushes the call button. "This thing is going to be slow. Let's take the stairs."

I can feel tears coming to my eyes as I follow him down the staircase. I dab at them with the back of my wrist, hoping more won't come. But I am so tired. I have to wipe them away again before we reach the bottom of the stairs. I shouldn't have gotten my hopes up. I feel ridiculous for thinking that a compliment and a blueberry muffin meant anything more than appreciation. I was just someone to take care of his girlfriend. I wish I'd gotten a ride from Will Grandin. I'm pretty sure nothing Will could say would make me cry.

We're in another hall now. Neil waits for me to catch up, then, without looking at me, resumes the lecture. "Normally, helping your sister would be a good thing. But Mary demands too much. You need to tell her no sometimes. And this guy offering you a ride—you don't even know him."

I know I should be defending myself—after all I've been taking care of his girlfriend for the past twenty-four hours. He should be thanking me. But talking would only make the tears come faster. I follow him out the door to the parking garage, dabbing a few more tears from my eyes. He doesn't look at my face until we get to his car and he opens the door for me to get in. I can't look back at him.

He puts my duffel bag into the back, then slowly gets in and starts the car. I turn my head to look out the side window. I feel so ridiculous. "Are you crying?" he asks.

I have to say something. There is no way out of it. "Do I have to tell the truth?" I can barely choke out the words.

He backs the car out of the parking spot. "No, you can lie if you want." He sounds a little amused. Amusement is better than pity.

"Then I'm not crying."

"Good because I've been a jerk."

Trying not to sniffle, I keep my head turned to the window. "No, you haven't."

"You can start telling the truth now. This whole weekend has been a disaster. This whole situation is just—"

"The truth is I'm really, really tired. And if I say anything else, I might regret it later."

Neil reaches into the back seat and grabs a pillow. "Here." He hands it to me. "Go to sleep."

I turn my head toward him. "I'll probably drool on this."

"I've always wanted a pillow you drooled on." Why does he flirt when he doesn't mean it?

I recline the seat, turn away from him, and rest my head on the pillow. I close my eyes to the souvenir shops and beach houses that fascinated me only yesterday. I listen to Neil fiddling with the stereo, trying to find something to listen to. I don't care what he listens to. Nothing could keep me awake. After a minute, he says, "About those things you might say that you'd regret later on—"

"I'm not saying anything else. Wake me up when you want me to drive."

Hours later, I'm jolted out of sleep, sensing that the car is no longer moving. I sit in near darkness and look up at Neil's face outlined by the lights from the dashboard. He has a two-day-old beard that probably feels like coarse sandpaper. He's looking at me, smiling. "Is it my turn?" I ask groggily.

He opens his door. The dome lights flood the car with a shock of light. I cover my eyes as he comes around and opens my door. He bends over me. "We're at Mary's house. I'm going to follow you to your apartment."

I drag myself out of my seat, walk over to my car, and try to find my keys. "I feel like I'm on a DUI," he says, reaching for my purse and digging out the keys for me. "Maybe I should drive you home."

"No, I need my car in the morning."

Backing out of the driveway, I cannot believe I slept the whole way home. It is 3:30 a.m. What if I snored? Or forget snoring, what if I talked in my sleep? He could have had a whole conversation with me, and I wouldn't know it. I have been known to do that sort of thing—to reveal my soul's deepest secrets to roommates while I'm asleep. And I wish I hadn't cried. He definitely saw more of my emotions than I intended.

As I drive down Mary's street, I see his headlights close behind. It is just like him to follow me home. Why does he have to be so polite? No matter what, I will not ask him into my apartment. That would be more than my emotions can take. Now that this weekend is over, I'm going to have to stay as far away as possible. The way he talks to me now is too much like the past. I know he's trying to be kind, but it fills me with such nostalgia. It is too painful to be around him, knowing I can't have him. His affection belongs to Lily. I have to remember Lily.

Neil's car follows me into the parking lot of my apartment building. I expect him to wave and drive off, but instead he parks and gets out of his car. I try not to say much as I lead him into the apartment building. Once inside the doors, I thank him and reach for my bag. He refuses my offer.

Although it is three in the morning, the elevator is as slow as it is during morning rush hour. I stare at the call button. "I hope I didn't snore or anything." I must look terrible.

"You didn't."

"You should have woken me up to take a turn driving."

"I needed the time to think."

"For seven hours?"

"I had a lot to think about."

The elevator arrives, and we get in.

I lean against the wall. "I didn't talk in my sleep or anything?"

He laughs. "No." What is so funny?

When we get to my door, I reach for my bag again. "Well, thanks for—"

"I know it's really late, but I was wondering if I could use your bathroom?"

So that's what this is about. I didn't count on him having any sort of basic human needs. "Oh, sorry, I should have asked you in. I'll show you where it is."

"Is your roommate here? I mean, do you have a roommate?"

"Yeah, she's probably asleep."

I lead him into the apartment, past the orange kitchen and the tiny living room into the hallway. I point out the bathroom for him and lean against the wall, wondering what I'm going to do with him when he comes back out. Marcy pops her head out of her bedroom. "Who's with you?" She must have heard a man's voice, which is always an occasion for surprise, at least if he's with me.

I step close enough to whisper. "Neil Wentworth." Marcy clasps her hands over her mouth and widens her eyes.

I shake my head. "He drove me home. It's really not what you're thinking."

Still, Marcy is impressed. "So what? He's in your apartment, isn't he?"

With the twist of the bathroom doorknob, Marcy disappears and I'm left standing alone in the hallway, as if I've been waiting there for him. "Would you like something to eat?"

Neil rubs the back of his neck. "That'd be great. I mean, if it's not too late. Usually, I wouldn't be in a woman's apartment this late. But you have a roommate, and I trust you."

What does he mean by that? I go to the kitchen and open my cupboard. He trusts me because I won't make a pass at him? There is an almost empty box of crackers, some rice cakes, and a box of raisin bran. Or does he trust himself not to be attracted to me? In the refrigerator,

I find jam, organic nut butter, and what looks like Marcy's leftover vegetarian beef stew. "I don't have a lot because I've been away so much," I explain. "Oh, I forgot—I always keep an emergency pint of ice cream." I open the freezer and extract Ben and Jerry's Brownie Batter.

He sits down at the kitchen table. "That sounds good."

"Except I forgot I ate half of it. And I ate out of the container."

He shrugs his shoulders as if he doesn't care. I hand him the container and a spoon. I sit down across from him.

He sticks the spoon in and takes a bite. "So this is your emergency ice cream. Do you give it to your roommates when you kiss someone?"

I put my elbows on the table and rest my chin on my hands. Why is he talking about kissing? Emergencies don't have anything to do with kissing. "No, it's more of a worry ice cream. I save it for when I'm upset."

Neil looks down into the container. "There's not much left. You must have been pretty upset."

I stand up to get the crackers. "Yeah, I was. The only reason I didn't eat the whole thing was because that would have made me even more upset."

"Is it anything I can help with?" He sounds like my home teacher. "I kind of owe you one."

I really don't want to say anything else on the subject since he is the subject, so I stick a cracker in my mouth and shake my head. After I swallow, I answer him. "You don't owe me anything."

Neil holds out the ice cream to me. "Do you want some of this?"

"That's okay. You can finish it."

Neil looks down at the ice cream. "I really appreciate all you did for Lily. After she's better, we'll have to get together for dinner or something."

I take a mental note of that statement. It proves that he's only paying attention to me because I helped Lily. "That'd be nice," I reply, but I know I am never going out to dinner with him and Lily. "I hope she gets better soon."

Once we finish off the box of crackers, Neil asks me how I liked my mission. Now there's a question I didn't expect. What does that have to do with Lily? I bring out a bag of rice cakes and some almond butter. Then I tell him about a couple of the highlights of my mission. I'm thinking he's going to leave at any moment, but he doesn't. He keeps talking. He asks me how my parents are doing. He asks about my roommate, my work, and my calling.

We linger, drinking glasses of water and speculating how soon it'll be before Lily is back to normal. Then we joke about how tired we'll be at work in a few hours. That must be why he is staying so long—he's too tired to get up. Finally, he looks at his watch and announces he'd better leave if he wants to make it to work on time.

I lead him to the door. "Thank you for driving me home."

He reaches his hand out and runs his fingers along the side of my cheek. His touch drives away every hopeless thought. I feel valuable and feminine. "Take care of yourself, Anne. I'll see you around."

I watch him walk down the hall toward the elevator. He is limping a little, his hair sticks out at the usual spot in back, and his hands are in his pockets. He reminds me of a little boy, and I wish I could be the one to take care of him. I even wonder if I might not be able to do a better job of it than Lily.

11

Saturday, July 6, 2002

*N*eil and Jack took me fishing down below Great Falls. We didn't catch a thing, but it was fun. After I got home, I looked up the definition of *love* in the dictionary. It said, "A profoundly tender, passionate affection for another person." That's about how I feel.

I took Mom shopping for a wig. It's still a couple more weeks before she starts chemotherapy, but they say it's best to pick the wig ahead of time. It was hilarious—the first time I've seen Mom laugh since this whole thing started. I wish I'd brought a camera.

Sitting in the beauty salon, Mom and I look like Halloween trick-or-treaters. With her hair done up in rectangles of aluminum foil and wearing a black smock, Mom looks like an alien. I've just gotten my eyebrows waxed, so I look like a punk with bright pink stripes above my eyes. We're sitting next to each other in pedicure chairs with our feet soaking in hot water.

It is lunchtime on the last Tuesday of August and I've been home from North Carolina for a day. Something tells me Mom is about to give me the third degree about the trip. Normally, I would take a deep breath, but the fumes of nail polish prevent it. So I grab a magazine—it happens to be one about cooking—and try to concentrate on an article. It isn't working. Mom is like a shark, going for my throat. "Mary tells me you had an adventurous weekend."

I start to explain the accident. Mom, just as I suspected, is shocked at Lily's behavior—wondering how anyone could be so careless. "I guess she got her comeuppance. It's too bad she couldn't have had a milder reaction."

I have to mention Neil, awkwardly reminding Mom how she knows him. It is easiest to look down at the magazine as I tell her this part. I can only look up again after I explain Neil's relationship with Lily.

"Do you mean to tell me that Neil Wentworth, who used to be so in love with you, is now in love with Lily?" The tone and volume of her voice reminds me a little of Mary's.

I force myself to maintain eye contact. "That's the way it seems."

Mom slaps her knee. "That just goes to show that I was right about him. He didn't have the brains to appreciate you, Anne. It's a good thing you broke it off. I know, you thought you were in love, but he wasn't good enough for you."

I stare at the red nail polish in my hand as I feel anger well up inside me. "I think you're wrong about him, Mom."

"Don't tell me you still like him. You know, if it wasn't for that church of yours, preaching abstinence, you could have gotten him out of your system a long time ago."

"What exactly do you mean by that?"

"I mean, if you'd gone to bed with him—or maybe lived together a while—you'd know for sure he wasn't for you. I chalk it all up to sexual repression."

"Mom, I'm perfectly happy living the way I do. It's the right way. Sex is for people who are committed to each other, and the way you show that commitment is by being married. There are so many things I don't have to worry about because I've chosen to live this way— unwed pregnancy, diseases, feeling used, to name a few. But that's not why I live the way I do. I live this way because I promised my Heavenly Father that I would keep his commandments. I know you don't believe in God, but I do. I know he's there, watching out for us. He loves us. He wants us to be happy. That's why we have commandments. And that's why I follow them. And, believe it or not, there are men that feel the same way as I do. There are men who wait until they're married."

The pedicurist working on my feet is staring up at me with a look somewhere between shock and disgust. Feeling flustered, I go on. "But that's beside the point. Neil and I have a lot in common. It wasn't just physical attraction. He's actually very smart. I think we could have had a happy marriage—even if we were young."

There's a long pause. Mom clears her throat. "So I guess you've met your father's new woman friend."

I'm too busy wishing my mother could have higher moral standards to hear what she says. Mom has to repeat herself. "I said, have you met your father's new woman friend?"

"What do you mean woman friend? Is Dad dating someone?" In all the years since the divorce, Dad has never dated anyone.

"Liz can't stop talking about her. It's Felicia this and Felicia that. I got the idea that this Felicia isn't much older than Liz. Beyond that, all I know is that she owns a small business."

"That sounds good . . . I mean, about the small business."

Mom raises her eyebrows. "I'll let you be the judge of that. Tell me what you think after you meet her."

I don't respond. I hate it when she acts like I'm her personal spy on Dad. I open the magazine again and try to talk about a recipe that sounds interesting.

Meanwhile, Mom must be preoccupied with our earlier conversation because she switches to advice mode. "Anne, forget about the past. It's time to move on. Break-ups are hard. I sometimes even regret the divorce. But you've got to learn from them and move on. You'll find someone new, who deserves you so much more."

Remembering the bad advice Mom has given me in the past, I can't take her words to heart. Logically, I know it's time to get over Neil. I've made a list of things to do to distract myself from thinking about him. I've even looked into online dating. Still, little things pop up that remind me of him.

After I get back to the office, I get an email from Charlie, explaining that Lily's condition is about the same. The most interesting part of it is Neil's email address listed at the top beside my own. I add it to my address book. Yes, he is dating Lily, but there's no harm in keeping his email address. You never know when you might need an email address.

Another email comes from Susan Wentworth. Again, I think of Neil and read it immediately:

Hi Anne. I was wondering if you'd like to join the stake choir with me. They're giving a concert at the visitor's center in October. Jack told me you like to sing. Practices are Tuesdays at 8 p.m. at the stake center. I'd love to have a friend go with me.—Susan

It could hardly be considered a distraction to go anywhere with Neil's sister-in-law, but I ignore my better judgment. That evening, I'm sitting next to Susan at choir practice, listening to the choir director complain about low attendance. Having sung in many choirs, the complaints seem familiar. I wish we could start singing. I need a distraction, not boredom.

While the director asks for opinions about how to get more people to come, Susan whispers, "I hear you had quite a weekend."

"It was kind of a disaster. But up until the accident, we had fun. Poor Lily—it couldn't have been much worse for her."

Susan glances at the director, then back at me. "Neil didn't tell us about it until last night. We went up to visit him for family home evening. There we were sitting in his favorite restaurant, trying to buy him dinner, and he's refusing everything. Finally, he tells us he's fasting for Lily. We felt horrible. He seemed so miserable. I wished he'd told us before we came." She looks up at the director, who is staring at her. "We'll have to talk about it after."

I try to focus on the hymn we're learning. It's about gratitude. I don't feel grateful; I feel agitated. Why didn't I notice that Neil was miserable the other night? Maybe I don't know him as well as I think I do. Maybe I'm spending too much time hoping.

When the basses and tenors are practicing their lines by themselves, I hold my hymnbook in front of my face and whisper, "I think Neil feels responsible for the accident, but it really wasn't his fault at all."

"Oh, I know. He's like that. But I'm sure everything'll turn out well . . . It sounds like you were a big help. Neil told us how you were the only one who didn't panic when it happened. And how you took such good care of Lily. He asked if I'd seen you at all. He said you were exhausted when he brought you home. It's no wonder, after all you did."

I'm trying not to get too excited about what Neil said, but I can't help it. As we start to sing again, I am smiling. I hardly know what I'm singing, but I sure feel thankful.

When the practice is over, we walk out into the parking lot together. Susan pauses before she gets in her car. "Neil will be happy to hear you're well. I don't know that we did much to cheer him up last night. He and Jack went over to the gym together—that's where they usually go to talk, just the two of them. Jack's a good brother, but he can be insensitive. When they got back, he kept laughing and saying things like, 'This is the kind of thing that happens when you're in love.' I'm not sure he was very helpful."

My optimism drains away as we said our good-byes. Jack's words hang in my mind: "This is the kind of thing that happens when you're in love." Even Jack thinks Neil is in love with Lily. I feel so blind. Am I the only one who doubts it?

I am so tired of all the teeter-totter emotions I have about Neil. One thought sends me flying up; another drops me down. It's too painful. Maybe Mom is right. It's time to get over him.

The next morning, as I walk into my cubicle at work, I'm surprised to find a vase of red roses sitting beside the monitor. My coworkers, who've already noticed them, gather around to witness my reaction. "You've gotta tell us who they're from, girl," someone prods.

Thinking of only one person, I'm reluctant to open the card. Surely, they aren't from him. He's in love with Lily. He wouldn't send me red roses. Neil is smart enough to know the meaning of a red rose. They're the color of passion, not gratitude. I strain my mind to think who could have sent them. They look expensive. I hope they aren't from Dad. In his financial situation, he can hardly afford such a luxury.

As my friends tease me, I think of someone else—they could be from the Musgroves. Maybe they're sending flowers to thank me for helping with Lily. Of course, red roses are an odd choice, even for the Musgroves.

My curiosity overcomes me. "I have no idea." I reach for the card and open it.

It reads, "I'd like to get to know you better. How about dinner Friday? Sincerely, Will Grandin."

Soon ten or twelve of the people at work are passing the card around and reading it as I try to explain how I know him. He's the guy I met at the beach, the guy with the Jaguar and the perfect suit. He offered me a ride home. All in all, he will be a very convenient distraction.

Tuesday, July 9, 2002

I was beginning to wonder if Neil would ever kiss me. Well, today it happened. It's probably a good thing he hasn't kissed me before this because I am way too attracted to him. It's hard to think of anything else.

Mom's doing better. Still no sign of her boyfriend.

I spent a couple hours yesterday helping Dad sort out his finances. I didn't realize how much debt he has. I didn't know a person could have so many loans. As soon as I get my degree, I'm going to help him pay it off.

Will Grandin doesn't mention that the dinner is a black tie affair until after I agree to go. That's when I learn the true meaning of the phrase, "I have nothing to wear." All my prom dresses from high school, and even a bridesmaid's dress, went to charity years ago. I doubt they would still fit if I had them anyway.

I spend several fruitless hours perusing the racks at the mall, searching for something that is modest enough to even try on. The one dress I find, a sequined jacket dress, would be great for a New Year's Eve party at the nursing home, but I doubt someone as sophisticated as Will Grandin will approve of it. Two days give me no time to order anything or have anything made. I don't even have time for alterations. By Friday, I've decided my only option is to borrow a dress.

I call Mary, who is still in North Carolina. She answers on the first ring. "Hi, Anne, guess where I am?"

"The hospital?"

"I'm on the beach. Valerie Harville's watching the kids. We take turns. She's the best. I wish I had a friend like her in McLean. And guess what else? I haven't had to cook once."

"How's Lily?" I'm anxious for good news.

"She's better. The doctor says she might get out of the hospital soon. Did I tell you I've got a great tan?"

"So who's taking care of her?"

"Janet. Jay's always there too. They don't leave much for us to do. Oh, and Hannah's usually there. Did I tell you Barry came down? But he's always at the hospital too, so we hardly ever see him, which is just as well."

"Listen, Mary, I have to go to a fancy dinner, and I need a formal dress. Do you have anything I could borrow."

"I have my formals from high school. You can look at them if you like."

Two hours later, I examine my reflection in Mary's bedroom mirror. I am wearing the only formal dress in Mary's closet that fits. Luckily it is burgundy, a subdued color. But I look like I stepped out of a high school yearbook from ten years ago. Can a man who wears Italian suits overlook such a thing? Shoes are another problem—I left my only pair of black heels in North Carolina. And there is nothing appropriate in Mary's closet. All the good shoes are in North Carolina.

What am I going to do? I only have fifteen minutes before Will picks me up at my apartment. I get in the car and dial Liz. Dad answers. Liz is at work, but he promises he'll find me some shoes and a purse in Liz's closet. He remembers the dress exactly and knows what would look best. "I'll get some scissors, too," he offers. "We can cut off that bow I never liked."

By the time I arrive at Dad's apartment, I have five minutes to spare. Dad opens the door before I even ring the doorbell. He's impressed. "You look great. What have you been doing different? There's something different about your face."

I rush in and grab the pair of very high slingbacks off one of the kitchen stools. "I haven't been doing anything different, Dad." I sit down on the couch and try on the shoes. They are bigger and higher than my shoes, but they'll have to do.

"Are you sure you haven't been doing anything different? Your skin looks clearer. Have you lost weight?"

"No." I stuff my cell phone, keys, wallet, and lipstick into Liz's sequined purse. "Nothing different."

"Well, whatever it is, keep it up. Liz and Felicia—you'll have to meet Felicia—they've switched to mineral makeup. Have you ever tried that?"

If there is anyone who can prepare me to meet Will Grandin, it's my dad. Sometimes I think he should have been a fashion designer instead of an accountant. He has me stand up while he cuts the bow off Mary's dress, then recommends a deeper shade of lipstick. He hands me the purse. "Why don't you call your date. Have him meet you here. You don't want to have to run across the complex. I've got Liz's curling iron heated up if you want it."

I call Will, then sit down for a moment to compose myself. That is when I begin to notice the array of new merchandise scattered through the kitchen. There are new pots and pans, flatware, decorations, and soaps. The place even smells different—there's a citrus fragrance in the air.

I remember the conversation I had with Mom about his new girl-friend. I guess there's no harm in asking. "So when am I going to meet Felicia?"

"She'll be here next Friday. You can come if you like. We're having a party."

Once the doorbell rings, I realize I should have practiced walking in four-inch heels. There is something so unnatural about the way I have to stick out my hips as I walk to the door. And the straps are too loose. I open the door, and there he is, looking even more handsome than I remember. I introduce him to my father.

Dad shakes his hand. "Will Grandin—that name sounds familiar."

Will flashes a smile. "You'd be surprised how many people say that. They must know something I don't."

Dad laughs politely. "What line of work are you in, Will?"

"I'm a lobbyist, actually. I lobby for agricultural interests."

This is enough to impress my dad, and he sends us off with a grin on his face.

Out in the hall, I struggle to walk as Will compliments me on the way I look. I confess that I borrowed both the dress and the shoes. Before we even get to the elevator, I'm kneeling down to adjust the straps on the shoes.

Will leans against the wall as if he's posing for the front cover of Money magazine. "I love your honesty. A lot of women, and probably even more men, aren't courageous enough to be honest. It was nice to meet your dad too. I've heard of him, you know."

"Really?"

"He's much more down-to-earth than I expected. I respect that. A lot of guys like him are like that—living simply in an apartment, no need for frills."

"Oh, the apartment is temporary while he's looking for a new house."

In the car, he asks me what I thought of the Outer Banks, and we compare opinions about the sights. He remembers seeing me with my friends on the beach. He went to North Carolina alone, on business, and when he saw us all together, he wished he could join in the fun. If he'd only known we were going to breakfast at the same restaurant he'd just left, he would have stayed longer—if only to eavesdrop.

I imagine that Will's manners are exactly what they ought to be. He is at once suave, polished, considerate, and agreeable. And I have to admit he is so easy to talk to that I can compare him to only one other man.

He asks about the accident, wanting to know all the details— how I felt, what it was like to call 911, what happened in the ambulance, what the doctors told me. He sympathizes with all that Lily has suffered, and even with what I've suffered in trying to help her. He pats my knee. "I hope this experience doesn't make you afraid to swim at the beach. It's unusual to get stung by jellyfish, and even more unusual to have such a bad reaction. I'm sorry it had to happen to your friend."

I thank him and explain that I'd like to stay away from jellyfish for awhile anyway.

Will points to a large hotel ahead of us. "Here it is." Everything about the place looks expensive—from the uniformed employees standing out front to the stately white columns around the entrance. I can feel my phone vibrating inside the little purse as we pull up for valet parking. I sneak a look at it as the car stops. It's Neil.

Will opens my door and leads me into the building. The marble floors and sumptuous carpets are all a blur. I follow Will past velvet couches and into a large ballroom filled with elegant people. Normally I'd want to compare Mary's prom dress to the black velvets and taffetas surrounding me, but all I can think of is the phone call. Jewelry sparkles all around me on fingers, necks, and wrists.

Why would he call me? He's never called me before. Is it something about Lily? It has to be about Lily. Is there something wrong? I have to call him back. I excuse myself from Will and head for the lobby restroom.

There, standing inside a marble stall, I dial his number. "Hi Anne," he answers, "thanks for calling back." He sounds happy, so it can't be anything bad.

I lean against the cold marble. "What's going on?"

"I wanted to let you know Lily's doing better. She ate some Jell-O tonight. I just wanted to let you know."

"That's great. Thanks for telling me." To tell the truth, I'm a little disappointed. I guess in the back of my mind, I was hoping he'd ask me out. Why would I hope for that?

"I think she'll probably get out of the hospital tomorrow. She's going to stay with the Harvilles for a few days until she feels up to the big road trip."

"I'm so glad she's doing better. I hope she can get home soon." There's one of those awkward pauses during which I decide that Neil is going to have to speak next. He does. "How are you? You seemed kind of down last time I saw you." He sounds like he really cares—or maybe it's wishful thinking on my part.

"Oh, I'm great. I was just tired, you know. How are you? Susan said you were a little down yourself."

The silence on the other end lasts for a few seconds. "You've been talking to Susan?"

"I saw her at choir practice. She said you were worried about Lily."

He stammers. "Oh, yeah, I was."

"I guess you'll be going down to North Carolina to see her."

"I don't know. My work schedule is real busy for the next few weeks. I've got Labor Day to deal with for one thing. It's always a big day for the police. But I call her every day. I'm hoping she'll be well enough to come home soon." He pauses. "So, do you have a fun weekend planned?"

"Actually I do," I respond with confidence. "I'm at a political benefit dinner right now. We just got here, but it looks exciting. It's kind of like visiting the great and spacious building."

He laughs. "Don't start mocking anyone, okay?"

"I'm not mocking now, but I might be tempted later. I haven't really gotten into it yet. What are you up to?"

"Grocery shopping. I'm all out of rice cakes." It almost seems like he's flirting with me again.

I giggle. "Yeah, I'll bet you are. Listen, I've got to go. My friend's waiting for me. But thanks for calling me about Lily. I'm so glad she's doing better."

We say our good-byes and hang up. I talked to him for three and a half minutes. Here I am on a perfect date, and he distracts me. Will is supposed to be distracting me from Neil—not the other way around.

Determined to forget about Neil, I turn the cell phone off and walk back out to join Will. I find him where I left him in the red-carpeted ballroom, standing underneath a crystal chandelier, holding two drinks, and chatting with another couple. "Anne," he says, "I want to introduce you to Delores. She's the president of PAW. And this is her husband, Greg."

"Nice to meet you," I reply, shaking hands and wondering what PAW stands for. People Against Warfare? Power And Women? It could be anything.

"Here." Will hands me one of the drinks. "I got you a Sprite."

"Thanks." I remember something I read about date rape drugs: you should never accept a drink from your date unless you see him pour it.

"We were just talking about their Welsh Corgi," Will informs me. "She's about to have puppies"

"Oh." I help myself to an hors d'oeuvre off a server's silver tray. "Isn't that the kind of dog Queen Elizabeth has?"

Delores is pleased to answer that it is, and goes on to describe how her dog is a Pembroke like the queen's. "We're so excited to be grandparents. You'll have to come by and see the puppies. They're gonna be adorable."

Will asks Delores to call him as soon as the puppies are old enough for visitors. Delores replies that she'll be sending out announcements to all her friends, and she'll be sure to include him. She is also planning a baby shower for the mother.

I sip my drink, checking for any strange tastes. What am I thinking? That he'll slip me a Mickey in front of a couple hundred people? He doesn't seem like the kind of guy that would do that sort of thing. He seems nice, actually.

Trying to bring my focus back to the conversation, I guess that PAW has something to do with dogs. Will winks at me. He really is attractive. Then, almost effortlessly, he excuses himself from the couple and escorts me across the room, whispering in my ear as we walk along. "PAW stands for People for Animal Welfare. Sorry I couldn't tell you earlier."

Now we're chatting with an older couple Will introduces as Karl and Mandy. Karl holds up his wife's hand, where a large diamond ring sparkles. "Look what I bought for the Missus."

Both Will and I bend over Mandy's outstretched hand to admire the quality of the stone. I really have no idea how to evaluate a diamond, but this one does reflect a whole kaleidoscope of color and light. "Isn't he the most wonderful husband?" Mandy gushes. "I had no idea he was planning it."

Karl puffs out his chest like a penguin. "We just had our fortieth anniversary."

I clap my hand to my chest. "Oh, that's so sweet." Okay, I know I'm not supposed to be thinking about it, but sometimes my thoughts go places without my permission. My engagement ring, the one I wore for one day, was white gold with three little diamonds in a row: one for Neil, one for me, and the middle one for the Lord. He said that the best relationships have God in the middle. I always wonder what Neil did with it after I returned it to him—probably he took it back to the store. I imagine he'll buy something totally different for Lily. After all, Lily is the type to pick out her own engagement ring.

Sometimes, when I have trouble falling asleep, my mind travels back to the middle of the high school football field. It was pitch black and I was supposed to be watching for shooting stars while Neil found Jupiter through the telescope. But I couldn't concentrate on the stars; something was different. I could feel him shaking when he held my hand. And some of the things he said seemed almost scripted—as if he'd thought them out beforehand. He was using the word "celestial" when he could have just as easily said "stars" or "planets."

It'd all been such a surprise, the whole relationship—to think that a man like Neil would ever fall in love with me. I wasn't good enough for him. Somewhere in the back of my mind, I was sure it wasn't going to last. How could something that good last forever? But there was Neil, talking about forever. He had me look through the telescope. When I couldn't see anything, he fiddled around with the lens. "Wait, I think I found the problem. This is blocking your view." He pulled out a ring box and held it in front of me. Then, he was on his knees, holding my hand, promising, "I will always love you."

Will is still examining the ring. "It never hurts to celebrate the diamond anniversary early. You have a good eye for diamonds, Karl. Next time I'm shopping for jewelry, I'll have to take you along."

Karl eyes me up and down. I'm unadorned, except for some pearl earrings. He chuckles. "Anytime."

Will proves himself to be a master at mingling. By the time we sit down to dinner, I've met several members of congress, an advocate for the disabled, and the CEO of a major corporation. "I'm surprised we haven't talked politics at all," I admit, as I move my fork toward the elegant salad in front of me. "I thought this was supposed to be a political event."

Will raises his brows. "Politics is definitely a topic to avoid at political events."

"That's a relief."

Will places an arm across the top of my chair. "I've been dominating the conversation for a while now. I should let you decide on the next topic. What do you want to talk about?"

"Oh, I don't know—people, places, books."

His lips curl with amusement. "All right, let's start with people.

I'd like to talk about you. We'll start with where you were born and go from there."

"I guess I left myself open to that."

Will listens with interest to my less than fascinating life history, sharing bits of his own background whenever we have something in common. Actually, we have more in common than I ever would have thought. We both have parents who are divorced, and we're both converts. Like me, Will studied liberal arts in college. He also likes to run. If I could write it all down on paper, we would look like a perfect couple.

"I hope you like dancing," he says as we're finishing up our salmon in basil sauce. "The Four Tops are playing. They're an older group, but they sounded good last year."

We are one of the first couples out on the dance floor. I like the way Will dances. He's somehow found the perfect medium between doing a two-step and flinging his body around.

"How did you learn to dance so well?" I ask him during one of the slow songs. "Did you take lessons?"

"Not really."

"You danced in front of a mirror?"

"I wouldn't admit it if I did. No, the way I learned was much worse than dancing in front of a mirror. I had an old girlfriend who taught me. She was ruthless."

How many girlfriends are there in his background? Is he the type that dates a woman for a long time, and then breaks it off? Or is he the type to date lots of women for just a few dates? It's obvious he's an accomplished flirt. No one could build up this kind of chemistry on the first date without some serious practice.

Will and I like to sing along as we dance. He's a good singer too. And he makes me laugh between the dances by imitating the American Idol judges and pretending to critique our singing. I'm impressed that a guy as good looking and talented as Will can also be funny. He seems too perfect to be real—or at least too perfect to be unattached.

We are still singing together as Will parks his Jaguar in front of my apartment building. I wait for him to open my door, then I get out and lead him into the building. I've always felt that men read too much into whatever happens on the doorstep. Yes, I'm comfortable with Will, but I hardly know him. I'll have to be gentle but firm. There is no way I'm inviting him in. I push the elevator button and start in on the good night lines: "Thanks for everything. I had a really good time."

He takes my hand. "I did too."

The elevator opens and we get in. With some pain, I remember the last person who accompanied me on this elevator.

Will reaches for my waist with his other hand. "How about one more dance?"

Perhaps it is too calculated, but I agree to it. We dance around in the small elevator. If I don't say something now, I know I'll be in trouble, so I let it spill out. "I should probably tell you that I never kiss on the first date."

He spins me around as the elevator doors open and catch me in an embrace, holding his face an inch away from mine. "How about next Friday then?"

13

Sunday, July 14, 2002

Neil told me he loved me today. He whispered it into my ear during sacrament meeting—right in the middle of the high councilman's talk on the Word of Wisdom. I should have said, "I love you too," but instead I said, "Really?" I said it a little too loud and the people in front of us turned around.

Liz was sitting on the other side of me, but she didn't hear. It's the first time she's been to church in at least a year. The only problem was her dress. She's got this thing where she follows all the fashion advice in magazines.

Will and I arrive late for Dad's party, but we're still first to arrive. Felicia, Dad's new girlfriend, meets us at the door with mugs of hot cider. I'm trying to figure out why she's serving cider. It's only September. Dad's apartment is decorated in a fall theme with various displays clustered on tables and counters. Why are they displaying vitamins and kitchen tools? And what is a toilet seat doing in the corner beside the couch? I notice that an assortment of catalogs lies fanned out across the kitchen island, each with the title "Feel Fantastic!" That's when I realize with a flutter of embarrassment that this is an entirely different kind of party than I imagined. I've brought Will to a selling party. Nobody brings dates to these things. What is he going to think?

I peek sideways at him. He's sipping cider and glancing around. Based on the fact that he's wearing khakis and a polo shirt, I guess that he anticipated a real party, perhaps one next to a tennis court.

Felicia chatters on about how nice it is to finally meet me. She is a petite, dark-haired woman who wears fuchsia lipstick, a thick coat of foundation, and long, false eyelashes that remind me of daddy long legs spiders. She's dressed in a hot pink Indian sari. Six or seven gold bangles clatter together on each of her wrists.

I set my cider down beside the catalogs and introduce Will. I'm hoping Felicia is going to mention where Dad is. "It's so nice to meet you, Will," Felicia gushes in a Southern drawl. "I'm so glad you could come to our Feel Fantastic Fiesta."

Will clears his throat. "I'm glad I could come too."

Felicia sways her arms around in a circle. "Have a seat wherever y'all feel most comfortable."

I take a seat on the sofa beside Will. "Thanks, but we really can't stay long."

She turns on some New Age music, and then sits on the floor with her legs crossed in the yoga meditation pose. "Come on," she instructs. "Get comfortable." She rests her hands, palms up, on her knees. Since I'm wearing a skirt, I'm not about to follow her example. Maybe Mom was right about Felicia after all.

Felicia exhales deeply then speaks. "Feel Fantastic products are all about achieving your wildest dreams. So we're gonna start with a little get-to-know-you activity. I want y'all to close your eyes." I feel like a kindergartner. What is Will thinking? "Now I want y'all to think of what you want more than anything else. Where do you want to be five years from now? Ten years from now? Twenty years from now?"

In five years, I'll be thirty-two. In ten years, thirty-seven. In twenty, forty-seven. Time is going by much too quickly. I don't feel old enough to be twenty-seven. Next month, I'll be twenty-eight. Is this the way it is for everybody? Do little old ladies still feel like teenagers inside?

I've never been one to map out my life. I never planned to marry by a certain age or have children by a certain age. As long as I get married sometime and have children sometime. I tell myself that I have plenty of time. There is nothing to worry about. But more and more, I've felt impatient and anxious about the future.

Will takes hold of my hand. I give his hand a squeeze, trying to communicate how sorry I am to drag him into this whole thing and how grateful I am that he is putting up with it all. He squeezes back. I think that means something like, "You're welcome."

I hear the door open. "Y'all can open your eyes now," Felicia says.

Liz is standing with her back to the front door, still wearing her power suit from work. She's breathing as if she ran all the way up the stairs. "I've gotta talk to you guys before Dad gets here. He's parking the car." She pats her chest and tries to catch her breath. "Oh, hi Will. I didn't know you knew Anne." She glances down at his hand, which is still holding mine. "What was I going to say? Oh, Dad lost his job today. His company's been having layoffs, and his number finally came up. He wants to be the one to tell people, but I thought I'd better tell you first, so you don't freak out on him." She looks at me as she says this last part. "Anyway, try to act normal. I don't want him to know I told you." She walks into the kitchen and pours herself a cup of cider.

"We won't tell," I promise. "But how could they lay him off? He's worked there for almost twenty years."

Will squeezes my hand again. "It'll be okay. We'll help him find something. What does he do?" There is something so comforting about him holding my hand and telling me everything will be all right.

"He's an accountant," I whisper to Will.

"There are lots of opportunities with Feel Fantastic!" Felicia mentions, batting her eyelashes. "Speaking of which, we'd better get on with our little exercise. Why don't you tell me your dreams, Anne?"

"Oh," I sputter, caught off guard. Since I don't know what else to say, I decide to say what I'm really thinking—even if it sounds predictable. "I guess I'd like to get married and have a family some day." I'm in a hurry to get over with this part, and not just because Dad is on his way.

Felicia claps her hands. "Feel Fantastic is the best business for women with families. It's so flexible, and you'll have everything you need for a healthy family lifestyle. I think Feel Fantastic is exactly what you need to make your dreams come true. Let me show you this." She walks over to the kitchen and pulls out a poster with little squares connected to each other in the shape of a pyramid. "Now what Feel Fantastic does is it eliminates the middle man. You get all your products at wholesale prices, then you sell them at a profit."

"I'll have to remember that when I get married."

"There's no time like the present to get started. Once you start building your business, you'll see your dreams all falling into place. Why, you'll have a husband and children in no time. You just have to sign on. But I almost forgot Will. We want to know about your dreams too, Will."

Will laughs. "Are you sure you're ready for this? My dream is to become a billionaire."

I try to keep my mouth shut. His greatest dream is to become a billionaire? Doesn't he want to get married or have children? Doesn't he want to help people? How could he want so much money when people are starving all over the world? Maybe he's kidding.

The door opens, and Dad ambles in. It seems he's aged ten years since the last time I saw him. He actually stoops and it looks as if his hair has finally tipped the scales from mostly blond to mostly gray. He's lost his home and now he's lost his job. I completely forget my promise to Liz. I run up and throw my arms around him. "I'm so sorry, Dad."

"I was only six months away from a great retirement package," he says, shaking his head. "I guess I should have expected it. I just thought it wouldn't happen to me."

There is a long silence. I try to fill it. "You'll find another job, Dad. We'll all help you. Accountants are always in demand."

"Who's going to hire an old guy like me?"

"You're not old. You're in the prime of life. And you look younger than you are anyway."

"You do look young, Walter," Felicia adds, wedging her way between us. She runs her hand through his hair and gives him a movie star kiss right there in front of everyone. I take a few steps away from them.

Dad smiles a little and looks up for the first time. But his smile fades. "I'll never find as good a job. The salary and benefits were really—"

"I can do some networking for you," Will offers, standing up from his seat on the sofa. "I've got a lot of connections up on the hill. I think I know a few people who could use your skills. I wish I had my laptop with me."

"You can use mine," Felicia volunteers, running into the kitchen.

Soon, Will is at the computer, drawing up an impromptu resume while Dad tells him about his experience. I'm sitting next to Will with my hand curled around one of his perfect biceps. It seems so long ago that I teased Neil about Will's biceps. Back then, Will had been nothing more than a good-looking guy with a Jaguar. Now he is fitting himself into my life like some sort of missing puzzle piece. What would I have done without him tonight?

Mary hobbles in as they're wrapping up. Her face is splotchy, as if she's been crying. "Am I too late for the party? I would have come sooner, but I had to go to my ultrasound. It took forever."

Felicia smiles and waves her arms around in something that resembles the flamenco. "You're never too late for a Feel Fantastic Fiesta."

Mary looks at her, a bit confused. "Oh."

"Have a seat, honey," Dad calls out. "We're working on something for a minute. We'll be done soon."

Mary sits down on a bar stool at the kitchen island and I join her. "You haven't missed much," I whisper in her ear. "How'd the ultrasound go? You don't look too happy."

"I'm having another boy," Mary utters, her voice quivering.

"Is everything all right? Is he healthy?"

Mary bites her bottom lip and nods. I rub her back and resist the urge to tell Mary how lucky she is to be having a healthy baby. I think of Susan and Jack, who would give everything to have a baby, any baby. "You must have really enjoyed North Carolina. I never thought you'd stay so long. How long was it?"

Mary sniffs and rubs her nose with a tissue. "Almost two weeks. We would've stayed longer if it hadn't been for the ultrasound, that and Charlie's work. He's got to catch up on a lot."

"How's Lily doing?"

"She's a lot better. But she's different. I don't know how to describe it. It's like she's paranoid. She has nightmares about swimming in the ocean. And she's all of a sudden afraid of driving in a car and being up high. She didn't even want to go on the elevator to get to the Harvilles' apartment."

I don't dare ask about Neil. "I guess she's had a lot of visitors to help her."

"No, not really. Janet and Steve are still there. Other than that, she just sees the Harvilles and that weird guy, Jay. By the way, Charlie thinks he likes you. It'd be too weird if he did. Didn't his fiancée die less than a year ago?"

"I think that's what Dave told me."

"Well, even if he does like you, I wouldn't trust him unless he waits at least a year before falling in love again. He's not worth having if he doesn't."

"I'll keep that in mind."

By the time we leave, it's too late for the movie we planned to see. That's fine with me. I'm in the mood for a moonlit walk. There is a touch of fall crispness in the air as we set out across the parking lot. We walk up the hill to a subdivision with rambling sidewalks and overgrown trees. A big, full moon hangs in the sky. As we saunter along, Will wraps his arm around my shoulders.

I am so full of gratitude for all he's done for Dad that I think I'll let him kiss me. I'm overdue for some romance. It's been at least a year since I've been kissed—and that was a peck on the lips from a forty-year-old I met on a blind date. The guy actually wore white socks with his suit.

I walk close to him. "I really appreciate the way you're helping my dad."

He takes my hand. "It's nothing. I do that kind of thing all the time. Besides, he'll be fine. A man like him—a man with capital, I mean—can get a job wherever he wants. I wouldn't worry about him."

"I'm sorry about the whole party thing. I didn't know it was going to be a Feel Fantastic Fiesta. How embarrassing!"

Will laughs. "I'm not sure what your father sees in that woman. He could do a lot better."

"Well, he likes her. That's what matters."

"She sure would make for an embarrassing step-mother."

I'm surprised I didn't notice Will's dislike earlier at the party. He treated Felicia in the same cordial way he treated everyone else. He even looked through two of her catalogs and complimented her on her presentation skills. "Thanks for being patient anyway," I tell him. Being a little judgmental myself, I can relate to his feelings. So what if he is a little critical? Most people are critical every once in a while.

Will takes a call on his cell phone as we wander through the dark streets. How can you avoid eavesdropping in situations like this? The conversation has something to do with a tile floor. I entertain myself by looking into the windows of the houses we pass. Almost every one displays the blue glow of a television set. Occasionally, when the shades are open and the lights are on, I can size up a decorating scheme. Mirrors and framed pictures seem to be the norm.

After about fifteen minutes, Will says good-bye to the tile floor caller. "Sorry about that. I didn't mean for it to take so long."

By this time, I've found a street that snakes back down the hill to my apartment complex. "I'd better be getting home. It's getting late."

He takes my hand again. "I didn't realize you had a curfew."

"Gotta get my beauty sleep."

When we get to my apartment, he leans in and kisses me. It's long and tender, but it leaves me wanting to wipe my mouth. Leaning up against my door, I tell myself I need a little more time to get used to him. I already have my keys ready. "Thanks for everything."

He tickles the palm of my hand. "I had a great time."

Where did I leave that lip balm? "Me too."

"How about next Friday? I've got tickets to a concert."

"That sounds like fun."

The next morning, I'm up early. I have to meet Susan for breakfast, then we're shopping for blouses. We're supposed to wear harvest-colored blouses for the concert. Since neither one of us owns—or wants—a yellow, orange, or brown blouse, we're trying our luck at the thrift stores.

I have no trouble at all getting dressed this morning. Thrift stores demand nondescript attire, something that won't get you noticed. I settle on a pair of old jeans and a white T-shirt. Then I slip into my running shoes, stick my hair in a ponytail, and head out the door.

I am five minutes early when I turn the corner onto my old street and catch sight of the house, its windows gleaming in the golden morning light. As I'm about to pull into the driveway, I notice the SUV right there in front of me. Neil is here. Instead of stopping, I keep right on going down the street, turn at the corner and pull to the side of the road. I flip down the visor and gaze into the tiny mirror. Whipping the mascara out of my purse, I pray that I'll stay calm. "Help me to get over him," I plead, but all the while I feel my prayer is in vain. A little blush, a little lipstick—it's all I can do. There is no logical reason to be so nervous. If I really want to get over him, I'm going to have to stop this kind of thing. I shouldn't care how I look. I start the car again and drive back to the house.

I don't think I'll ever get over the smell of the old yard—that strange mix of mossy oak trees, boxwoods, mud, and wet grass. Inhaling, I think of childhood tea parties in the grove of trees to the side of the house. I walk up the flagstone path, climb the steps to the porch and knock. Ringing the doorbell would be too bold for the way I'm feeling. If no one answers, I'll sit on the squeaky, old porch swing for a few minutes. I'm about to do just that when the doorknob twists and the door swings open, revealing the first and last person I want to see at the moment.

It is obvious that Neil was not expecting to see me. He stands, looking at me for a moment in confusion before he returns my greeting. I congratulate myself for having more self-composure than he does—now that's a first. It gives me a little jolt of pleasure to see the redness rising in his face. "Hi Neil, can you tell Susan I'm here?"

He clears his throat. "Jack didn't tell me you were coming. He just asked me to get the door. I'll go get Susan." He closes the door, then opens the door again to invite me inside. I tell him I prefer to wait outside.

I try not to smile too much as I push myself back and forth on the swing. He was embarrassed. There are only two possible reasons for this. It could be a symptom of pride—maybe he was ashamed of the shabby old jeans he's wearing. Or he's attracted to me. Do I dare to hope?

After a minute, Neil reappears on the porch wearing a nicer pair of jeans, providing me with at least a partial glimpse into his psyche.

He explains that Susan is still getting ready, then he stands in silence beside the swing. Finally, he says, "Those boxwoods sure smell good."

"I was thinking the same thing." I scoot to the side of the swing. "Why don't you have a seat?"

He sits beside me with a certain stiffness, completely unlike himself. Is he already engaged to Lily and embarrassed to be seen sitting out on the porch with another woman? I scoot further to my side of the swing. "How's Lily?"

"She's doing better. There's nothing to worry about anymore."

"That's good."

He looks at the seat of the swing and runs his finger along a patch of peeling paint. "You were really amazing, Anne, during the whole thing."

"It wasn't that big of a deal. Most people would've done the same thing."

Our eyes meet. "Anne, I know how most people are during emergencies. You weren't like most people."

"I didn't know what I was doing at all. There were a few times in the ambulance when I thought she was going to die."

He is still looking into my eyes. "I was afraid too."

I look away, pretending to be distracted by a squirrel running up the big oak beside the porch. "Well, I'm glad she's okay. Now you two can be happy."

"Yeah?" he says as if it's a question.

I don't know what to say to keep this going. He's looking at me, and I have nothing in my mind except the awkwardness of being in love with him still. The conversation is too heavy to carry. I feel like an economy car trying to cross the Continental Divide with four hundred pounds of sand in the trunk. I already betrayed myself once—crying in his car on the way out of the hospital. Now, I'm going to be strong and silent like a man. I am determined not to let my imagination trick me into thinking that he might have feelings for me. I have to remember that he's dating Lily.

He shifts sideways on the swing, so he's facing me. "You miss it. Don't you?"

It takes me a while before I realize he means the house. I can handle talking about the house. "Yeah. I guess there's something magical about the place where you grow up. There are a lot of good memories." It is so strange to be talking with my ex-boyfriend in front of the house that is no longer mine.

Neil stares at me as if he can look right through my eyes into every corner of my mind. I feel so transparent. "It's okay to miss the way things used to be." He is pulling me back into another whirlpool of wishful thinking. "I sometimes feel the same way."

Why does he have to say things in such a vague way? I grasp for something more concrete. "How are your parents doing?" I never met Neil's parents. They were on a mission in Spain while we were dating.

"I guess I never told you. My father passed away—it was a little while after they got back from their mission." I catch a glimpse of Susan peeking through the window at us. "He had pancreatic cancer, but they never really knew about it until the last month of his life."

That must have been shortly after we broke up. "I'm sorry." I fight the urge to touch him.

"My mom's remarried now. They live out in Utah. My stepfather's a nice guy, but it's not the same. I have four stepsisters now. Every time I visit, I end up going on three or four blind dates."

I laugh. Susan leans out the door to promise that she is almost ready. I wait for Neil to speak next. After what seems like a long time, he says, "I'm glad we've gotten to know each other again."

I'm sure I'm blushing as I look at him. "Me too."

Whatever Neil reads in my eyes, Susan must be able to read it too. "Neil's quite a catch," she says as we pull out of the driveway. When I don't respond, she adds, "He's the kind of guy who needs clear signals from a woman. So many women chase after him that he's never sure when someone's interested. I'm not saying he's conceited because he isn't. I'm only saying that a woman has to be bold. Do you know what I mean?"

"I think so. Lily's that way."

"She is, but I don't know if she's right for Neil."

"Why do you say that?"

"It's just a feeling."

I keep her words in my mind, letting them roll around like a handful of pebbles in a rock tumbler. If there is any hidden message behind them, maybe time will reveal it.

14

Saturday, July 20, 2002

This morning, Neil and I drove until we got ourselves completely lost. By the time we stopped, we were way out in the country, where they still have rolling green fields and woods that go on and on. There was a country store, kind of a mix between a farmer's market and a craft shop. That's where we got our lunch—strawberries and peanut brittle.

He's been telling me he loves me for seven days now, but I honestly don't feel any pressure to say, "I love you too." I wish I could be as confident about my feelings as he is. I want to be in love with him, but I'm waiting until I'm sure. He deserves me to be sure.

It is a blue-sky day at the end of September. Apples shine red on the trees. Flocks of geese honk as they fly south. The morning is cool enough that I need a cardigan as I walk across the dewy, morning fields with Will on the way to our balloon ride. The muddy ground sucks my sneakers in with each step. One red, yellow, and blue balloon is already in the air, floating above us. The other balloon—I guess it's the one we'll ride—is waiting for us on the ground a few hundred yards away.

After a few minutes of instruction from the pilot, we board the envelope. The burners roar, heating the air and lifting the balloon high into the sky. The wind pushes us along over the fields, but we don't feel it. We are one with the wind, floating and drifting.

Once the balloon gets high enough, the pilot turns off the burners and pours champagne glasses full of sparkling cider. Will must have arranged the alcohol-free twist ahead of time. I admire him for it.

Everything is silent. We look down on woods full of trees, houses on hills, farms with horse pastures, orchards, and towns. Will stands behind me and holds me around the waist.

It's only Will, the pilot, and me. In some ways, it might be more private if we had a couple more passengers. Three is definitely a crowd on a balloon.

I should be feeling romantic. Here I am with a handsome man, drinking from stemmed crystal, looking at beautiful scenery. We've been dating for a month. Shouldn't I be feeling something by now? I can't think of a reason not to fall in love with him. Why don't I fall in love with him? I enjoy spending time with him. We have great conversations. He's helping Dad get a job. He's sent me roses twice. He's smart. And he smells great. But somehow all these little things that should add up to an emotional attachment never manage to evolve into anything greater than a jumble of thoughts in my mind.

Will rests his head beside mine and whispers. "I missed you while I was away." He was gone all last week on business.

"I missed spending time with you, too." It's true. I missed going out with him. His dates are always extraordinary—a concert at the Kennedy center, lunch at a French restaurant, sailing on the Chesapeake Bay. I can't deny that I enjoy them. But they're the kind of dates you go on to celebrate an anniversary or to propose marriage— high-pressure dates. And I'm beginning to feel the pressure.

I shy away from relationship talk. "This is a great way to start General Conference weekend."

"To tell the truth, babe, I wasn't thinking about General Conference."

Babe? "I wonder who's going to be sustained as the new apostle."

"Did I tell you how beautiful you look this morning?"

"I think you did."

He kisses me. It is such a long kiss that I want to open my eyes and check if the pilot is watching. Once it's over, I break away from him to point out a stream we're passing over. I try to keep him busy that way, pointing out the sights for the rest of the trip.

Luckily, our hour in the air ends sooner than I expected. We land with a couple of bumps in the middle of a farmer's field. During all the jostling, Will takes the opportunity to hug me tightly. Once we stop, he helps me out of the envelope, lifting me in the process. Then he insists on carrying me over the puddle we landed in. I feel like a cavewoman thrown over the back of a Neanderthal. "Really, Will, put me down. I don't mind getting muddy."

"And I don't mind carrying you, babe," he responds, breathing heavily.

During the van ride back to Will's car, he tells me about all the networking he's doing for Dad. He's managed to line up a couple of interviews for the next week. Maybe if he'd told me this before he kissed me in the balloon, it would have made a difference.

My cell phone is ringing as we get into the jaguar. It's Liz. I know as soon as I hear her voice that it can't be good news. Liz never calls before noon. "I've been trying to call you all morning, Anne. We're over at the hospital. Dad's had a heart attack. The doctors are doing a coronary angioplasty on him right now. It's that thing where they put a little balloon in his artery to open it up."

Listening to my conversation, Will must sense what's going on. He's already racing along the little country road. For once, I'm glad Will likes to test out the speed and accuracy of his car, along with his state of the art, illegal-in-the-state-of-Virginia radar detector.

As we race along, I run through the worst case scenario in my mind. Dad could be dying in the hospital. Then comes the guilt of what brought it on. Selling his house, selling his possessions, and then losing his job. It was too much stress for him to take. I should have realized it before. He is getting to be an old man after all. Maybe he had to sell the house, but did I have to persuade him to sell all those other things too? And the other day, I dropped by with a copy of a book about job hunting. I could have just as easily taken him out to dinner.

Once on my mission, I visited a dying old woman, lying with her eyes closed under a dark blue sheet. The old woman breathed slowly, each breath raspy and long. There was a smell in the little cinder block house I can only describe as sweet and bubbly. The woman's daughter knelt beside her, singing and mopping her mother's face with cool water from a white plastic bucket. There, in Cape Verde, I wasn't an intruder on death. I knelt beside the daughter, held the woman's hand, even learned to sing part of the song. It was almost peaceful, and I think the old woman looked forward to it.

I haven't had to be around death for years. Now, here it is, taunting me again. Dad isn't even sixty yet. I don't know the first thing about planning a funeral or picking out headstones or calling mortuaries. We've never even discussed the possibility. "Please don't let him die," I plead in prayer. "I'm not ready."

15

Monday, July 29, 2002

Mom was back in the hospital today. She collapsed at work, and they called an ambulance. Liz and I went over as soon as we found out. It was so hard to see her so pale in that horrible hospital gown, unable to eat anything. Before she got cancer, she always seemed kind of immortal to me. Now, it's like she's barely alive. I asked her if she'd like a blessing, but she refused. I wish that she could take comfort in the gospel the way I have. Even now, seeing her this way, I feel a kind of peace, a reassurance that life doesn't end with death. No matter what, everything will be okay in the end. I wish I could help Mom see things the way I do.

Less than an hour after we left the balloon, Will is leading me through the halls of another unfamiliar hospital. I hate the smell, this strange mix of plastic and antiseptic. It makes my stomach cramp, remembering the frightening hour spent with Lily in the emergency room. But this is worse. This is my father, the man who raised me almost single-handedly after Mom left.

Will locates the room. We enter and see Dad covered with wires and tubes—oxygen through the nose, monitors on the chest, and an IV on his arm. Dad smiles at us in his usual way and apologizes, "I didn't mean to worry you, Anne. I just thought I'd better come in and get things checked out."

"It's a good thing you did," I respond.

"They've got me fixed up now. That angioplasty wasn't as bad as I thought. I was in and out in about an hour. The doctor said I should be back to normal in a few days. I won't even have a scar." He is pale, but otherwise the same. Liz is standing beside him, talking on her cell phone.

I sink down into a chair beside his bed, then the words tumble out of my mouth. "Dad, I'm sorry I've been so hard on you lately. You've been a great dad, and I'm so proud of you. I've been so bossy. I hope I haven't stressed you out." There is more I want to say, but putting it all into words at this moment is out of my power.

Dad looks at me with his tired eyes. "Stress is a part of life, Anne. It's not your fault."

I reach for his hand. "I love you, Dad."

Liz snaps her phone shut. "Did I hear Anne admit that she's bossy?" she asks. When no one answers, she looks up at Will, standing behind me with his hands on my shoulders. She sighs and gets back on her cell phone.

Dad lets go of my hand, reaches for the remote control, and turns on the television. "I wonder if we can get the game here." Thus ends my attempt at a heart-to-heart. It was the wrong time. He's afraid of dying, and I've given him the "here's what I want to tell you before you die" speech.

Felicia drifts in, covered in a yellow chiffon flapper dress. She is wearing a big, floppy hat to match. "Don't I look like a big, yellow daffodil?" she questions in her saccharine sweet Southern drawl. She plants a kiss on the patient. He responds in a whisper, then the kissing continues. Felicia tops the football game in a way no one else can.

Will squeezes my shoulders. "It looks like your dad's okay for now. Why don't we go get something to eat?"

I stand up and announce that we'll be in the cafeteria, but no one hears me.

"I'm not sure that's the best thing for his heart," I whisper after we've left the room.

Will puts his arms around me. "How could kissing be bad for your heart?"

"I guess you're right."

"This probably isn't the best time to bring this up, babe, but I think she's after his money."

I suppress a laugh. That is one thing I really don't have to worry about. With Dad as penniless as he's ever been, without a job or a house, Felicia has to be attracted to something less tangible than his money. "From what I've seen, I think Felicia has more money than he does."

"Wow, I would've never guessed."

We sit in the stark cafeteria at a cramped booth, eating ham and cheese sandwiches on white bread and watching a news broadcast on a television that hangs from the ceiling. Ham and cheese is not the worst choice we could have made. Other choices include fried chicken, shriveled hot dogs, and nachos. Will tastes his sandwich and struggles to swallow it. "Why don't I go get some take-out?"

"If you leave, I'll have to stay here by myself. Why do they serve such unhealthy food at hospitals? Isn't it supposed to be a healing environment?"

"I guess they have to strike a balance between healing and comfort."

I feel guilty that I didn't ever teach Dad to cook. I always meant to do it, knowing it would save him money. Now, I'm not only going to have to teach him to cook, I'm going to have to teach him to cook low fat, low salt, and high fiber. Maybe if he hadn't eaten so much fast food and take-out, he wouldn't be in the hospital at all. How much is it all going to cost? Does he even have insurance? I really shouldn't be thinking this way. I should be happy he's alive. I should be grateful.

Will looks over at the television. "I wonder how the game's going." He stands up to change the channel on the television but just ends up cycling back to the news channel. "I guess this is the best thing on."

As we're finishing our sandwiches, my mother walks into the cafeteria. Her hair is a perfectly styled blonde poof. She wears a pair of jeans with a crease ironed down the middle of each leg, red loafers, and a red blazer. Her reading glasses hang from a chain around her neck. She is talking on her cell phone with a client as she walks in. I motion for her to sit down with us. I introduce her to Will while she's still on the phone. "Saturday is a busy day for Mom," I explain. "She's a real estate agent."

Will seems to understand. He shakes her hand and says as much as he can to a person talking on the phone.

After another few minutes, Mom finally snaps her phone shut, rolls her eyes, and apologizes to Will. "You'll have to excuse my talking on the phone. Another agent's covering for me, but this particular client—well, I've been working with her now for almost a year and she's finally found a house she wants to buy, and, of course, someone else made an offer on it this morning. Could there have been a worse time for Walter to have a heart attack? Poor Walter. He's always had bad timing. And what's with that girlfriend of his? You'd think she'd know to lay off all the kissing when his ex-wife is in the room. I couldn't stand it. I had to get out of there. But enough about me. I'm so glad to finally meet you, Will. Anne's told me so much about you."

In reality, I haven't told Mom anything at all about Will. I only mentioned that I was dating a lobbyist I met in North Carolina. But it doesn't seem to matter. The two hit it off immediately. They both make their living by being agreeable, so together they achieve what they must consider to be introduction nirvana. Will asks about the real estate market in Virginia and mentions that he owns rental property in North Carolina. Mom asks about the market in North Carolina. They discuss the challenges of renting out properties, then go on to discuss Will's latest remodeling project.

I feel like I've dialed the wrong number. If I could, I'd apologize and hang up on the whole conversation. My eyes wander toward the television, where two news anchors discuss the football game. The word stream running across the bottom of the screen mentions Baltimore. "Three off-duty officers shot in Baltimore," it reads. My chest tightens. Three officers? Does that mean police officers? I keep reading the streamer, but I can't find anything else about the three officers. How can anyone learn anything about the news from those things?

Will and Mom are talking about granite countertops. My eyes are glued to the news. Surely they have to say something else about the officers. I want to be moving, doing something. I bounce my legs up and down under the table. There is a weather forecast, a commercial break, news about a bill in the Senate, and a story about a lost dog. What if Neil is one of the officers? What if he's dying? I want to fly out of this room, access the Internet, and find out what happened. Still, I wouldn't find out the most important detail—who was shot.

"Are you all right, Anne?" Mom asks. "You don't look well. Why don't you get her some water, Will?" Will dutifully walks off across the cafeteria, digging his hand into his pocket—he isn't the tap water type. I'll definitely have to pay him back. Mom leans across the table. "I really like him, Anne. He's the best thing that's happened to you in a long time. And to think, I came expecting only bad news, but I've found something to be really happy about."

I don't get a chance to make a phone call until we're back in Dad's hospital room. While the others are watching the game, I drift out to the lobby. With trembling fingers, I find Neil's number on my phone and push the button. It rings seven times—I'm counting. One more ring and I'm going to hang up.

"Hi, Anne. What's up?" The sound of his voice makes my knees wobble.

It strikes me now how vulnerable I must seem, calling because of a news report. "I saw the news. I wanted to make sure you were okay."

"You were worried about me?" He sounds surprised. Maybe I shouldn't have called.

"Well, yeah. I mean, there were three officers shot in Baltimore, and the news didn't exactly say who they were. I thought I should call. You know, to make sure you're okay. That's a pretty high percentage of officers, isn't it? Three out of—how many are there?"

"About three thousand," Neil responds. I calculate in my head—less than one percent. "But it's nice of you to think about me. Listen I've got someone on the other line."

"Oh, I'll get off. I wanted to make—"

"No, just let me say good-bye to the other person."

"I don't want to interrupt anything. I really only just wanted to—" What did I want to do? I'm digging a deeper and deeper hole for myself.

"If you're going to argue with me, I guess I'll have to leave her on the other line until she hangs up."

Her? "Are you talking to Lily?" Of course he's talking to Lily. Why did I even ask?

"Yeah, but we're through talking. Hang on a sec."

"No, really, I've got to get going. I'm at the hospital with my dad. I should probably get back to him."

"Is everything okay?"

"Yeah. He had a heart attack, but he's all right now."

"I'm sorry."

"He's doing better now . . . You should really get back to Lily. I'm sorry to bother you. Bye."

"It really wasn't a bother."

"Bye," I repeat, resolving never ever to call Neil Wentworth again.

"Bye."

I turn to go back to Dad's room and run right into Will. How much of our conversation did he hear? "Who was that?"

"Oh, a friend. I was explaining about Dad."

16

Wednesday, July 30, 2002

I can't deny it anymore. I'm in love with Neil Wentworth. I don't know quite how to explain everything I'm feeling. I know that being with Neil is right for me. He makes me a better person. It's not just an emotional feeling. It's spiritual too. I know Heavenly Father approves it.

The fact that my mother disapproves still worries me. I think she's wrong about Neil—I think he has plenty of ambition. I have to convince him to give up this whole police officer idea. He's so smart, he could be anything he wants.

Things start to fall apart around the second week of October. First, it's my refrigerator. It makes a loud, whirring sound, almost like a helicopter. I decide I'd better repair it before the neighbors start to complain. Then, it's my car. It gets so anemic that I can't accelerate to more than twenty-five miles an hour. I suppose that's what I deserve for owning a ten-year-old car. I make the mistake of telling Will about it. I don't know what it is about him and cars, but he's determined to take it to his mechanic—all the way in Gaithersburg. So I let him.

It's only after I get the refrigerator fixed (Marcy is out of town) that I find out how much the car is going to cost me—$2500. Maybe it wasn't such a great idea to use Will's mechanic. Since I can't afford both the repair and a rental car, I'm stuck getting rides to and from work—sometimes from Liz and sometimes from Will. I know I should have rented a car, but if watching Dad has taught me anything, it's to spend less and save more. I've been doing better at saving lately. I have enough to cover the repairs. Still, by the end of the week, the stress of carpooling is taking its toll. It starts as a cough and sore throat, then proceeds to a fever and headache.

I cancel my Friday night date with Will—we'd planned to go to a dinner theater. Even though I would have liked the play, I'm almost relieved not to have to spend more time with Will. I can't justify my feelings or explain them to anyone very clearly. I feel, though, that there is something I can't trust about him. He is too congenial. He always says the right thing. He never slips, never says anything tactless or impolite. Everything about him is calculated to impress. It's as if he's always on stage, always playing a part. He's one way with Dad, another way with Mom. What's he like when he isn't around me? Do I even know the real Will?

The single life is a life of uncertainty. I'll always wonder if or when I'll get married. But I remind myself that everyone has to deal with uncertainty. Some people worry about having a job or whether they'll ever have children. Others have disabled children and worry for their future. My particular uncertainty is marriage. Yes, I want to get married, but not to just anyone. I want the right person. Romance—it's one of those things that seems so unimportant, yet, in a way, it is at the center of everything.

I lie on the couch, wearing sweats, watching old movies and blowing my nose for most of Friday night and Saturday. I don't want to think about Will or Neil or anyone else. For now, Cary Grant will do.

Around four o'clock on Saturday, right in the middle of *That Touch of Mink*, Janet Musgrove calls. I answer it. (I've gotten into the habit of keeping my phone charged.) "Hi, Anne," Janet croons, "it's so good to hear your voice. How are you doing? I haven't seen you in so long. It seems like forever."

I try not to cough. "I'm fine." Why is it that I always say I'm fine when I'm not? Maybe I have more in common with Will Grandin than I realize.

"That's good. We're having a little get-together tonight: dinner and dessert. And we were wondering if you'd like to come. We haven't had everyone together since before the accident. Of course, Lily's still down in North Carolina. But she's so much better. Steve and I thought we ought to do something to celebrate. And you were such a big help with Lily, we had to invite you. Of course, it's all thrown together at the last minute, but we were hoping you'd be free."

"I'd love to, but I think I'm coming down with the flu. I'd better sit this one out."

"Why didn't you say so, honey? You should always tell me when you're sick. I'll have Steve bring you over something later. How's that?"

"That's so sweet of you, but really I'm fine. I have plenty to eat here."

"He'll be over there around five."

At four thirty, the doorbell rings. It's the florist, bringing another vase of red roses from Will. I set them in the middle of the kitchen table. The card reads: "Hope you're feeling better. Love, Will." I'll call to thank him after the movie. It is the third vase of red roses he's sent in a month. I'm beginning to feel guilty. Will has spent a lot of money on me, and he isn't really getting much of a return on his investment.

At five, right as Cary Grant comes down with hives, the doorbell rings again. Janet Musgrove has to be the most punctual cook on the planet. My voice is hoarse, but I still manage to call out as I sit up from my nest of blankets and pillows on the sofa. "Come on in, Steve. It's open."

I hear the doorknob twist while I'm looking for the remote to pause the movie. "You shouldn't leave your door unlocked," Steve says, but it isn't Steve. His voice is different. "Anyone could walk into your apartment."

I look up to see Neil, standing there in jeans and a blue flannel shirt. He carries a paper bag full of food. "Did I scare you?" I'm too stunned to answer the question. I can't breathe. He closes the door. "I should have called ahead."

I get up to turn off the television, but Neil holds out his free hand to stop me. "I'll get that. You sit there." Even with the flu, I can smell the sandalwood. He turns off the television, then walks back to the kitchen to put down the bag of food. "Nice flowers," I hear him call from the kitchen. "Who gave them to you?"

"A friend." My voice sounds husky and a little squeaky.

He pokes his head out from the kitchen. "How long have you been dating him?"

I'll have to tell the truth, but hopefully not all of it. "A few weeks."

He walks over and put his hand on my forehead. "You do have a fever."

"You shouldn't get too close. It's probably contagious."

"I'll be fine. Have you taken anything for it?"

"No. How's Lily?"

His hand is still on my forehead. It feels cool and soft. "Better than you are. I think you need to go to the doctor."

"I'll be fine. I just need some rest."

"If it's okay with you, I'll bring you something to eat. Janet sent over some chicken soup."

I hear Neil talking on his phone in the kitchen. "Hey, I'm here at Anne's. She's pretty sick. I think I'll be here a while. I'm gonna see if she'll let me take her to the doctor." What is it with him always having to rescue me? Is it his way of proving his superiority? Is it some sort of revenge? Or is he still trying to pay me back for helping Lily?

"Neil," I call after he's hung up. "We have to talk."

"Okay," he says, walking back into the room and sitting on the opposite end of the couch from me. He leans back against the cushions. "Let's talk."

"I wish you didn't feel like you always have to rescue me. I'm really fine. I don't need you to rescue me. I can take care of myself."

"You can't dump your ex-boyfriend. That's the one good thing about it."

"I mean it, though. It's becoming a pattern."

"I'm not trying to rescue you all the time, Anne. You need to be rescued all the time." He stands up again and walks into the kitchen. I hear him opening cabinets and starting the microwave. I lie down on the sofa and close my eyes. "Do you need anything from the store? Looks like you could use some Ben and Jerry's." I should never have told him about the ice cream.

I stand up and walk to the bathroom to wash my hands. While I'm there, I take the time to brush my hair and put on some inconspicuous makeup. He won't notice. As long as it's not overdone, men never notice subtle things like mascara and blush. I dig around in the medicine cabinet until I find my old bottle of coconut oil perfume. There is still a little left in the bottom. Do I dare? I dab some on my wrists. It's what he deserves for wearing that sandalwood stuff all the time.

I walk across the hall to the bedroom and change my clothes. Maybe I won't seem so pitiful if I'm wearing better clothes. And it won't hurt if I look really good in them. No, I can't compete with Lily in the curves department, but at least I can hint around that I have some. I settle on a pair of jeans and a purple T-shirt that drapes nicely over my waist and hips.

Neil is sitting at the table waiting for me when I come out. He's set the table for two with Marcy's good china. He's surprised. It's completely obvious from his full-tooth smile and the way his eyebrows rise. I push the flowers to the side of the table. He still hasn't said anything. He's looking at me. I ask if he'd like to say the prayer, not even guessing he'll pray for me to feel better. Listening to him pray sends me back eight years. He hasn't lost that missionary spirit.

The soup is one of my favorites. Janet Musgrove makes thick, homemade noodles. The chicken is soft. The broth is simple with a hint of garlic. The carrots and celery are always slightly crisp. I feel better the moment I taste it.

Neil still hasn't tasted it. He's just looking at me with half a smile. "Can I tell you a secret?"

He is going to tell me something about Lily. He is going to propose to Lily. I'm going to have to spend the rest of my life watching them be happy together, and I'm going to be the first to know about it. I'm going to have to congratulate him.

I wrinkle my nose. "If you want."

"You act like it's a bad thing, but it's not. I'm all fired up about it, and I haven't been able to tell anyone." Of course he's all fired up. He's about to marry Lily. He leans toward me. "But I know you won't tell anyone. And you're friends with the people involved." It's true.

I'm friends with Lily. I should be happy for her. "Do you want to try and guess what it is?"

I shake my head and eat another spoonful of soup. I can't bring myself to talk about it.

Neil leans back in his chair and draws in a breath. "It looks like I'm going to be an uncle. The adoption agency called Jack and Susan about it yesterday. It's a little girl. She's due in a couple of weeks."

My feverish brain takes a minute to process the information. "Jack and Susan are getting a baby. That's wonderful." I reach my hand out and pat Neil's. "Congratulations." He puts his other hand on top of mine, making a hand sandwich. Then he wraps his fingers around my hand and squeezes. He isn't looking at me, though. He's looking at the vase of flowers.

After a while, he lets go of my hand and nods toward the flowers. "So, how soon is this guy going to join our club?"

"What club?"

"You know—Charlie and me and all your other ex-boyfriends."

He really is bitter. How am I supposed to answer that? I look down at my soup. I take another bite and chew, trying to think of a response. My nose is starting to run again. I dab at it with a tissue. "I didn't realize you had a club."

He laughs. "I didn't mean to upset you. I was just wondering—"

"How's Lily?"

"You already asked me that. She's fine."

The doorbell rings. I'm only too glad to step away from the conversation for awhile. Swinging open the door, I see that it's Liz, wearing a short-sleeve black angora sweater with black leather pants. She's teased her hair into an eighties style. "Anne, I'm having the strangest problem. All my checks are bouncing. But I swear I haven't been spending too much. I've been writing everything down in the register like you said."

"I'll get the laptop. Why don't you have a seat. You remember Neil, don't you? He came over to bring me some food from Janet Musgrove. I've had the flu."

Neil stands up to shake her hand. Liz looks him up and down. She puts one hand on her hip and winks at him. Then she takes his hand in hers. "Of course I remember you, Neil. You are looking really good."

I set up the laptop across the table from Neil. I know Liz's account number and password better than my own. Liz smacks her lips. "You don't look sick to me."

I stare at the computer screen. "I have a fever."

Neil still hasn't said anything. He's standing up with his arms folded.

Liz giggles. "It's a good thing I never get sick or I'd be out of here. Who sent the flowers?"

"Will," I answer. "Why don't you two sit down?"

Liz sits down and scoots her chair toward Neil's. "Will Grandin is sure a catch. I don't know how you did it, Anne. I've been trying to capture him for years. Maybe I needed to be a little more boring."

"Thanks," I say. Neil looks at me and laughs. It's a déjà vu moment. We've found humor in Liz's conceit before.

Liz leans over to smell the roses. "I didn't mean it that way. I just meant. I don't know what I meant. I meant that maybe I need to think about boring things more often. You know, the stuff you read in newspapers. Maybe Will is one of those guys who likes brainy girls."

"Brainy women," I correct her.

"I don't know when I'd find the time to read the paper. I've already had to cut back on my beauty routine. My hairdresser will kill me if I cut back anymore."

I struggle not to laugh. "Just be yourself, Liz. You don't have to read the paper if you don't want to."

Liz walks her fingers across the table toward Neil. "I'm surprised you're still single," she purrs. "If you ever want to get to know someone new, I know a lot of eligible women, including myself." Why is she flirting with him?

"I already have someone in mind," Neil replies.

"He's dating Lily," I explain.

"Oh," Liz exclaims, "she's really cute. I can see why you like her."

I cut in. "I think I found your problem. Some place called 'Post-Dated' is taking $200 out of your account every week."

"Are you serious? I've never used a dating service in my life. Oh wait, that's one of those money stores. I borrowed some money from them, but I didn't borrow that much. Have you seen their ads? You give them a canceled check and your car title. Felicia told me she uses them all the time—never has any trouble. I borrowed it for a good cause. I've started investing. Felicia's showing me how."

I let out my breath slowly. "Those check-cashing stores charge a high interest rate. That's why you have to pay back so much. Did you keep the papers you signed?"

Liz shakes her head and points out a cockroach crawling along the top of the kitchen wall. This is the sort of thing that seems to happen every time I'm around Neil. Even the bugs conspire against me. Neil, once again slipping into his knight-in-shining-armor mode, has the honor of squishing it.

My phone rings. This time it's Marcy. I'd forgotten that today is the day she arrives home from a month-long business trip. She needs a ride home from the airport. "Liz," I beg with my hand over the phone, "is there any way you could pick up Marcy at the airport? My car's still in the shop."

Liz twists a lock of her hair. "I wish I could, Anne, but I've got a lot going tonight. You know, I'm not your chauffeur."

"I can get her," Neil offers. "Just show me her picture."

Liz puffs out her lips and tilts her head toward Neil. "You'll never be able to find her. I'll have to go along with you."

"I thought you said you had a lot going on tonight," I interject.

"Don't worry about it, Anne," Liz responds. "I can rearrange my schedule." She stands up and turns to Neil. "My sister is such a worrier." She grabs his arm. "We better get going."

Neil smiles at me as they head out the door. "See you in a little while . . . if you're not asleep."

I am filled with so much euphoria that I hardly notice my stuffy head and achy legs. As illogical as it seems, Neil wants to be around me. And some of the things that happened just now make me highly suspicious—the way he looked at me, the way he held my hand, and the way he said, "I've already got someone in mind." There is no way I'll be able to sleep tonight.

17

Thursday, August 1, 2002

I had my first fight with Neil today. It was about his whole obsession with becoming a police officer. I think it's such a bad idea, but he can't seem to see things from my point of view. I tell him it's dangerous; he says it's not as dangerous as everyone thinks. I tell him he'll hate the hours; he says he'll enjoy the flexibility. I tell him he could do so much more with his life; he says the country needs good men to be officers. I tell him that people will hate him; he says popularity is overrated. It was like arguing with my family, except we didn't yell, and Neil didn't seem very angry.

If only things could stay the way they've been this summer, and I'd never have to worry about guns and criminals. I can't believe I have to go back to school in three weeks. Then Neil and I'll have one of those long distance relationships people are always talking about. I really hope he decides not to become a police officer—maybe if I pray really hard.

I wake up face down on the sofa with my hair in my mouth. I can hear voices. Liz and Neal must have gotten back from the airport with Marcy. There is someone else too. Liz is making introductions. I'm too tired to move and too scared to know what I'll look like if I do move. As Liz continues the introduction, I realize with horror who the fourth person is. It's Will. If anyone tries to wake me, I'll have to fake a coma. The only thing worse than having Will and Neil in the room together would be having to talk to both of them at the same time.

I never imagined that everyone in my life could get so mixed up together. There was something so satisfying in having Neil wonder about the mystery man who sent the roses. Now he recognizes him as the guy from North Carolina, the one he doesn't trust.

Marcy must already know Will too. They're talking about their work on the hill. Will says something about a resume he's working on for Dad. Liz offers to take it to him. They're whispering. I can't hear everything they say. Liz mentions the flowers. Will asks her what she thinks of them. Liz assures him that they're excellent in every way. Then she says something about his jacket. Liz's voice is getting nearer and nearer. Until she sits down on the sofa—right on top of my head.

Liz squeals, hopping back up to her feet. "Anne, I didn't know you were there. Why were you sleeping on the sofa, anyway? There were so many blankets piled up on you I couldn't tell you were there."

I roll onto my back and pull the blanket over my face. "Are you okay, Anne?" Neil asks. It's the first thing I've heard him say since they arrived. I'm reminded of the scene in *Ben Hur* when Judah goes to visit the leper colony to find his sister, who tries to hide under a blanket. In the movie, Judah pulls the blanket off her face while she cries, then he embraces her. I imagine Neil ripping the blanket off me, then kissing me and carrying me off to some more romantic setting—away from Will and Liz and even Marcy. Someplace with palm trees would be ideal.

"Are you okay, Anne?" This time it's Will asking.

I sit up and open my eyes. I see Neil standing over me, but I feel myself blacking out almost immediately afterward. "I think I'm going to . . ."

Liz shrieks. "Don't throw up on me. I'm wearing leather."

"I think she's feeling faint," Neil says. "She sat up too fast."

Will rushes to the sofa. "I can take care of her. What can I get you, Anne? Shouldn't you have your head between your knees."

Lying down again, I open my eyes to see Will's face right above mine. "I'm fine," I insist. "I wasn't expecting company. I mean, I wasn't expecting all of you to come at once." What am I saying? "I really don't mind having everyone. I just didn't mean to fall asleep here." Will is coming in closer. I think he's going to kiss me. "You don't want to get too close. I'm really sick. I don't want you to get it."

He kisses me on the forehead. "It's worth the risk, babe. You smell great."

Did he have to call me "babe" in front of Neil?

Neil backs up a few steps and looks at his watch. "I really should get going."

I try to sit up again. "Neil, I really appreciate all you've done—really. Thanks for bringing the dinner and getting Marcy."

He glances toward the door. "It was nothing. Don't get up. I'll see you around." He gives me a little, closed-lip smile.

"Keep in touch," I call out as he leaves. "Bye." Why isn't he looking at me? I must look terrible. "I really do appreciate your help." But he is already out the door.

Liz looks from Will to Marcy. "I guess I'd better go too." She follows Neil out the door like a tiger going after its prey.

Marcy is still looking at the door. "Mmm, that is one fine man. I can see why—" She breaks off in the middle of her sentence and stares at Will with her hand on her hip. She shakes her head, then carries her luggage to her room, leaving me alone with Will. "I better get unpacked."

Will is telling me something about my car, but I can't focus on his words. Why did Neil leave so soon? It's not like him to hurry off like that.

"I'm going to pick you up after work to go and get it. Do you think you'll be better by then?" Will asks.

I feel like a kid in school caught by the teacher's question. "Sure."

"Are you all right, Anne? You seem really out of it."

"I'm fine. I just need to rest. I should probably get to bed."

"Mind if I use your restroom before I go? I need to wash my hands." Maybe he wants to wash his lips too. I'm glad he's not interested in sticking around.

"Go ahead."

While he's in there, I lie back down with the blanket over my face. No use risking another kiss. As he's heading out the door, he says, "I'll see you Monday then."

"Okay . . . what time are we meeting again?"

"I'll pick you up after work, remember?"

Marcy seems more subdued than usual when she sits down at the end of my bed that evening. "So, a lot has happened while I was away—a lot that you haven't told me."

"What do you mean?"

"Well, for one thing, you're in love."

I sit up and lean toward her. "Is it that obvious?"

"No, not really. Liz told me all about it while we were driving home from the airport." Marcy looks away.

I gasp. "In front of Neil?"

I can't think of anything else to say. I'm mortified. How could Liz betray me like this? "In front of Neil . . . Why didn't you tell me?" Marcy folds her arms. "I can't say I exactly approve of your choice. But if you see potential in him, who am I to judge? Maybe you'll be good for him."

I lean back against the headboard and exhale. "Why don't you approve of my choice?"

Marcy sits down on the end of my bed. "I don't know if you want to hear this, Anne, but I think if I were in your position, I'd want to know. I've known Will a long time, and there are some things about him that aren't right. He lobbies for tobacco companies for one thing. I don't think it's right for a member of the Church—or anyone really—to help tobacco companies."

"What does Will Grandin have to do with this conversation?" I ask. Then I gasp again. "You don't think I'm in love with Will Grandin, do you?"

Marcy stares at me, then breaks into a smile. "You're not in love with Will?"

"No."

Marcy claps her hands together and bounces on the bed. "Hallelujah. Liz sure had me worried."

"That is good to know about the tobacco companies, though. Stop bouncing. I have a headache."

"Oh, I forgot you're sick." Marcy climbs off the bed and starts to leave the room. Then she turns. "If you're in love, but you're not in love with Will, then why are you dating Will?"

"I was trying to forget Neil, but it didn't work. I'm still in love with him, and I was starting to think—oh, never mind."

"Never mind what?"

"I was starting to think Neil might—I don't know. Do you think maybe he still has feelings for me?" I feel like I'm reading the words from a script. It is so unlike anything I'd normally say.

"Well, let's see—he comes to visit you when you have the flu, goes to pick up your roommate at the airport for you, then gives your sister the third degree about Will." Marcy plops back down onto the bed again. "Of course he still has feelings for you."

"Really?"

"Definitely."

"But he's dating Lily."

"And you're dating Will."

"What exactly did Liz tell him about Will and me?" I ask.

"Well, I'll put it this way—she had me totally convinced that you're head-over-heels for him."

"That's not going to help my chances with Neil, is it?"

Marcy gives a short laugh. "No. But the ball is definitely in your court. Sometimes a little jealousy is what a man needs."

I sit up, then lie back down. "I don't want to get my hopes up. What if he's just being nice? What if he's going to marry Lily like everyone says?"

Marcy puts her hands on her hips and wiggles her neck. "You don't want to get your hopes up? What's that supposed to mean? If you want him, girl, you better get your hopes up. You gotta be a little more optimistic if you wanna get married anytime during mortality. Men—they walk around like they're confident, but inside they're like a seventh grader with braces and acne. We women have to be confident enough for both sexes. That's all there is to it. For sure, you'd better get your hopes up. Have you given him any hint of how you feel about him?"

"I kind of assumed he knew how I felt about him."

She lets out another short laugh. "You shouldn't assume anything with men. You have to be straightforward."

"It's not like I can just call him up and ask him out. He's dating Lily. She's Mary's sister-in-law. If he does marry her, I'll never be able to show my face at Mary's house again. It's embarrassing enough as it is."

"I didn't mean you had to ask him out. There are other ways to get the message across. Use some body language. Call him up just to chat. Cook him something. Things like that. Let him know you think about him. Don't be so prideful about the whole thing."

"I'm not—" I begin, but before I can finish my thought, I realize Marcy's right. I have been prideful. For the past five months, I've been trying to prove that I don't want him, don't need him, and I'm perfectly okay with him dating Lily. I only talk to him if I have to. And, for the most part, I only look at him if I have to. I've never given him any reason to think that I regret breaking up with him. I haven't really considered that he might be hurting, too, or that he might be looking for a signal from me. I've been acting as if he dumped me when, in reality, it was the other way around.

I see now that I'm stuck on step one of the repentance process: regret. Sure, step one is necessary, but I need to move past it. Regret isn't the purpose of repentance. Change is the purpose of repentance. I need to apologize—even the people at Alcoholics Anonymous know that. I should tell him I'm sorry for the way I treated him. But I can't just call him up and say, "Hey, by the way, I'm really sorry I dumped you." I'll have to get him alone again, the way we were tonight. I could have apologized tonight. I should have apologized tonight.

18

Friday, August 2, 2002

I had another long talk with Mom about Neil. She thinks I shouldn't get too serious with anyone who doesn't have a college degree or a full-time job or money. In other words, she thinks I should break up with Neil. I don't think I'll ever be able to please Mom. She doesn't like the food I make, my friends, my clothes, or my church. Why should she like my boyfriend? Everything about Mom and me is so complicated right now. I want to please her more than ever now that she's sick, but I also don't want to give up the person I've become.

Sometimes I wish God would let me see the future. At least then I could know which decisions to make.

Tonight is Lily's welcome home party. I couldn't be more nervous if I were competing in a beauty pageant. Before I leave for work, I try on three outfits. They all look too formal, so I pack a bag with jeans and a sweater. I'll change after work. While I'm packing, I throw in some makeup and my coconut oil perfume. I check my purse for breath mints. Then I decide I might need my hot rollers. Then there's that pan of cinnamon rolls I baked last night. I end up carrying two huge bags out of the building when Liz comes to drive me to my office. She asks if I'm going on a business trip.

It's a slow day on the market. There's not much to do at work, so I try to fill up the time organizing my cubicle. While I sort through my in-box, I mentally rehearse what I might say to Neil when I see him. Then, as I look through a pile of annual reports, I conjure up plans to get Neil away from the rest of the party. I'll ask him to walk me over to Susan's—we have choir practice tonight again. Or I'll ask him for a ride.

Mrs. Fonseca calls, asking if her stocks are at risk. Everything is going up right now, and she wants to know if she should sell. I try to break it to her softly—everything's a risk. You either have to live with the risk or get out altogether. As for me, I'm learning that a little risk can be a good thing. I'm investing in my future—and not only by setting aside more money for my retirement fund.

I'm going to talk to Neil—that's certain. It's just that my plan seemed simpler last night. Now that the party is only hours away, I feel less bold. I can see myself slipping into my familiar role while he slips into his. As the babysitter and the boyfriend, we may never get a chance to talk. There'll be at least ten feet between us at all times. We'll be typecast. I imagine him, sitting on the sofa with his arm around Lily while I chase Daniel and Joseph around the kitchen table. I'll have to force my way in to talk to him. If I have to, I'll sit between him and Lily on the sofa.

It's so unlike me to steal someone else's boyfriend. Or even to think that I could succeed. Yes, it's against the rules, but it's not like I'm going after someone's husband or fiancé. The only real danger is embarrassment. And I could make some enemies. Still, the possibility that I might succeed makes it worth the risk.

Another problem is that I haven't actually broken up with Will yet. I had it all planned out for last night. Then he got the flu. So our break-up date, as I think of it, is postponed until Thursday. That's when I get my car back too. So Thursday is Independence Day for me.

Jan from the office drops me off at the Musgroves', but I can't bring myself to walk up their steps. I'm tempted to take a run around the block, just to calm my nerves. My stomach feels like a popcorn popper. Maybe Lily's homecoming party isn't the best time to talk to Neil.

I walk over toward Mary's house, where I hide behind a tree and say a prayer. I can't wait forever to tell Neil how I feel about him. If

I'm going to do it, I'm going to do it tonight. I pray for determination and confidence. He needs to know how I feel. He deserves to know how I feel. If I was the right woman eight years ago, don't I deserve a chance now?

I march back up to the Musgroves' and ring the doorbell. In the time it takes for Hannah to answer, I almost turn back again. Once she answers, I'm stuck. She hugs me like a football player making a tackle. "Did you hear the news?" she asks, flashing an engagement ring in front of my face.

I smile and hug her again. "You and Barry are a great couple. I'm really happy for you."

"We're going to have a double wedding. You should see Lily's ring. It's gorgeous."

I almost drop the cinnamon rolls. "Lily's engaged too?"

Hannah nods and pulls me into the living room. "She's out doing a little shopping. They should be back soon. You've gotta see the ring."

I drop down into the sofa beside me and rest the cinnamon rolls on my lap. I am not going to cry. I should have known this would happen. Everyone expected it. How could I not have seen it coming?

"We're getting married in April, all four of us. It's going to be gorgeous at the temple in April with all the azaleas and dogwoods blooming. Mom's going to make us matching dresses. Do you think that's tacky?" When I don't answer, she proceeds. "Really, you can tell me what you think because I don't want everyone to think we're tacky."

"No, I think that'll be fine." I try to smile. In situations like these, you have to be happy for people.

"We're all so surprised about Lily. I guess I'm a little hyper today, having Lily home and all. I was so afraid—" She chokes on her words. It's my turn to say something comforting, but I can't. She sniffles and reaches for a tissue. "I'm glad she's better."

I force myself to utter, "Me too." I want to throw the pan of cinnamon rolls across the room. How could he flirt with me one day, then turn around and propose to Lily the next? How could he talk about missing the past? Why did he touch my hand the way he did? I will never, ever understand men.

We sit in silence for a while before the door opens and the rest of the Musgrove family enters, along with Jay Bentley. At least Neil isn't here yet. If I hurry, I can leave before he gets here. "Oh, Anne," Lily cries when she sees me. "I'm so glad to see you." She doesn't run to me like she usually does. She walks as if she is an old woman, holding onto Jay's arm for support. Jay actually looks joyful. Wasn't it just a couple of months ago that he was lamenting he'd never be happy again?

I stand up to hug her, then I say what I know I should. "Congratulations." But I can't keep the tears from spilling out onto my cheeks. I'm glad Neil isn't here yet.

Lily laughs and sits down on the sofa. "Oh, Anne, you're so sweet. Look, Jay, Anne's so happy for us she's crying."

Jay sits down beside Lily and grins. "There's a lot of that going around . . . ever since we got engaged."

Why is he saying "we?" Is he really so close to Lily and Neil that he includes himself in their engagement? And why is he holding her hand? As he leans in to kiss her, it dawns on me. Lily is engaged to Jay, not Neil. I smile, and then, not knowing what to say, I sit down to listen. Lily thrusts her left hand in front of me. "Look at the ring Jay got me. Isn't it gorgeous?"

The diamond is dim and small. I take her hand to examine it. "It's beautiful. I love it. I'm so happy for you. I have to say I'm so surprised."

Jay kisses Lily. "I'll admit, I surprised myself at how quickly we fell in love. I couldn't help myself. Lily is the perfect woman for me."

I realize now that I'm sitting on my pan of cinnamon rolls, but I don't care. Neil is free. I slide the pan out from underneath me and decide not to ask whether he's coming to this little event. In the few minutes I sit there, no one mentions his name.

A half hour later, I am carrying my pan of cinnamon rolls up Jack and Susan's front steps. Brimming with questions, I ring the doorbell. Jack answers. He smiles and holds the door wide open for me to enter. "Hi, Anne. I was just thinking about you. What are you doing in our neck of the woods?"

"Choir practice. Is Susan around?"

Jack chuckles. "Oh, I forgot about that. We're forgetting everything today. Remember how I told you we've been trying to adopt?"

"Yeah."

"The adoption agency called this afternoon. One of the birth mothers picked us, and she's due any minute. Susan and I have been running around like chickens with our heads cut off."

"That's wonderful!"

"Yeah." Jack glows with happiness.

"I guess Susan won't be going to choir practice then."

"No. We're heading out to do some shopping. We've got to get a crib, a car seat, clothes, and a whole lot of diapers. I hope you didn't drive all the way out here to pick her up."

"I was out here for Lily's welcome home party."

Jack grins and shakes his head. "Oh yeah, I heard about that one. That was the other good news we heard today. Neil told me this morning."

Jack is standing there with a silly grin, so I go on. "I guess it would be pretty upsetting to have one of your best friends get engaged to your girlfriend."

"Yeah, you'd think so." Jack chuckles.

"So is he taking it pretty hard?"

"Nope. Not at all."

"So he's not angry with Jay?"

Jack half winks at me. "He seemed pretty happy for him."

I am trying not to smile, but I can't help it.

"What's in the pan?" he asks me.

Now I'm embarrassed. "Cinnamon rolls."

Jack nods, waiting for me to explain why I've carried them into his house.

"I didn't know Lily was engaged to Jay. So I was thinking Neil would be there tonight, and I owe him for bringing me dinner when I was sick and for driving my roommate home from the airport. So I brought cinnamon rolls to the party. I was going to give them to him to thank him, but he wasn't there." I take a breath. I think I've really said too much. "I wanted to do something to thank him."

I didn't think it was possible for Jack's grin to get even bigger, but it has. He reaches into his pocket and whips out his cell.

"You're not going to call him."

"Why not? It'll cheer him up."

He's punching the number. Now he's listening. "He must be at work. I got his voice mail," he tells me. Then he speaks into the phone. "Hey, Neil. I'm here talking to Anne. She just got the news. Wants to congratulate you."

"Jack!"

"She made you some cinnamon rolls."

"To thank him for—"

"She says she's sorry she didn't get to see you tonight. Here, Anne, why don't you say something."

I think my face is as red as Felicia's fingernail polish. I reach for the phone. "Hi, Neil. Jack told me about the baby. I'm so happy for him. Um. I hope to see you soon. . . . Oh, and I wanted to thank you for all your help the other night. I really appreciate it. Bye." It wasn't exactly what I was hoping to say to Neil that evening, but what can you really communicate in a voice mail?

19

Saturday, August 3, 2002

Neil and I went up to the temple today to do baptisms for the dead. It was the perfect day for me to go. I've been so agitated about everything with Mom, and I really needed to feel the peace there.

I don't feel at all ready for this summer to be over. Everything here is just beginning. How can I go back to school?

It's Friday, and I still don't have my car. Now that I've broken up with Will, I'm wondering why I ever thought it was a good idea to use his mechanic. I called the guy this morning, asking why it was taking so long. He said it'll probably be done on Monday. They're waiting for a part.

So Dad and Felicia drive me to the temple visitor's center for our concert. It's a big day for Dad. He finally got a job offer, thanks in part to Will's networking. I have to admit I feel a little guilty about that: I break up with him one day, and he helps my Dad get a job the next.

I don't exactly expect to see Neil at the concert, but I'm keeping an eye out anyway. In the five days since I saw him last, I've steeled myself to talk to him. I'm ready to let my feelings out of their hiding place—maybe not all at once, but a little at a time as I see how he reacts.

Sure enough, I catch a glimpse of Neil walking into the visitor's center as we drive into the parking lot. He's alone. I feel a little feverish, as if that flu is returning.

I check myself in the little mirror on my lipstick case—no glaring problems. I thank Dad for getting me there on time, then leave him and Felicia to find their way into the building on their own. It seems they prefer their privacy anyway.

Neil is standing in front of a painting with his hands behind his back when I find him. The little flap of hair that always sticks up at the crown of his head is neatly combed in place. He doesn't notice me until I touch his elbow. Then he startles, smiles, and—wow—blushes. This time I'm sure of it. "Hi, Anne."

"Hi." We stand there smiling at each other for longer than is probably normal. I remember my promise to show my true feelings. "You look nice." Well, it wasn't too much of a risk, but he does look handsome in his suit.

He looks me up and down, then his eyes settle on my face. "You look beautiful."

I run a finger through my hair. "Well, much better than last time you saw me."

He laughs. "No fair trying to get me caught in that one. So you heard about Lily and Jay?"

"Yeah." I'm standing close enough to get a whiff of sandalwood. "I saw them both at Lily's welcome home party."

Now he's looking at my lips. "Surprising, isn't it? I didn't see it coming at all."

"I hope you weren't too disappointed."

"No, just surprised. Don't get me wrong. Lily's a sweet girl. She's a lot of fun to be around. I just didn't ever picture Jay with someone like her. Jay's always reading, always trying to improve himself. I wish you could have known Wendy, the woman he was going to marry. She was extraordinary." He shakes his head and looks straight into my eyes. "A man doesn't recover from losing that kind of woman. At least he shouldn't." His voice falters as he says this, as if he's trying to restrain his emotions.

I am stunned. In this moment, I understand more of his feelings toward Lily and more of his feelings toward me than I thought I could learn in weeks. I reach my hand out and touch his forearm.

He inches closer. "Are you doing anything after the concert?"

I can't believe this is happening. He's coming back to me. "No . . . I mean, yes. My Dad's taking us out to eat. He got a new job today. We're going to celebrate. You can come along with us if you want."

"Sounds good."

I feel someone touching both my shoulders and turn to see Will. What is he doing here? "Will. I didn't know you were coming."

Will slips into charming mode. "Wouldn't miss it for the world." He holds a hand out to Neil. "Good evening. Neil, isn't it?"

The enthusiasm drains from Neil's face. "Yes." He takes a step away from me, but I still hold onto his arm. This is not good.

Will grips my shoulders. "The director's looking for you, Anne. He wants everyone in position."

I cannot disguise the irritation in my voice. "Tell him I'll be there in a minute."

Will releases my shoulders and takes my arm. "You don't have a minute. You're late, you know. They're waiting for you."

I step toward Neil and squeeze his arm. "We'll have to talk later."

He's looking at Will. "Sure."

Will escorts me across the visitor's center. "I have to tell you, Anne, I don't think I can accept what you told me yesterday. I think I am the right man for you. You know there's something between us—an electricity. We're meant to be together. I know you haven't been feeling well, so I'm willing to forgive you for the things you said last night."

I swallow and look past my shoulder to where Neil follows a few yards behind us. Can he hear? I snatch my arm away from Will. "I'm not going to change my mind about this."

Will whispers as we approach a crowd of people who've gathered to attend the concert. "I've known from the moment I saw you, that you're the woman for me. You owe it to me to give me another chance"

Now he's got my attention. "I owe it to you?"

His mouth twists into a smile. "I know more about you than you think. You're not going to get rid of me. I'm completely dedicated to you."

A shiver runs through me. What does he mean that I can't get rid of him? I climb up the risers to take my place in the soprano section. Maybe I'm misunderstanding. I'm getting carried away. Still, I can't shake the creepy feeling I just got. The director hands me my music and glares at me. Instead of feeling guilty, I transfer the glare in the direction of Will, who's sitting on the front row, and then to my father, who's sitting next to him. Doesn't Dad know I don't want Will here? I told him this morning that we broke up. Of course, with Felicia practically sitting on his lap, I doubt he's thinking about me at all.

Scanning the crowd, I see Neil standing off to the side. I try to catch his eye. But he's not taking the bait. Instead, he's staring at Will and my dad, who are both oblivious to him.

While we sing the first hymn, I try to recall the conversation I just had with Neil. He took all the risks—calling me beautiful, stumbling through sentences about losing an extraordinary woman, and asking what I was doing after the concert. Did I say anything to reciprocate his feelings? No, he gave me reason to hope, but I gave him nothing. I was carried along by his conversation, never jumping out of it to explain how I feel. I should have at least hinted that I've broken up with Will.

During the next three songs, his stare is unwavering and always focused on Will. He's jealous. I wish it were a good thing. But considering what I've already put him through, it's not. Finally, on the fifth song, he looks at me. I smile at him and wink. Surely, that will help. Instead of smiling back, he looks away.

As soon as the performance is over, I jump down from the risers, squeeze past the front row and chase Neil through the visitor's center then out the front door. It's starting to sprinkle. I catch up with him as he walks beside the reflecting pool, now filled with little raindrop-induced circles. He looks up at the temple and scratches the back of his neck. "Listen, Anne, I think I'm going to pass on the dinner."

I stand between him and the temple, trying to catch his eye. "Neil, I'm really sorry. It's not the way it looks. I didn't know Will was—"

He tips his head to the side and whispers. "Boyfriend approaching from the left."

I roll my eyes. "He's not my boyfriend."

He starts to walk toward the temple. "Maybe you should tell him that." I follow him out into the parking lot. He stops in front of his SUV and opens the trunk to retrieve his temple bag. "I've been meaning to get to the temple. If I hurry, I can make it to the next session."

I sit down on his bumper and fold my arms. It's getting cold. "I wish you would let me explain."

He reaches up to close the back door. "Maybe another time, Anne. I've got to get going." He turns his head and looks past his shoulder. "And if you want to talk to someone, Jaguar man over there seems like he'd be interested. Now, are you going to get out of my car, or should I leave the trunk open?"

I look back at Will, who's standing three cars away, watching us. Without saying anything, Neil slings his bag over a shoulder. I sigh and stand up. "Will you at least call me after you get out of the temple?"

He turns on his heel and walks away. "I'll think about it."

There's finality in his voice. My stomach sinks. This is the way it was eight years ago. I told him how I felt, and he walked off. The next day, I boarded an airplane to go back to school in Denver, vowing that it was best for both of us to be apart. When I finally started to regret my decision and called him, he'd changed his number. I'm not going to let that happen again. I shout to him. "I'll call you then."

I watch him as he navigates across the parking lot and disappears into the temple entrance. I was right about him being jealous of Will. It's the only explanation.

I hear footsteps, then Will's voice. "Are you all right?"

I fold my arms. "Yeah."

He puts his arm around me. "That guy's pretty intense. I don't think you should spend so much time with him."

I shrug off his arm. "I better get back to Dad."

"Oh, he already left. Felicia was hungry. You know how she is— always having to have her needs met."

"I was hoping to ride with them." It's starting to rain harder now. For a moment, I consider running to the temple, but I know Dad's looking forward to this dinner. And I'm probably overreacting to the things Will said before. "So do you know where we're going?"

He takes my arm again and starts walking. "My car's right over here."

Reluctantly, I climb into Will's car. He turns on the engine. "You sounded great, Anne. I could hear your voice over all the others'."

I gasp. "I didn't mean to sing that loud. I thought I was blending in." That'll teach me to get so distracted while I sing.

"I'm sure, to everyone else, you were blending in. But as far as I'm concerned, you'll never blend in."

I put my hand to my forehead and lean back in my seat. I don't want to hurt Will's feelings after all he's done for me. But it's obvious he didn't get the message yesterday. He reaches for my hand. I pull it back. "Will, this isn't a good idea."

"I'm not going to give up." He really is starting to sound like a stalker.

I fold my arms and scoot against the door. "What do you mean by that?" Rain is pounding down on the hood of the car and streaming down the side windows.

"I'm willing to wait for you to sort through your feelings. I'll do whatever I need to do to get you back."

I pull out my cell phone, wondering if Dad will be able to figure out a text message. There's no way I'm letting Will drive me home from the restaurant. "My feelings are sorted, Will. I've made up my mind. I appreciate all you've done for me. I've enjoyed the time we've spent together. But I'm not right for you. I'm sure there's someone else who can make you happy."

He steps on the gas as we exit the parking lot. "You make me happy."

I look at the speedometer. He's twenty miles over the limit. Doesn't he know the roads are slippery? "Where are we going to dinner?"

He hesitates before answering. "A seafood place. I can't remember the name, but I know exactly where it is."

My cell phone rings. It's Felicia. I answer right away. "Hi, Felicia."

"Hi, Anne. Y'all left before we discussed where we're going to eat. Is Tivoli okay? It's Walter's favorite."

That shiver is back. Why did I believe Will when he said Dad had already left? And obviously Will didn't know where we were supposed to go either. Tivoli is not a seafood place. "Umm, that sounds fine to me. We'll see you there." I hang up. "That was Felicia. We're going to meet at Tivoli. Do you know where that is?"

Will turns the music up and nods. When we get onto the beltway, he turns the wrong direction. Another shiver. I turn down the music. "Tivoli's the other way, Will. We'll have to turn around."

He turns the volume back up. "We're not going to Tivoli. If you don't want seafood, fine. But we're not going to Tivoli."

Since we're going eighty miles an hour on the beltway, I might as well be locked in a cage. The music is loud, but I can still feel my heart beating. I plug my ears and pray. "Heavenly Father, please help me get out of this."

I grip my cell phone and decide the best strategy is to play along. If he knows I'm afraid, I'll only be in more trouble. My fingers tremble as I touch his shoulder. "You know, there's a great place a few miles from here. I can't remember the name of it. It's Szechwan." I don't really know anyplace like that, but there are always so many Chinese restaurants, I'm taking a chance on it. "It's over near the University of Maryland. Or maybe you'd rather have Italian." If I can get him to stop the car where there are other people around, even if it's at a stop light.

He snorts. "You want to go someplace near the University of Maryland?"

I've been reading the exit signs. "It's close. Aren't you hungry?"

He doesn't answer.

"I love the University atmosphere. It's so fun. You'll like it." I'm still praying for help in between every sentence. "We'll have to get off at the next exit."

He doesn't turn off.

20

I got Liz, Mary, and me on a three-way call to talk about what's going to happen with Mom after I go back to school. Mary is still up in New York and doesn't get what a big deal all of this is. I don't know if we'll be able to count on her at all. It ended up with Liz being mad at both of us. I feel so stuck. If I stay here, Mom will be upset that I didn't go back to school. If I leave, Liz will be the only one helping Mom. Sometimes I'm still angry that Mom left Dad in the first place. If she'd stayed, we'd all be in the same house, and Dad would be taking care of Mom.

Neil and I spent the last week helping Mom remodel her exercise room. She's not really using it right now because she's been so sick, but I guess it gives her hope to know the room will be waiting for her when she feels better.

I lean closer to Will so he can hear me over the music. "I think we can get to that Szechwan place from the next exit." At least, I hope we can since I've never actually been there. I whip out my phone and type in a text message to Mary. "I think Will is stalker. Call me."

Will glances down at my phone. "What are you doing?"

I shut the phone and put it back in my purse. "I got a text from Mary. I'm answering her. Here comes that exit I was telling you about."

Will sounds uncertain, as if he doesn't believe me. "Are you sure this is the right one? I don't remember seeing any restaurants down this way."

Uh-oh. "I'm sure this is it. I'll show you how to get there." I feel like Nephi, not knowing beforehand how I'm going to get where I'm supposed to go.

He takes the exit. I feel my cell phone vibrating. It's probably Mary. She'll have to wait. From the looks of our surroundings, we're not exactly in the best part of town. We pass a run-down mall then rows and rows of apartment buildings. I slip off my heels. It'll be easier to run without them, especially with all the rain. I slowly zip up my purse and loop it around my shoulder. Will shakes his head. "Are you sure you know where you're going?"

As Will stops at a busy intersection, I prepare for my get-away. "I sure do." I unlock the door, open it, and scramble out. I don't know if this is the right thing to do, but I'm scared enough to do it anyway. Hopefully, I'm right about him not wanting to leave his car there in the middle of the intersection. I take off running between the other cars stopped beside us then in between the apartment buildings to the right. I'm running faster than I thought I could. Someplace to hide—I need someplace to hide. If I don't find a place soon, he's sure to find me.

I round a corner. Ahead of me, in the parking lot, there are three young African-American men working on an old Buick. They're all wearing hooded jackets because of the rain. "Can I hide in your car?" I shout as I approach them.

They stare at me without answering. It's probably not every day they see a woman in a skirt running barefoot through the rain in the parking lot.

As I get closer, I ask again. "My ex-boyfriend's chasing me. Can I hide in your car?"

"Sure," the taller youth answers, opening the back door for me.

I jump inside. "Thanks. Pretend I'm not here, okay?"

The three youth walk back around to look underneath the hood while I crouch down in the back seat beside a calculus textbook. The rain is pelting the car, leaving me unable to hear anything except my own heaving breaths and the rain. After a minute or two, the short one comes to sit in the driver's seat. Without turning to look at me, he asks. "Ma'am, does your ex-boyfriend drive a Jaguar?"

I crouch down lower and try to stop shaking. If there was ever a time I needed that blue fleece blanket, it's now. "That would be him."

"He passed by a minute ago."

I sit up a little bit. "Thank you so much for your help."

He turns to look at me. His dark eyes show sympathy. "You need a ride somewhere? A woman like you shouldn't be out alone here at night."

I look at my watch. It's eight thirty—only a half hour after the concert ended. It seems like it should be later. I let out my breath. "Is there a metro station around here?" If I catch a train soon, I should be able to make it home by midnight.

"There's one a couple miles away. That guy won't look for you there?"

"He's not the type to ride the metro."

"I'm Tyrone, by the way." He reaches his hand out to shake mine.

I sit up on the back seat and shake hands with him. "Nice to meet you. I'm Anne."

He leans forward and looks to the right, then the left. "We'll have to walk over to my car. This one don't work."

Bent down low, I slowly open the door and creep out. Looking down, I see my toes peeking out from holes in the bottom of my nylons. "Oh, I forgot I left my shoes in Will's car." I guess I should feel lucky it's not worse. Who knows what I could have stepped on here?

Tyrone holds up his finger, signaling for me to wait. "I've got something in my apartment that'll do."

He comes back with a huge pair of purple flip-flops, which I slip onto my feet. I'll definitely be flipping and flopping around the metro stations with these on. He, his two friends, and I squeeze into a rusty hatchback that has to be at least twenty years old. Then Tyrone drives us all over to the metro station. I offer to pay for the gas and the shoes, but they won't take my money. "Just consider us to be your good Samaritans," Tyrone tells me.

I step out of the car. "I'll do that."

Logically, I know I'm safe now, but I keep an eye out for Will anyway. My hands are so shaky, I can't even work the machines to get my pass. I have to ask a little old lady for help. She looks up at me and pats my shoulder. "Having a bad day, honey?" I nod. She grips her bony fingers around my shaking hands. "I'll say a prayer for you."

I sit on a cold, concrete bench and wait for the train. It's then I notice that my cell phone is full of messages: five from Mary, three from Felicia, one from Will, and two from Dad. With a jolt, I remember the text message I sent to Mary. They must be worried. I spend the next few minutes, before the train comes, trying to reassure everyone that I'm all right. So much for Dad's celebration dinner. Good thing I didn't give him another heart attack.

After I get on the train, I get a call from Will, which I don't answer, then another call from him, then a text message. Leaning back in the yellow vinyl seat, I turn the phone off. In another few minutes, we'll be underground, and blessedly free of cell phone reception. I'm not even going to think about my car or my shoes or how I need to change the locks on my door.

I watch the people around me, mostly young students, as I would a documentary on PBS. There's a girl with pink stripes in her hair. A boy wears tight black jeans that emphasize his narrow calves. An older woman dons a clear, plastic rain hat and carries a purse that swells with knitting supplies. A young woman taps her pointy toed high-heels and types away on her laptop. A man stands next to me with long salt and pepper hair. His gray parka smells like cigars.

I retrieve the breath mints from my purse and start to chew away. I didn't realize how hungry I was. The cinnamon flavored gum goes down too. Even the strawberry lip balm is starting to look yummy. Must be all the adrenaline. Too bad there aren't vending machines on the metro.

It takes another hour and a half before I'm above ground again and ready to use my phone. There are only a few passengers left. Remembering the call I promised Neil, I walk to the middle of the train where others are less likely to overhear.

The phone rings seven times before he picks up. "Hi, Anne." He sounds tired and maybe a bit impatient.

"Did I wake you up?" My calculations for when he'd get home from the temple must have been wrong.

"No. It's just been a long day. I haven't slept since yesterday afternoon. Work, you know."

That makes his coming to the concert even more remarkable. "Look, I owe you an explanation about the dinner. Will and I broke up yesterday, so I wasn't expecting him to come. I know it looked really bad, me inviting both of you to dinner. Actually, it was my dad who invited him."

"Are you back together now?"

"Hardly."

"Sorry about that."

"There's nothing to be sorry for. It wasn't working out. I really would have rather gone out to dinner with you." Silence. Okay, maybe that wasn't the right thing to say. I swallow.

"I didn't catch that last part."

Oh please, do I have to repeat it? "I said I would have rather gone to dinner with you."

"That's what I thought you said." Another silence. "Maybe some other time, huh?" He doesn't sound too enthusiastic.

"I'd like that."

My reception starts to break up as he responds. I can only hear every other word he says. "Neil, I can't hear. The signal's breaking up." I don't know if he can hear me, but I go on. "I hope I can talk to you again soon. Bye." Chalk that one up for another less-than-successful phone conversation with Neil. I lean back in my seat and take a few deep breaths to calm my nerves. If anyone's going to call back, it's got to be him this time. I've had enough risks for one day.

The sound of my phone ringing gives me a thrill. "Hello."

He doesn't sound quite so tired this time. "Anne, I'm so relieved. I was worried about you." Why would he be worried? "I hope I didn't scare you. I think we need to talk." That's progress. "Maybe I could bring your shoes by later and—"

"My shoes?" Oh, no. It's Will. Why didn't I check to see who it was before I answered? I clap my phone shut and hold it to my chest where my heart beats a fast staccato. Okay, maybe he wasn't trying to abduct me and maybe he's not a stalker. But he is a liar, and liars can't be trusted.

By the time I get to Falls Church station, I am starving. Marcy's waiting on the platform. She hands me a can of mace as soon as I get off the train. "I thought you'd better be prepared—just in case."

I put the can in my purse, wishing she'd brought me food instead. "Thanks." How long am I going to have to carry mace around? I don't even know how to use the stuff. "Will always seemed so normal. It's hard to believe I might have to use this on him."

Marcy smirks. "From what Mary's been telling me, Will is not normal. He's crossed the line."

21

Monday, August 19, 2002

I had family home evening with Neil and Jack tonight. They didn't believe me when I said I could make cinnamon rolls in 90 minutes, so I proved it. We played some board games and read scriptures. Then Neil and I played tennis against Jack. He beat us. It was the first time I went to a family home evening and actually felt like I was part of the family.

Whether or not Will is stalking me, I'm determined to have a normal Saturday. Thanks to Marcy being on an all-day excursion with another one of the guys from the ward, I even have her sporty little hybrid to drive around. All I have to do is get down to that car and put some distance between myself and any place Will expects me to be. For the first destination, I'm visiting the gym. Yes, it's not exactly normal—I usually run in the park, but my nerves are a little too raw for a solitary run.

I feel like an actor in a murder mystery as I hold the bottle of mace with my finger right over the button. I'm ready to fire. Looking through the peephole in my front door, I see nothing. I crack open the door and look in all directions. Still nothing. Since Will is the type of guy that always takes the elevator, I take the stairs, all the while carefully checking in all directions. When I reach the ground floor, I hesitate. What if he's waiting for me at the bottom of the elevators? There's no way I'll be able to see him from the doorway. I say a prayer to calm myself.

Holding the mace at the ready, I crack the door open and peek out—nothing. I creep out into the lobby. The coast is clear. Then the elevator doors open. I back into a corner and pray it's not Will. Nope, it's an elderly gentleman. I let him pass. It's a hundred feet or so before I can get into Marcy's car. If I run for it, I'll make it in a matter of seconds.

Here I go. I fling open the door and take off down the sidewalk. All I have to do is round one corner, then Marcy's car should be right there. But right as I'm turning the corner, I hear someone shouting my name. He's here all right, waiting for me outside. Speeding up, I press the unlock button on the key fob. The lights on the car flash. I'm almost there. He's still shouting. "Anne, hold on. I need to talk to you."

I just have to get to the car and get in. I can hear footsteps behind me—running footsteps. I think he might be faster than I am. I've still got the mace. I jump into the car and close the door, but how do I lock it? Never mind. I'll just turn it on and get out of here. I press the button to turn on the ignition. It won't start. Still got the mace, though. When I look up and see a face staring at me through the driver's side window, I spray for all I'm worth. Then I realize, it's Neil. And there's mace dripping down the inside window of Marcy's car.

He's laughing, of course. I open the door. "Why were you chasing me?"

Now he looks apologetic. "I came by because you haven't answered your phone since I talked to you last night. Susan wants you to come by and see the baby. I was getting out of my car when I saw you running past. I didn't want to miss you."

I blow my breath out. "Oh."

"You're carrying mace, now?"

I look down at the can I still grip in my hand. "Yeah."

He takes the can from me. "I think you've used this one up. You better wash your hands in case it got on you. Has there been an increase in crime around here lately?" He sounds like a police officer.

I stand up out of the car. "Sort of."

"We better go back up to your apartment, so you can get it off your hands. Then I'll help you get it off the window."

As much as I hate for him to rescue me, this time I'm relieved. I stare at the middle of his chest and wish I could press my face into it.

He stoops to meet my gaze. "Are you okay? I didn't mean to scare you." He reaches out to touch my shoulder. "You're shaking."

"I am so embarrassed." I move to put my hands to my face.

"Don't do that." He grabs my hands as they reach my chin and holds onto them. "Now I'll have to wash my hands too." He smiles a little half smile with only his top teeth showing.

"I'm so sorry about this."

Letting go of my hands, he shuts the car door. "I have a feeling you shouldn't be."

While we're on the elevator, he asks me when I started carrying mace. I swallow. "Not too long ago."

When we reach my door, I find an envelope with my name on it—in Will's handwriting. I guess I didn't notice it before. Neal removes it while I unlock the door.

I take the note and toss it onto the kitchen table on my way to the bathroom. "You can wash your hands in the kitchen." I scrub my hands for a full minute, then grab some Windex and paper towels.

When I step out of the bathroom, I find him examining the envelope. He squints at me. "Did he threaten you?"

I might as well answer since he's assuming the worst anyway. "No." I hold up the Windex and paper towels. "I got the stuff to clean the car."

He's still holding the note. "You'll need rubber gloves."

I grab some from the kitchen, then I snatch the note away from him and throw it in the trash. He takes a step toward the trash can. I step in front of him, my hands on my hips. "Oh no, you don't."

"Okay, Anne, it's none of my business what's going on between you and, uh . . ."

"Will?"

"Yeah, but I think you'd be wise to let me read that. I do this for a living you know." He winks at me. "Or I'll wait and go Dumpster diving later in the week."

I roll my eyes and let him pass. He plucks the envelope off the top of the trash. "Any more notes in here?"

"No."

"Messages on the phone?"

I sink down into the sofa. "Yes, but I haven't listened to them."

He opens the envelope and unfolds the letter. "Don't delete them."

I put my head down in my hands. He sits down beside me. I groan. "Do you have to read it in front of me?" Should I be letting him do this? Could Will say anything I don't want Neil to know? Except for the kissing, there's really nothing.

He reads the letter, then stands up and puts it in the back pocket of his jeans. "Let's go take care of your car."

I follow him to the door. "Marcy's car. Mine is still in the shop. Do you think I'm overreacting?"

He opens the door for me. "I know you too well to think you're overreacting, Anne." Then he runs his finger down the side of my face, the way he did the night he brought me back from North Carolina. I look up into his eyes and feel myself melting down into the floor. I'd like him to kiss me. Instead, he keeps talking. "Where were you planning to go?"

I step out into the hallway. "What?"

"Where were you going when I chased you down?"

I push the button for the elevator and look down at the sweats I'm wearing. "The gym. I wanted to go running. I usually go in the park, but—"

"Mind if I come along? I could use a workout."

Is this a date? Maybe not. If he didn't feel sorry for me, I might not be here in the passenger seat of his car. I'm here, though, so I make the most of it. I ask him about Jack and Susan's new baby. He turns down the song on his stereo. "I held her this morning. Her eyes were open, looking all around. She has fuzz on her ears. And little wrinkles all over. She's beautiful. You'll have to come see her." He looks in the rear-view mirror, then glances over at me. "Do you have any plans for this afternoon?"

"Nope, you?"

"I'll take you to see the baby if you want. I've got the whole weekend off, so I have all day. I traded for Halloween."

I check in my purse for a breath mint, only to remember that I ate them all on the metro. "I'd like that."

We stop at a light and he reaches over to get his GPS navigator out of the glove compartment, brushing my leg in the process. "Jack tells me you made me some cinnamon rolls the other day. Sorry I wasn't around to eat them. He said they were good."

I'm sure I'm blushing. "I'll have to make you some more. I wanted to thank you for bringing me dinner and driving Marcy home. "

He looks up from the navigator he's examining. "Thanks. It was sweet of you." The light changes, and he hands me the navigator. "Do you mind if we stop somewhere on the way to the park?"

"No." I'm kind of relieved he wants to stop, actually. It'll give me a chance to put on the makeup I forgot to wear this morning. (Will I ever learn?) And if we're near a store, I can restock on breath mints.

Five minutes later, he pulls up to a police station, puts the car in park, and jots down something on a note pad. This must have something to do with his job. When he comes around to open my door, I tell him I'd rather wait in the car.

He bends down so his eyes are level with mine. "I didn't want to freak you out, Anne, but that Jaguar's been following us since we left your apartment. I need you to file a report." He takes my hand and pulls me reluctantly from the car.

We sit side by side in beige plastic chairs backed up against a wall of the police station, a wall without any pictures. His elbow touches mine on the armrest, and I'm tempted to inch my foot over closer to his, which seems to be inching closer to mine. He shifts in his seat, and, there it is, our feet touch. I'm quivering. He notices. "You cold?"

I sit up straighter, breaking contact with him. "No. I'm fine."

Rising to his feet, he touches my shoulder. "I'll be back in a sec."

A minute later, he comes back with his jacket and scriptures. "I'll trade you these for your cell." He helps me into the jacket before I answer, then hands me the scriptures, which are soft in my hands. "I'm waiting." His hand is reaching out, palm up beside me. He wiggles his fingers as if he's asking for a piece of candy.

My fingers grip the top of my purse. "Why do you want my phone?"

"I'm going to listen to the messages." He clears his throat. "If you're embarrassed, I'll get someone else to listen to them. They're evidence."

I let the scriptures fall open on my lap and see that he's been reading 3 Nephi 17. His notes are all over the margins. I flip over to the Doctrine and Covenants, where the pages open to section 121. He's underlined the part about letting virtue garnish our thoughts.

I extract the phone from the bottom of my purse, where it's been since last night. "I am embarrassed, but you can listen to it if you want. It's not like I did anything wrong."

He rubs his hand across the back of my shoulders. "I'm looking for something he's guilty of, not something you're guilty of."

I bend down over the scriptures. "Just remember that he doesn't always tell the truth. That's one of the reasons I broke up with him."

"And the other reason?"

I let the question pass. Now's not the time to go into the particulars of why I'm not attracted to Will, especially since they have so much to do with Neil.

We sit in silence, me exploring Neil's psyche through the notes on the margin of Doctrine and Covenants 121, him exploring my recent past by listening to the twenty-seven messages Will's left on my phone since last night. I'm halfway through the chapter when Neil cracks up laughing. "Sorry. He keeps calling you 'babe.' You must hate that."

I can feel myself blushing. "I know. I'm not really the 'babe' type."

"What's the deal with your shoes? Why were they in his car?"

I'm forced to rehash the entire story of last night's ride on the beltway and my escape at the stoplight in College Park. He listens, without making any comments. By the end of it, his teeth are clenched, his eyebrows scrunched. I try to lighten the mood by telling him about the big purple flip-flops. He laughs, then goes back to his serious expression. "If I'd known, I wouldn't have left you alone with him."

I shrug my shoulders. "I didn't know either. I still wonder if I'm overreacting."

"My gut tells me you're not. Twenty-seven messages? That's over the top."

It's two hours later when we finally leave the police station. Will hasn't done anything unlawful, but the officer tells me I did the right thing by filing a report. She says sometimes it takes years to catch a stalker. Could Will Grandin really be desperate enough to follow me around for years? I doubt it. Not only is he good-looking, he's charming enough to get a new girlfriend.

As we drive out of the parking lot through the back exit, Neil keeps an eye on his rearview mirror. "I wouldn't blame you if you didn't want to go back to your apartment tonight. In fact, it might be a good idea for you to stay at Jack's. You can stay in the guest room. I'll sleep on the futon downstairs."

I shift in my seat. "I don't know if that's a good idea."

"You're not scared of me, are you?"

"It's more like I'm scared of myself, being in the same house with you all night long." The minute I say it, I regret it. What was I thinking to let that come out of my mouth?

I look straight ahead, but, out of the corner of my eye, I see that he's focused on me, not the road. I turn to see his wide grin. "Remember, you're driving."

His eyes drift back to the road. "I'll keep a can of mace under my pillow, in case you attack. No, seriously, Anne. Jack and Susan will be there all night, and we'll be on different floors. Has he been to Mary's house?"

I turn my head to look out the back window. No Jaguar in sight. Maybe we've lost him. "Yes. He's been to Mom's too."

Neil looks at the rearview mirror. "How about that run in the park?"

I lean back into my seat. "If your knee's up to it."

"It's much better. I hardly feel it anymore."

Fall leaves crunch beneath our feet as we jog along the wide, asphalt pathways of Meadowlark park. It's a still, crisp day, perfect weather for jogging. Neil lets me set the pace—I'm sure he goes much faster when he's on his own. I can't even hear him breathing. I lead him up and down all my favorite paths. First I take him through the woods where we can hear the birds. Then we run past the herb garden. We stop to smell a few of my favorite herbs, lavender and sage, then lemon geranium and spearmint. Circling down around the pond, we try to avoid the duck droppings, which seem to be everywhere.

As we head back uphill, I break the silence. "I feel really bad about what's happening with Will." Neil doesn't say anything, so I plunge ahead. "It's really my fault. I knew he was starting to care about me, and I kept dating him—even though I didn't feel the same way. He seemed like a great guy, and I needed a distraction." Neil raises an eyebrow. And I realize, once again, that I've said the wrong thing. So I look down at the pavement and keep explaining. "I really wanted to like him. I just couldn't. I liked going out with him, but it was mostly because he spent a lot of money on me. I guess it was selfish of me not to break things off sooner."

He moves off the pavement to run on the grass. "Selfish might be too strong of a word. It sounds like you were enjoying yourself."

"At his expense. I'm really not good at dating."

"That makes two of us . . . Listen, Anne, you're better than you think you are. You shouldn't beat yourself up about this. Dating is a risk. I think most guys with half a brain realize that. Just because a guy spends money on you, it doesn't mean you have to fall in love with him. If you want to end it, it's over. He has to accept that. It's the way things work."

I stop and kneel down to tie my shoe. If I'm ever going to apologize to him for the past, now would be a really good time. "It doesn't seem fair that other people have to suffer because of the mistakes I make." Neal removes the sweatshirt he had on over his T-shirt, and my eyes linger on his arm muscles.

He notices. "They're the same size now." He grins at me.

I feel as transparent as the canning jars that line Janet Musgrove's food storage shelves. I always know exactly what's inside those jars: peaches, green beans, pickles, beets, pears, or applesauce. And right now, Neal knows exactly what's inside my head. I start to run again.

"Every time I wanted to skip my workout, I remembered that guy with the Jaguar whose biceps were perfectly matched."

I shove his shoulder and laugh. "I was kidding about that."

I know this whole thing is more of a pity party than a date. Even so, I hope it can morph into a date, complete with a good night kiss.

Either way, I have Will to thank for all the attention Neil's showing me. That wasn't exactly what I'd wanted.

When we finish lap one, Neil takes a detour to his car for a bottle of water. Running back, he holds it out to me. "You first."

I drink what I judge to be about a quarter of it, though I'm much thirstier than that. I wipe my lips and hand it back to him. "Thanks."

He drinks another third and gives it back to me. "Go ahead and finish it."

I pause. "I don't want to drink more than you did."

"What's the matter? Are you afraid of my germs?"

"No."

"Don't you remember you're already inoculated against me?"

It takes me a while to figure that one out. He's talking about the kisses we once exchanged. Could it be that he's testing me? I put the bottle to my lips. "That was eight years ago. Your germs are all different now, not that I'm afraid of them." I drink the rest.

He takes the empty bottle from me and corrects, "Eight years and two months, but who's counting?"

Thursday, August 22, 2011

Neil proposed to me tonight, and I said "yes."

Neil's arm isn't exactly around me. It's resting on the back of the sofa behind my head as he bends over the baby I hold in my arms. No matter how many times I've held a newborn, each time I'm surprised to think that anyone could be so small. The little girl, named Faith, is asleep now. We watch her chest rise and fall, witnessing the miracle of life—that a little body so perfect could grow from a couple of cells. Neil takes her little hand, clutched into a fist. Not wanting to wake her, he whispers. "Look at her fingernails."

I lift her other hand with my pinkie. "Such tiny hands."

His face is right next to mine, but he's looking down at the baby. "She has a lot of hair for a baby, don't you think?"

I rub a finger on the dark curls. "I love baby hair."

Jack observes from the far side of the room. "You look good with a baby in your arms, Anne, especially when you're beside my brother."

That was a little more of a hint than I was prepared for, even from Jack. I don't dare to transfer my gaze from the baby to Neil, but I'm guessing he's burning red to the tips of his ears. Neil puts his hand beneath the baby's foot and turns his face to mine. He speaks quietly. "You'll have to excuse Jack. He's anxious to get me married off."

I look up into those blue eyes of his and discover he's not blushing at all. As much as I'd love to savor the moment, which could actually be romantic, that water I drank an hour ago is demanding attention. "Could I use the bathroom?" I hand the baby to Neil, who takes her with an eagerness I envy.

Jack starts to show me where the bathroom is, then remembers I already know. As I open the door, I catch Jack's voice again. "You gotta remember she said yes before she said no." I'm startled. Did he intend for me to hear that? He always was a little too loud.

Even though I really shouldn't, I stop to hear Neil's response, which comes at a much softer volume. "The last thing she needs right now is another ex-boyfriend chasing her around. She needs me to be her friend and that's what I'm going to be."

I can't say I'm not disappointed. He wants to be friends. And it's because of Will. I promised myself that Will would not ruin my day, but he's done it. I've become a service project.

As I stare into the mirror, a thought flutters into my head the way a bird might land on a tree branch: Neil's thinking of me and what I need. Am I thinking of what he needs?

Does he need me—someone whose makeup from last night is still smudged at the edges of her eyes? Someone who dumped him eight years ago because she was too scared to get married? Someone who hasn't quite ended a relationship with her last boyfriend?

With a wet Kleenex, I try to repair the damage to my eyes. It doesn't help—just makes me look like I've been crying, which may happen again if I think any more about him being my "friend."

Automatically, as if I still live here, I kneel down on the pink tile floor. It chills my knees through my sweats, but I stay. Letting the words pour out of me, I tell my Heavenly Father everything I feel about this man and everything I feel about myself. I tell him about Will, including how angry I am at how he's behaving. I tell him how scared I am and how embarrassed and how frustrated. I ask him if I might be the right woman for Neil. Then, I quit talking and wait for the inspiration. Though the thoughts don't come, the feeling does, that feeling of his pure love flowing all through me. I'm warm despite the tile floor. Whether or not I get together with Neil, whether or not Will stops bothering me, whether or not I ever get married, everything will be okay.

Exiting the bathroom, I face a wall of photos. Jack kissing Susan on their wedding day. Susan standing with two other women who must be her mother and sister. Jack and Neil with their parents. Jack on his motorcycle. Jack's graduation from medical school.

Then, there, to the far left is Neil, my Neil, the one I dated. I recognize the faded blue T-shirt and the tan from his long days working at the country club. I step closer. He looks so happy. Even his eyes seem to be smiling.

I scan the background of the picture for clues: picnic tables, trees, and a water marker. It looks like Great Falls park. Didn't I go to Great Falls with Neil and Jack one time? The Spirit's warmth engulfs me, telling me this is my answer: I was there. He was that happy because we were together.

I must have been gone too long because when I find Neil in the kitchen afterward, he gives me a long, serious look. "Okay?"

"Yeah."

Not satisfied with my answer, he persists. "Feeling sick?" He's looking at me as if he suspects some sort of feminine problem. That piece of hair at the back of his head is sticking up at least two inches.

I walk over to the counter where he's making sandwiches. "Praying."

Judging from his wink, he likes that answer. "I guess that means you're feeling better?"

I know I probably shouldn't do this, but the faucet is already on. My hand is under the stream of water. "I hope you don't mind, but I have to fix this," I tell him. I stand on tiptoe, rest one hand on his shoulder and wet down that piece of hair that's been driving me crazy ever since I saw him at the garage sale. Yes, there's something inside me that tells me I shouldn't be doing this, that I'm not his girlfriend anymore or his mother, but looking at his old picture changed something in me. It's almost as if the old Neil is urging me on, daring me to remind the present Neil of the way things used to be, the way I used to fix that piece of hair nearly every time I saw him.

I watch for the blush, which I'm sure will arrive. And here it is— cheeks first, then nose, then ears. His smile is shy, as if he's wondering what it means. He'll have to keep wondering since I'm not about to explain.

He starts to spread mayonnaise on a piece of bread. "Thank you."

I tilt my head to the side. "You're welcome."

He keeps spreading on the mayonnaise until it looks like frosting on a cake, then he tops it with meat, cheese, a pickle, and lettuce. I take the sandwich over to Jack, where he's holding the baby on the sofa. Jack opens it up to examine it. "How much mayonnaise did you put on this, Neil?"

Neil, who's carrying two sandwiches to the kitchen island, doesn't seem to hear him. "Do you want to wake up Susan for lunch?"

Jack puts his sandwich back together. "No. Let her sleep. She was up a lot last night."

We say a prayer, then dig into the sandwiches. Unlike Jack's, mine has the right amount of everything. "Thanks for the sandwiches. I didn't mean to invite myself to lunch."

Jack calls out from the couch. "You're welcome here anytime, Anne. Oh, and your purse has been singing to me for the last five minutes."

"Sorry, I thought I turned my phone off."

Neil stands up before I do. "Anne doesn't exactly get along with cell phones." He retrieves the purse and brings it to me. "I turned it on when I was checking your messages."

Reluctantly, I pull out the phone and check who's been calling— four more calls from Will, and one from Dad. "Oh, yeah, I've got to return this call from my dad. The last thing he needs right now is to worry about me. I think I almost gave him another heart attack last night."

I walk into the corner of the kitchen as the phone rings. On the third ring, he answers. "Anne, I'm glad you called me back. I need to talk to you about Will."

"Will?"

His voice is gruff and reminds me of the lectures he gave me in my teen years. "I've had a long conversation with him."

"And?"

"I think you're wrong."

"You think I'm wrong?"

"You shouldn't have run away from him yesterday. He's a nice guy, Anne, the best you could hope for. He has looks, money, a good job. I think you should reconsider. I've told him—"

My voice starts to break. "Dad, he lied to me. He told me you'd left when you hadn't. He told me we were going to Tivoli, then he turned the wrong way."

"It was all a misunderstanding. Now that I've heard the whole story from his point of view, I can understand how he got confused about the dinner plans."

I huff.

Dad exhales. "Hear me out, Anne. The man cares about you. You've made him look like some sort of criminal when all he wanted to do was talk to you. If you've got any sense, you'll reconsider."

I can feel Neil's hand against the small of my back. "I'm not going to reconsider. I've talked to him twice now. Isn't that enough?"

"Anne, he got me a job."

His words drop like an anvil on my chest. My knees wobble. Neil grabs my elbow. I take a breath and hope my voice comes out smoothly. "I forgot about the job, Dad." I press my hand to my lips to keep from sobbing.

"I don't want to have to go into the office on my first day with this hanging over my head."

"Yeah." A one syllable response is all I can manage.

"Will you talk to him? One more time?"

"Okay."

"That's my girl. I knew you'd be reasonable about this. Let me put down the phone a minute. I'll arrange a time for you two to talk."

I hear voices in the background—Dad's and Will's. Dad obviously trusted Will enough to let him into the apartment. Could it be that I'm wrong about Will? Am I overreacting?

Dad picks up the phone again. "Will says he'll meet you at Anita's restaurant at 6:00. He'll have a table reserved."

I dig my nails into my palms. If I weren't in Jack's home, I would yell. "I am not meeting him in person. I'll talk to him over the phone."

"Honey, I think it would be best if you talked to him in person. After the way you've been behaving, you owe him a face-to-face."

"After the way I've been behaving?" I must be shouting now because Neil opens the door that goes out to the garage and pulls me through it.

Dad waits a moment, then clears his throat. "Would you prefer to meet him someplace else or is Anita's okay?"

I haven't been to Anita's for almost a decade because the wait is so long and it's across town. "I'd prefer someplace else. I'd prefer a telephone conversation."

Dad sighs. "You name the place then."

I can only think of one fast place. "McDonald's. I'll meet him at McDonald's." At least I'll be in and out quickly.

"All right 6:00 at McDonald's. How about the one on Maple near Tyson's Corner?"

I hold the phone in front of my face and shout into it. "Fine."

Neil grabs the phone and turns it off before I can hurl it across the garage. "You look like you're about to break something."

I cover my face with my hands and sit down on the wooden steps leading into the garage. "Dad wants me to talk to Will."

Neil sits beside me and puts his arm around my shoulder. "I heard."

"I wouldn't have agreed to it, but Will got Dad a job. Monday's his first day. And he just had a heart attack, so I don't want to upset him."

Neil sticks my phone in his pocket and clenches his jaw. "I guess there's a good reason you never answer this thing." Yes, good old Anne, the one who's always caving into the desires of her parents, like she did eight years ago.

I look off to a corner of the garage. "I'm supposed to meet Will at 6:00 at McDonald's. I can't believe Dad is taking his side."

Neil looks at his watch. "That gives us five hours." He leans back against the top step. "You should know that it's normal for family members to think you're overreacting. It's not unusual for people to side with the stalker instead of the victim."

Jack's voice comes from the doorway. "What if you tell this guy you're dating Neil?"

I turn to look at Jack. What am I supposed to say to that? Am I dating Neil? Was our little run in the park a date?

Neil stands up beside me. "I don't think that would work. The best thing would be to break off all contact, but I guess that's not going to happen." Somehow this wasn't exactly the answer I was hoping for. He looks at his watch again. "Do you mind sticking around here for a while, Anne? Maybe you could take a shower and relax. I've got some things I've got to get done. If I leave now, I'll be back in time to take you over there." He gives me a hug, the kind he might give his mother, then he holds me by the shoulders and looks in my eyes. "Don't worry, okay?"

"All right."

I don't think I've ever had a guy actually recommend that I take a shower. Do I look that bad? If I weren't so stressed out about Will, I might take the time to be insulted by that comment. And what exactly does Neil need to get done? That came up rather suddenly. Have I lost him again?

The upstairs bathroom that now serves as the guest bathroom used to belong to Mary and me. It's small and white with only a shower, toilet, and pedestal sink. During our teenage years, it was littered with cosmetics, shampoos, brushes, combs, curling irons, and every other teen beauty necessity. Now it looks starkly simple with all surfaces wiped clean. Neil's razor sits on the edge of the sink beside his toiletries bag.

I lock the door behind me, and, feeling particularly modest, I undress behind the Battenberg lace shower curtain. Why am I doing this? It's not like Neil's razor is going to be watching me. I set my purse down on the floor beside the shower and make a mental note to start carrying shampoo, soap, and conditioner in case this ever happens again. I pick up the Johnson's baby shampoo that happens to be in the shower. Does Neil use Johnson's baby shampoo? It doesn't really seem to go with the Dial soap.

I turn the knobs and water shoots out of the old fashioned showerhead. Soon my mind is replaying bits and pieces of conversations with Neil as I stand under the warm high-pressure flow. I help myself to the shampoo and soap. Wishing there was time to linger but remembering I don't own the hot water, I shut the shower off as soon as I'm rinsed. As I reach for the towel, I'm startled by a tap at the door. I catch myself before I trip over the edge of the shower. It's Susan. "Do you need anything, Anne? Jack told me what's going on. I'm so sorry. What can I get you?"

Wrapping the towel around me and making a huge puddle on the floor, I call back to her. "I need just about everything, I'm afraid. All I have is what's in my purse. I am really going to owe you one, Susan."

"Okay, so everything would include . . . ?"

"A hair dryer, curling iron. Do you happen to have an extra toothbrush?"

Pretty soon I'm sitting on the hardwood floor of the guest room (Mary's old bedroom) while Susan sits above me on the bed and blow dries my hair with her round brush. Normally, I would not put up with this. But both Susan and I know that this is what I need. I guess it's one of those Relief Society moments when a sister does exactly the right thing.

Once it's all dry, she reaches for the curling iron. "Why don't you let me curl it too?"

"Don't you want to get back to the baby?"

Susan clicks the iron to a strip of hair. "She's asleep, and Jack's holding her anyway. I used to curl my sister's hair all the time growing up. I kind of miss it."

"I didn't know you had a sister."

She rolls the curl up. "And I didn't know that you and Neil had a history."

I bite my bottom lip and smile. "Jack didn't tell you?"

"Nope. Neil's love life is off-limits. They have a pact."

"Oh."

Susan unrolls the curl and starts on a new one. "Liz told me. She was over here with Neil about a week ago and let it slip."

I moan, wondering how much damage Liz can do in one night.

"I think she has a little crush on him."

Why do I feel nervous about that? She isn't his type at all—at least I didn't think she was.

Susan pats the top of my head. "Of course it's an unrequited crush."

That makes me laugh a little. "Poor Liz."

"Are you going to fill me in? Or do I have to keep after Jack?"

I swallow. "We dated during the summer after his mission."

"I thought so. Tell me more."

"I have to warn you that it's going to make me look really bad. I wasn't really—"

"You must be the one Jack used to call you 'the heartbreaker.' That was before the pact."

I guess the name fits. Still, it hurts to have to admit it.

Susan rubs the top of my back. "How'd you meet?"

"He sat by me one day in Sunday School. We talked a little afterward. Then, after Relief Society, you know how all the little kids stand right outside the door, waiting for their moms? Well, he was right there with them, waiting for me. He invited me to go to a fireside with him that night. After that, we started eating lunch together. He was working at the country club, and I was down the road from there working at the library. Then we started meeting after work. I really didn't mean to break his heart. I liked him a lot." I take a long breath and wonder if I'm talking too much.

"How old were you?"

"Nineteen."

"That's young to get so serious—for most people, at least."

"I guess I was young. I hadn't really worked through my feelings about my parents' divorce. And my mom and dad both disapproved of our relationship. Neil hadn't started college yet. I think they would have liked him better if he'd already finished school."

Susan picks through a curl and sprays my hair. "I can understand that."

"I might have been too young for marriage but not too young to fall in love." I scrunch my shoulders. "Is there any chance that Jack can hear this conversation?"

Susan turns to look out the door. "He's downstairs watching TV. You can check if you want to."

I shake my head. "I'll take your word for it."

She sprays some more. "So you loved him?"

"Yeah."

"Then why'd you break it off?"

"I got scared. I wasn't ready to get married, which is what he wanted. I think you probably know the rest of the story."

She hugs me around the shoulders. "Men can't take rejection, can they? Even if it has nothing to do with them." She fluffs my hair.

I steal a peak at the doorway to make sure Jack isn't standing there, then I go on. "Neal kind of has this—I don't know what to call it—but he's always rescuing me. Last week, he brought me dinner because I had the flu. This week, he's protecting me from Will. I think we've played out the damsel in distress scene about six or seven times by now."

"Is it working?"

"I'm not doing it on purpose. He seems to be waiting for me to get myself in some sort of mess, so he can swoop down and be my hero. I asked him about it—why he always feels he has to rescue me."

"What'd he say?"

I lower my voice and quote him. " 'I'm not trying to rescue you all the time, Anne. You need to be rescued all the time.' "

Susan laughs. "He obviously still cares about you." Letting her words sink in, I sit in silence. Then she fluffs my hair again. "All done."

I stand up and look in the mirror. "Thanks, Susan. After I finish my makeup, I want to do something for you. I feel like I've invaded your house. You're the one with the new baby. I should be doing something to help."

"I really don't need any help, Anne. I didn't go through labor and delivery."

Grabbing my purse, I start to pull out the blush, mascara, and lipstick. "Don't try to tell me you haven't gone through any pain because I know you have, even if it's all emotional."

She looks down, pretending to examine her fingernails. "You're right. I guess if you count all the emotional pain, I've been suffering for five or six years. Even this week, when we found out we were finally getting a baby, I was so worried that I wouldn't be able to bond with her because I'm not her birth mother. And I was worried that her birth mother would want her back—that type of thing happens so often. I couldn't sleep at all the two nights before we brought her home. Then Jack gave me a blessing. I felt the Spirit tell me that I really am her mother, even if I didn't give birth to her. It helped so much."

"I'm really happy for you, Susan."

"Thanks . . . You know, if you feel like you might want a blessing, you can always ask Jack . . . or Neil."

"It's been so long since I had a blessing. I think the last time I had one was when I was on my mission."

"All you have to do is ask. I'm sure Neil would be happy to do it."

"You don't think it would be awkward? I mean, so much has happened between us, I think he'd feel self-conscious about the whole thing. What if he felt inspired to say something about—I don't know—about marriage or something."

Susan rolls her eyes at me. "He has the priesthood. He's used to saying what Heavenly Father wants you to hear. I don't think he'll feel awkward at all."

"I'll think about it." I dig around in my purse some more. "So are you going to let me help you? I can clean the house—not that it needs it—or cook dinner or help with the laundry."

She looks at me sideways and smiles. "Do you have time to make some cinnamon rolls?"

I'm putting the glaze on the cinnamon rolls when Jack ambles in, having taken a nap. "Are these for Neil?"

I put one of the rolls on a plate for him. "They're for everybody. Susan wanted me to make them."

He takes the plate and sits down on a bar stool. "Do me a favor and tell Neil you made 'em for him."

I laugh and shake my head. "Why do I have the feeling that you want us to get back together?"

He takes a bite, smiles, and nods. "Gotta keep this kind of baking in the family. You're a domestic goddess, Anne."

I finish glazing and take the bowl to the sink. "It's about the only bread recipe I can make."

"We'll take you anyway." He looks toward the corner, then back at me. "You like him, don't you?"

Why do I have a funny feeling about this conversation? "Of course I like him."

He wipes his face with a napkin. "You want him back, don't you?"

I turn on the water and squirt dish soap into the sink. "Jack, if Neil wants to ask me that question, he'll ask me himself."

Jack's still smiling and shifting his gaze from me to the corner.

Pushing the dirty dishes down into the soapy water, I finally understand what's going on. "He's standing right behind me, isn't he?" I hear Neil's deep chuckle coming from the doorway in the corner and turn to see him, standing there in a freshly laundered, white button-down shirt. "How long have you been standing there?"

Neil digs his hands down into the pockets of his khakis. "Not too long."

Jack stands up and shoots Neil a look that tells me he was probably there longer than he wants to admit. "I think I'll go watch a little TV, and leave you two to discuss whatever you might want to discuss." He gives Neil another meaningful stare.

Wiping off the countertop, I turn to bat my eyelashes at Neil. "I made you some cinnamon rolls."

He laughs. "Yeah, I heard the whole domestic goddess thing. They smell good." Instead of walking toward the rolls, though, he heads toward the sink, where he grabs the dishcloth and starts to wash the dishes.

"I can do that, Neil. Why don't you eat?"

He washes a bowl and puts it on the other side of the sink. "There aren't very many."

I rinse the bowl. "You're all dressed up. Did you have a hot date this afternoon?"

Another laugh. He takes his time answering. "I'm taking a girl to McDonald's later."

I think back to my earlier conversation with Susan and decide now is as good a time as any to ask him about a blessing. I take a breath and swallow. "Neil, can I ask you something?"

He hands me the last dish. "If it's about Jack—"

"It's not about Jack. I was wondering if you'd consider giving me a blessing."

"You want me to give you a blessing?"

Maybe Susan was wrong about this. "You don't have to. I can ask someone else."

His hands are back in his pockets. "No, I want to do it. Let me get Jack."

Usually, the first thing anyone does when he gives me a blessing is ask my middle name. It's Alaina. Then I have to coach him a little on pronunciation—Uh-lay-nuh. So I'm about to recite my whole name to Jack when Neil says, "It's Anne Alaina Elliot." His pronunciation is perfect. This, in itself, is enough of a distraction to keep me from listening to the anointing.

As soon as Neil starts the blessing, the Holy Ghost fills me up and surrounds me. I feel warmth and peace and truth all at once. Tears are dripping off the end of my nose, so I'm already using the tissue Susan handed me a minute ago.

The words of the blessing fall down on me like water in the desert. I want to remember all the promises and all the counsel. It shouldn't surprise me how well it fits me, but it does surprise me. The blessing reaches deeper than the events of the last few days. I am stunned.

Heavenly Father loves me. He knows what I'm feeling. He's pleased with me. I get a sense of eternity that is so much bigger than my usual idea of past, present, and future. My car, my job, my worries about Will are all fading away. They all seem so unimportant.

Life is not a series of deadlines to be met. The Lord took things day by day when He created the world. I can take things step-by-step, day-by-day, asking for inspiration as I go. Doing things in order doesn't mean that I'll always know exactly where I'm headed. Sometimes it means choosing what I think is the best, favoring the things of God over the things of the world.

Faith, hope, and charity all depend on positive thinking. Faith—the ability to believe that Christ suffered for me and loves me. Hope—knowing that through Christ I can overcome all things. Charity—thinking no evil and loving unconditionally.

When the blessing ends, the room is still. I figure it's probably up to me to break the silence, so I stand. Following the protocol, I reach out to shake Jack's hand, but he pulls me into a big, bear hug. With my face pushed up against his collarbone, I mutter, "Thanks, Jack."

He lets go of me and, grinning, tilts his head toward Neil, who is staring at the floor with his hands in his pockets.

I step toward Neil. Our eyes meet. I reach for his hand. "Thank you. That was just what I needed."

He takes my hand in both of his. "It wasn't me, you know."

It is so hard to say anything with him looking at me this way. "I know, but you should at least say, 'you're welcome.'"

Amusement dances in his eyes. "You're welcome, ma'am. Now, how about a cinnamon roll?" Playing the role of a proper Southern gentleman, he loops my hand around his arm and escorts me back to the kitchen, where he helps me into a chair.

I watch him pour us two glasses of milk. "I really do appreciate all you're doing for me, Neil."

He sets the glasses down and dishes up two cinnamon rolls. "Why do I sense another 'please don't rescue me' lecture coming on?"

I pat the chair beside me. "Sit down. I'm not going to lecture you."

He sits down and takes a bite of his roll. I sip my milk and unroll the outer edge of the roll. "I really don't want to go to McDonald's."

Neil swallows. "This is delicious, Anne. Thanks." He takes another bite.

"You're welcome. I really did make them for you." I try to maintain eye contact, but I find myself looking down at my cinnamon roll again, which is now completely uncoiled. I tear off a piece and eat it.

Neil finishes off his roll. "So, would you consider a change of plans?"

"What kind of change of plans?"

He leans back in his chair and sits up straight. "I've been talking to Marcy and Valerie Harville. They're planning a sleepover for tonight."

"In North Carolina?"

"The Harvilles are staying up at my house for the week. Before you say no, let me explain why it's a good idea, okay?"

I bite my bottom lip. "Okay."

"No one in your family knows where I live. I'm not listed on the directories. I even keep a P.O. Box, so criminals can't locate me."

"Neil, I don't think it would be appropriate for me to stay in your house."

"The Harvilles are there. Marcy will be there. I'll sleep somewhere else. You can lock me out in the backyard if you want to."

I roll my eyes. "Are you sure this is really necessary? Maybe if I talk to Will one more time—"

Neil stands up and motions for me to follow him. "Come here." He takes me into the dining room, where the shades are drawn. When he parts the shades an inch, I see the Jaguar waiting for us across the street.

23

Saturday, August 24, 2002

I don't think I'll ever forget the look on Neil's face when I told him I couldn't marry him. It was devastation. That's the only way I know how to describe it. I think it was the hardest thing I've ever done in my life.

I did it because I love him. He deserves to have a good marriage, and everyone knows I don't have a clue about a good marriage. I had a long talk with Mom and Dad last night. It's the first time in a long time the two of them have agreed on anything. They both think I'm too young and inexperienced. They said the fact that we don't have any money and the fact that he wants to be a policeman will only make it worse. If anyone knows how hard marriage can be, it's them. They're both so successful in every way, and I'm so much like them. How could I have a successful marriage when all I've experienced is failure? I can't let my family problems become Neil's family problems.

Today I'm heading back to school. I'm on the plane right now. The man sitting next to me asked if I was going to a funeral. I probably look terrible from all the crying. In a way, it is like a death, seeing this part of my life end.

Seeing Will in his Jaguar in front of Jack's house has turned the smoldering embers of my rage into a roaring fire. Because of Will, I spent last night on the metro instead of at a restaurant. Because of

Will, I sprayed mace at Neil. Because of Will, I spent an hour and a half in the police station this morning. Because of Will, Neil and I are "friends." Because of Will, I've once again caved in to the will of my father. I march to the front door and fling it open.

Neil is right behind me. "What are you doing, Anne?"

I'm halfway across the lawn. Neil reaches for my arm. I snatch it away. "I'm just going to talk to him. You're welcome to come along."

"I thought you were afraid of him."

I've reached the street. I'm crossing it. "He's the one that should be afraid."

Neil is right beside me. "Fear really is a good thing sometimes, Anne. It's God's way of protecting you. Talking to him will only encourage him."

I stop beside the Jaguar. Will opens the door and steps out, but I am the first to speak. "You have got to stop following me everywhere, Will. I appreciate all you've done for me and all you've done for my dad. But as far as you and I go, it's over." Trying to emphasize my point, I poke him in the chest with my longest fingernail and stomp my foot. "You have absolutely no chance of getting me back. I don't know how to say it more clearly."

Will rests an elbow on the top of his car. "Anne, I think you misinterpreted what happened last night. I only wanted to talk to you."

There's no use arguing with him about it. "Last night has nothing to do with this. I told you on Thursday that it's over, and I meant it. Do you have anything else you want to say to me?"

Will rubs his Adam's apple. "Would it make any difference if I told you I loved you?"

I fold my arms. "No, Will, it wouldn't."

He steps toward me. "Anne, it's not like you to be so unfeeling. After all I've done for you, I don't think you should give up on me so easily."

As if on cue, Neil steps out from in back of me and stands between us. Confused, Will glances up at him, then slips into his charming mode. "It's Neil, right?"

Neil stands with his feet apart, his hands at his waist. "It's 'Sir.'" He reaches into his back pocket and pulls out some folded papers. "Listen, I don't want this to get ugly, but I have something I'd like to discuss with you, Will, if you don't mind." He unfolds the papers on top of Will's car. "First of all, when did you start dating Anne?"

Will opens the door of the car. "Around the beginning of September."

"That's strange. I have some information here that says your divorce wasn't final until about two weeks ago." He shakes his head. "That really doesn't make you look good. Does Anne's father know about this? He seems to think his job is on the line because Anne broke up with you."

Will gets into his car, but Neil prevents him from shutting the door. Will sneers. "Listen, I don't know where you came up with that lie—"

"Public records, and I'm just getting started. There are other things about you that I don't like as well."

Will turns the key in the ignition. Neil shuts the door for him, then waves as he pulls away from the curb. My mouth hangs open while we watch his car disappear around the corner. Then I reach for the papers Neil holds in his hands, but he's too quick. Before I can grab them, he's folded them up again and placed them in his back pocket.

As we walk back up to the house, I wipe my lips with the back of my hand. "Does that mean that I dated a married man? I kissed a married man?"

He looks at me sideways with a sly grin. "So you kissed him?"

I grab the papers that are still sticking out of his back pocket. "I didn't know he was married."

"Was he a good kisser?"

I wrinkle my nose. "Too wet."

Neil laughs. "Not quite the distraction you were looking for, then?"

Scanning through the stack of papers, I moan. "He didn't tell me he was divorced . . . or married. I thought he was single. He never said anything about a wife. What's this? He declared bankruptcy?"

"Yep."

"He's been spending a lot of money on me."

"So that's how he did it," Neil teases.

I give him a shove on the side of his arm and hand the papers back to him. Walking up the front steps, I get a whiff of the box-woods. Neil puts his arm around my shoulder and squeezes me in. "I meant to tell you about all this before I talked to him, Annie, but you kind of jumped the gun."

I stop and look at him. Did he just call me Annie? I search his face for a hint that he knows his tongue slipped. Nothing. Why is it that he seems to read me so well, and I have no idea what he's thinking?

I've heard that in Greek, there are three different words for love—one for romantic love, another for friendship love, and still another for the way you might love your mother or your dog or mint chocolate chip ice cream. I'm not sure how I'd describe what's going on with Neil and me. There's a sort of pity love because he feels sorry for me, then there's the obligation love because I helped Lily, and obviously there's friendship. But there's also a little of the attraction of the past.

I still haven't made up my mind about staying in Baltimore. Neil is changing the lock on my apartment door while I'm locked in my room, trying to pack. Not knowing exactly where I'm going or for how long makes the task seem daunting. After ten minutes of indecision, I go out to the living room and plop down on the sofa. "I don't know what to pack. I don't even know where I'm going."

Neil puts down the screwdriver that he's using to install the dead bolt. "You got some flowers." He steps out into the hallway, then reemerges with one of Will's signature rose bouquets, complete with the big red bow around the vase. Someone must have delivered it while I was in my room.

It's the fourth one he's sent. "I don't ever want to see red roses again."

Neil removes one of the roses from the top of the bouquet and holds it out to me. "This one is from me."

Seized with a desire to kiss him, I smile and take the rose. "Thank you."

"What do you want me to do with the rest?"

I hop up and take the bouquet from his hands. "It's not their fault they came from Will." Heading down the hallway, I open Marcy's door and set the vase on her dresser. Neil's rose gets a more prominent place in the middle of the kitchen table. Back in the living room, I sit back down on the couch.

Neil is back at work on the dead bolt. "Do you remember that night I brought you home from North Carolina—how you promised you'd go out to dinner with me?"

I remember, but somehow in my memory, it's all tied up with Lily. "Yes, but really Neil, you don't owe me anything. I think you've paid me back enough."

There's a trace of exasperation in his face, as he sets down the screwdriver and looks at me. "Do you want to go or not?"

"I want to go. I don't want you to feel obligated."

He lets his breath out all at once as if he's lifted a heavy weight. "I don't feel obligated." He picks up the screwdriver again and starts to remove the doorknob. "There's a place in Baltimore I want to take you. I think you'll like it."

"What kind of place?"

"It's on the formal side."

A shock runs through my spine. "Oh."

"That red dress you wore the night Lily tricked you into going to the singles' ward dance—it would be about right."

He remembers what I wore. Am I really awake? I go to my room and pinch myself. Yes. Yes. Yes. Once I get the red dress on, it doesn't take long to pack at all. I am saying a grateful prayer and singing and smiling all over.

I think this is it! White linen tablecloth, a candle in the middle of the table, more than one fork, stemmed goblets, and Neil is wearing a tie. How could it not be a date? I open the menu, looking forward to the northern Italian cuisine. Then I notice the prices and catch my breath. I lean toward Neil. "What are you going to order?"

"Last time I got trout, but they've changed the menu since then."

Does that mean they've raised the prices since the last time he came? "Maybe I'll just get dessert. "

Neil looks at me over the menu. "You should get real food, Anne. You haven't eaten anything healthy all day." Anne again, not Annie. It must have been a mistake earlier. Or maybe I imagined it. He looks back down at his menu. "I think I'll get the polenta with quail."

"I don't think I could eat a quail. They're too cute with that little thing bobbing along on top of their heads." He smiles, and I realize I've said the wrong thing again. "I'm sure it'll be good though." I look back down at the menu. "Where is the polenta with quail?" I want to see how much it costs.

He laughs. "It's not really on the menu. I just wanted to see your reaction. I think I'll get the swordfish." He points to the bottom of the menu. "*Pesce Spada alla Livornese* or however you say it."

I look at the price. Next to the lobster, which I know he doesn't like, it's the most expensive item on the menu. I squint at him. "Do you really want the swordfish, or are you ordering it so I won't worry about the prices?"

He winks at me. "I know what I want. All you have to decide is what you want."

Is he talking about the menu or our relationship? I look at the menu and try hard to focus on it. All the chicken dishes have wine in them. That leaves red meat or fish. "Maybe I'll try the lamb chops."

Once the server brings out the salads and bread, I realize how truly hungry I am. I devour the mixed greens drenched with balsamic vinaigrette then move onto the crusty bread. "I could eat this whole loaf."

Neil slowly butters a piece of bread. "I'll bet you could. When was the last time you had a real meal?"

I take a minute to think. "Probably last week when you brought Janet Musgrove's soup over. It's been pretty hectic without my car." I pop another piece of bread into my mouth.

He fingers the stem of his goblet. "Anne, there's something I need to get off my chest." Why does this make me nervous? He looks up from the goblet long enough to explain. "I owe you an apology. At that dance last summer, I wasn't very nice to you."

I remember how angry he was when we danced together and how he was always looking at Lily instead of at me. Is this why he's brought me here—to apologize? I put down the bread I was about to eat. "I think I kind of deserved it. I'm the one who should be apologizing to you."

His eyes are back on the goblet. "No, you didn't deserve it. I've felt bad about it ever since. Do you think you could forgive me?"

I hate it when people answer a question with a question, but it seems like the best thing to do now. "Do you think you could forgive me?"

I can see my reflection in his eyes. He reaches across the table and takes my hand. "I'm working on it." I swallow hard. Does he know what his touch does to me? My head feels like it's filling up with helium.

The server comes along to refill my water, and Neil lets go of my hand. "I also feel bad about last night. I wish I'd stuck around and gone to dinner with you."

I take a sip of my water. "If I'd known what was going to happen, I probably would have crawled into the back of your car."

"You almost did."

I laugh. "That was because I didn't want you to leave." Why don't I think before I blurt things out? We're here because he wanted to apologize.

"So, how's your dad doing?"

"He's better. It helps that he has a job now—less stress, you know. I worry about him a lot."

His eyes are back on the goblet. "Whatever happened between your mom and dad? I mean, why aren't they together?"

"They fought a lot—mostly about money. To me, it was just the way things were. It seemed normal for Mom and Dad to fight every once in a while. Then one day, we came home from school and Mom had moved out. She didn't say anything to anyone. She just left. I couldn't believe it when it happened. It was like I was numb. I guess I was in shock."

"How old were you?"

"Twelve."

"Hard age."

I brush the crumbs off the linen tablecloth. "I always felt like it was my fault. That year, I'd done a lot of things to give my parents grief. I used to complain about everything—the food, my clothes, having to share a bedroom with Mary, school. I used to sneak out at night just to sneak out. I fought with Liz a lot of the time, and when I wasn't fighting with Liz, I was fighting with Mary. The day before

Mom left, I'd gotten a report card. It was all C's except for a D in home economics. I really thought that Mom's leaving had to do with that report card. I thought that if I'd been a better student and a better daughter, I could have kept the family together."

Feeling hungry, I eat another piece of bread.

Neil leans forward. "So, you thought if you were perfect, you could have prevented the divorce?"

I feel the attraction taking over. If I keep looking into his eyes, my brain might as well be tapioca pudding. I want to explain things in a way that he'll understand. And if there's anything he needs to understand, it's this. I shift my focus back to the bread before going on. "After Mom left, I tried to get my act together. I worked hard in school, and I tried to be better at home. But I never really felt I was good enough. I guess somewhere in the back of my head, I thought that if I was a little bit better, Mom would come back. It helped when Liz and I started going to church."

"That was when you were fourteen, right?"

The way he remembers this little detail makes me smile. "Right. I don't know how teenagers make it without the church. I don't think I could have. I was really hungry for it. I needed it so much, and not just for social reasons. I needed to feel like I could start over. And I needed the Holy Ghost. How does anyone live without that?"

"So, you don't feel guilty anymore?"

"I don't know. I guess I feel guilty sometimes. But the older I get, the more ridiculous it seems that a twelve-year-old could break up a marriage. My parents had problems. As far as I know, they could have solved them if they wanted to." I pause while the server places our entrees in front of us. Once she leaves and Neil digs into his swordfish, I continue the thought. "I guess it's not my place to judge them. Divorce probably was the best thing for my mom. I just don't want my kids to ever have to go through the kind of stuff I went through."

I slice into my lamb chops and slip a piece of the tender meat into my mouth. It's much better than I was expecting—must have something to do with those fresh herbs. While I'm still chewing, Neil leans back in his chair. "You probably wouldn't want your husband to go through the stuff your dad went through either."

I draw my breath in and swallow. I don't mean to swallow the meat I'm chewing, but I do, and it goes down the wrong way. I'm coughing, my eyes are watering, and I can see the couple at the next table turn to stare at me. Why do these things happen to me? I wish I could stop coughing. Now people on the other side of the room are looking, including one of the servers, who's heading our way.

Pounding the top of my chest with my hand, I gasp for air. I reach for my water, but it's empty. Neil calmly pours the rest of his water into my goblet, but I'm coughing too much to drink. The server rushes over to inform me that she knows the Heimlich. Neil tells her not to worry, that I'll be fine. I cough some more. Finally, it dislodges, and I gasp for air. The server, looking almost disappointed at my recovery, refills my water glass and retreats. I gulp down the water and wipe my eyes. "Sorry. How embarrassing!"

Neil smiles. "It happens to everyone. Don't worry about it."

I fold the napkin and place it back in my lap. "What were we talking about?"

"I was about to ask about your plans for the future."

I sigh. "Isn't that kind of hard to say? I mean, nobody knows what's going to happen."

His eyes are back on his goblet, now empty. "Well, where do you want to be?'"

"I guess I want to be married to someone I love. And I want to have a temple marriage. Is that what you mean?"

He nods.

"I really don't want to get divorced. Even if there aren't any children. Unless we have much bigger problems than my parents had." I shouldn't have added that last part, but it's the truth. What if I married someone, and he turned out to be a big faker like Will? Of course, Neil isn't at all like Will. I take another bite of lamb and imagine what it would be like to marry Neil and have his child—to carry his baby inside me, to sleep beside him at night.

Neil strokes the back of my hand with his finger. "Care to fill me in?"

I look up into those blue eyes of his. "What?" I really should remember that he brought me here to apologize. It's not a real date.

"What were you thinking about just now? I wouldn't ask, but it's the happiest you've looked all day."

"Oh, nothing."

"I'll give you a bite of my swordfish," he tempts.

"You're not going to let this go, are you?"

He takes a bite of fish and shakes his head.

"Okay, I was thinking about marriage."

He shakes his head again and swallows. "You've got to be more specific if you want a bite of this."

"All right, if you must know . . . I was thinking of how nice it would be to . . . well, to have a baby with my husband."

Neil's fork is suspended halfway between the plate and his mouth. He's holding it there and staring at me. Maybe I shouldn't have been quite so honest.

"Do I get my bite of swordfish now?" I ask.

He startles. "Oh . . . yeah." The piece of fish slips off his fork and falls into his lap. Ignoring it, he cuts another piece. Then he holds the fork up to my mouth, and I claim my prize, still wondering if I really should have shared my thoughts with him. He gives a breath-filled laugh. "You really are hard to predict sometimes, Anne."

I chew and swallow. "That was really good."

"Do I get to taste yours?"

A devious laugh escapes my mouth. "That depends."

"On what?"

"Whether I get equal access to your thoughts."

"Okay."

We eat in silence while he thinks. Under the table, my legs are bouncing. I feel like a puppy who can't keep her tail still.

I'm halfway through my lamb-chop when he speaks. "Okay, I'll make a confession."

"As long as it's not another apology."

"It's not an apology . . . Here goes. I've been counting all day how many times I can make you blush. So far, we're up to eleven, not counting the three times that Jack did it. But—" He looks at me and waits. "I think we've made it to twelve. That's the most I've ever gotten in one day." He leans back in his chair, grinning.

I cover my face with my hands. "So you have a goal to make me blush?" Am I some sort of game to him? It sounds like he's done it before too.

He pulls my hands away from my face. "It's just that you're so cute when you blush. I can't resist."

Who does he think he is—my babysitter? I stab my fork into the meat. "I'm almost twenty-eight years old, Neil."

"I know you've gotten older, Anne, but you haven't changed that much."

A tiny wave of excitement ripples through my body. Isn't this the same guy who said he almost didn't recognize me at the garage sale?

"So are you mad at me?"

I take another bite and let him wait for the answer. Then I remember how I fixed his cowlick. "I got you to blush once today."

He raises an eyebrow and grins. "So I'm not the only one who's guilty, then?"

I shake my head and we dissolve into giggles.

The server wants to know if we want dessert. There is no way I can stuff anything else into my stomach, but Neil orders Spumoni ice cream with two spoons. He sets it in the middle of the table and hands me the second spoon. Chocolate, pistachio, and cherry—I love that combination. And the ecstasy on Neil's face as he tastes it tempts me even more. I dip my spoon into the chocolate. It's so deep and dark, I might not have to eat chocolate again for a week. Neil observes me. "Is it as good as Ben and Jerry's?"

I nod. "It might even be better . . . Thanks for dinner. I really enjoyed it. I'm glad you brought me here."

"Now, I'm supposed to say you're welcome, right?"

Once we leave the restaurant, Neil takes me on a walking tour of Baltimore's Little Italy. The streets are narrow, lined on either side with three-story brick buildings wedged side by side. There are no alleys. Every block has two or three restaurants, advertising themselves with neon lights, murals, and green awnings. In between the restaurants, older people sit out on their front steps chatting.

Neil walks along with his hands in his pockets. "I used to work here when I was going to school. I waited tables, mostly on the weekends."

I walk close enough so he can reach for my hand if he wants to. "It seems like a fun place."

"I didn't like it much then, but it's grown on me."

"Was that when your dad passed away?"

He looks over at an Italian flag hanging from the building next to us. "Yeah, it was right after that. I started here when I was in my second semester of college. I had a pretty heavy schedule. Looking back, it seems like all I did was work and go to school. I took Sundays off, but that was about it."

So this was what it was like for him the year after we broke up. Not exactly the life I'd imagined he'd lived that year—one full of social interaction and fun. I wrap my hand around his forearm, and look up at him. "Sounds lonely." He doesn't answer right away, so I let my hand drop again.

Removing his hands from his pockets, he glances at my face, and then down at my hand. "They have outdoor movies here during the summer."

"Italian films?"

"Sometimes. You still like foreign films?"

My hand bumps into his. "Lately, I like Indian films best."

He throws his head back and laughs. "Bollywood?"

"What's wrong with Bollywood?"

He looks ahead, down the road. "I always laugh when I think of their little dance numbers. Have you seen the one about the cricket game?" He stops walking and stares ahead, his hands at his waist.

I halt beside him. "You mean *Lagaan*. That was good."

He reaches an arm up my back and hunches over. "Get down," he commands. Responding to the pressure of his hand on the back of my neck, I bend forward. He pulls me, still hunched over, to a shadowy corner next to someone's front stoop. Though I was hoping for a little more physical contact, I can do without the policeman grip.

I squat against the brick wall with Neil close beside me. His arm still rests across my back, but his eyes are on the road in front of us. "What's going on?" I ask. This has to be something to do with his work.

Still looking at the road, he leans even closer to me. "I'm afraid if I tell you, you'll take off again." He pauses as his eyes follow a passing car, then he stands and watches it drive off. Something about the way he's standing reminds me of an old cowboy movie. But that thought passes as another fills my mind. Could Will have found us here? Is that why I'm hunched up against a cold brick wall?

24

Sunday, September 19, 2004

I've been thinking a lot about where I'm headed and where I want to be headed. It's been over a year now since everything ended with Neil. I look back a lot and wonder if I made the right decision. I dated a guy last summer, Charlie Musgrove. My parents liked him. But I couldn't make up my mind. I don't know why—whether it's because I know I'm not ready for marriage or because we're not compatible. I still think a lot about Neil. I try not to.

I need a change of pace. I can't spend my whole life thinking about the past. I'll be twenty-one next week, which means I could go on a mission. One of the returned sister missionaries at institute told me I'd never regret it if I did. I want to go. I want to make a bigger commitment to living the gospel and becoming the person I want to be. I need to find out what Heavenly Father wants.

A breeze blows across the pavement, scraping a dry leaf around in a circle beside us. Crouching there, I remember another night I hid—this time in the spring. Back then, I hid in the space between the lilac bush and the shed at our old house. The last few blooms of lilac still hung above me, drenching the air with their scent, while a cold spring wind chafed against my bare legs and arms. I was wearing the Easter dress Mom gave me, not even caring about the wet ground beneath me. How could I spend my whole spring break with Mom? She left me. Why should I want her back now?

Mary and Liz were already sitting in Mom's sedan. I could hear Dad calling me, sometimes inside, sometimes outside. After I'd gotten cold enough for my teeth to chatter, Mom came around the side of the house and spotted me. "Anne, honey, you've gotten your dress all muddy."

"I'm staying with Dad. If you want me to come with you, you'll have to bring him too."

Mom put her face in her hands. "Anne, you don't understand—"

"I'm not as dumb as you think, Mom."

She bent down and pulled back one of the lilac branches. "Sweetie, no matter what happens between your father and I, I want you to know that I love you."

I always thought she got that line out of a book. How could she love me when she'd rejected me? I wasn't the daughter she expected— one that got good grades and had perfect hair, one that would never sit down in the mud in her new dress. She said she was divorcing Dad, but it felt like she was divorcing me too.

Neil squats back down against the wall with his phone to his ear. "Your boyfriend is following us again."

I scoot away from him. "He's not my boyfriend." He should know that by now.

"I guess I'm a little possessive of my ex-boyfriend title. I don't think he deserves—Hey," he speaks into the phone. "This is Captain Wentworth. I need a couple squad cars down here in Little Italy. I'm at 55 Blackmore Street. It's a personal situation. I'm on a date and her ex-boyfriend is stalking us." The word "date" skips across my skin, leaving goose bumps, as Neil gives the dispatcher details about Will's car.

Neil looks over at me and keeps talking. "Not that it's any of your business, Gladys, but she's my ex-girlfriend. We dated a long time ago, and we've gotten to be friends again. This guy has a couple of unpaid tickets, so it'll be easy to bring him in." He winks at me. "No, I'm not the ex-boyfriend that's stalking her." Then he tilts his head toward me and covers the mouthpiece of his phone. "You don't think I'm stalking you too, do you?"

Laughing, I shake my head. "You can stalk me all you want."

He touches the tip of my nose. "I don't know. You're kind of dangerous with that pepper spray." He pulls my phone out of his back pocket and hands it to me. "You'll want to double-check with Marcy about tonight."

Less than a minute later, one police car arrives, and then another. Neil scans the street up and down. Then he takes my hand and leads me to the first car. "This is where we part ways."

I stop. "What?"

"I'm going to have these officers drive you up to headquarters. I'll catch up with you there after we're through."

"Wouldn't it be better if I took a cab? I don't want to waste their time."

He gives my arm a tug. "Your safety is not a waste of time." The tone of his voice tells me there's no use arguing.

"Thanks for dinner," I mutter as he opens the back door of the first police car.

I tilt my head up automatically, as if I'm expecting a kiss, but Neil's head is turned to the officers in the front of the car. "If you could take her down to headquarters, I'll do all the paperwork when I get there." Our date is over; he's back on the job.

I slide into the back seat, the material of my dress slipping easily over the vinyl seat. Never having been in the backseat of a police car, I notice the plexiglass window that separates me from the officers up front and the indentations in the seat backs for people wearing handcuffs. The officer in the driver's seat, a husky African-American man, extends his hand through the hole in the Plexiglas. "I'm Sergeant Hall." He nods toward the female officer at his right. "This is Officer Chavez." She nods at me.

I shake Sergeant Hall's hand. "Nice to meet you. Thanks for your help."

Neil shuts my door and waves as Sergeant Hall pulls away from the curb. The Sergeant says something into his radio, then turns his attention back to me. "Let me get this straight. You were on a date with Captain Wentworth when someone started stalking you?"

"Well, he's been stalking me all day, actually."

Sergeant Hall slaps his leg. "That's rich—a stalker following the captain's woman. He doesn't know what he's in for."

"Captain Wentworth is tough on stalkers, then?"

Officer Chavez smiles knowingly at the Sergeant. "He has that reputation."

Sergeant Hall holds up his hand. "I'll put it this way, if it concerns a lady, you can be sure the captain is going to put everything on the line. He's soft on the ladies." He shakes his head. "I only wish I could stick around to see it."

Staring out the window, I wonder why Neil brought me here. Is it some sort of trap he worked up to get Will? Is he using himself as a target? That would be just like him to take me on a date to rescue me.

The scenes we passed earlier are now rushing by my window. The big Catholic Church with the round window that looks like a sliced pizza, the group of old ladies gossiping, the green and white murals, the neon signs, and the restaurant where we ate all slip into the past. Neil's SUV is ahead of us, parked halfway between two street lamps, in a darker section of the street. The spot is dark, except for underneath the car, where a dim light shines. "Why is there a light under Neil's car?" I ask myself.

I don't mean for anyone else to hear my question, but Officer Chavez responds, "Pardon me?"

By this time, we've already passed his car. "Oh, it's nothing. I was wondering why there's a light under Neil's car. Maybe I imagined it."

Sergeant Hall slows to a stop while Officer Chavez calls in to headquarters, notifying them of their change of plans. They leave me in the car alone while they investigate. Within seconds, another police car pulls up behind us. Neil waves to me as he exits the back—a policeman wave—then walks around to join the others near his car.

Unbuckling my seat belt and kneeling on the seat, I try to figure out what's happening. What if Will is trying to wreck Neil's car? I don't know much about it, but he could probably poke a hole in the gas line or cut through some wires. Or what if he's put a bomb on it? Please don't let it be a bomb.

I've got my head in my hands, praying about bombs when the two officers get back in the car. "How 'bout that," Sergeant Hall says as he takes the car out of park. "You nabbed your own stalker." He laughs. "That boy was all the way under the captain's car when we walked over there. He was so surprised to see us cops looking at him that he bumped his head. Got a big, greasy bump on his forehead now."

"What was he doing?"

"You got me. The captain's kneeling down in his dress pants with a flashlight right now trying to figure it out."

"What happened to Will?"

"He's cuffed."

"So he's going to jail?" I've never even known anyone who's been in jail.

"Most definitely."

I hate to admit it, but the emotion I'm feeling is not relief or pity or embarrassment; it's disappointment. With Will in jail, there'll be no excuse for spending time with Neil. Worst of all, I won't need to stay in Baltimore. I can go back home. There won't be any use at all for the dress I packed to wear to Neil's ward tomorrow or my best pair of jeans I was going to wear while we ate breakfast. Instead of spending the day with Neil, I'll be far away, enjoying the quiet monotony of a Sunday in my apartment.

The police headquarters is a plain-looking building that, from the outside, appears to be made entirely of cement, except for a few windows slapped here and there. The inside is not much different. Officer Chavez leads me up a set of stairs, down a hall, and into what she calls the break room. I'm sure she's brought me here because she thinks I'm the captain's girlfriend. I should probably explain that I'm not, but I don't.

Unlike the rest of the building, the break room attempts to be peppy and fashionable. The walls are burgundy and the metal tables and chairs are black. Stainless steel light fixtures hang from the ceiling, throwing subtle lighting on the three vending machines that take up a prominent place along the wall. It smells of stale coffee, a smell that reminds me of long road trips.

I sit as far away from the television as possible and prop my legs up on one of the chairs. Though I'd like to avoid it, it's time to call Marcy. "The slumber party is off," I tell her.

"Are you kidding me?" Her voice is so loud that I have to hold the phone half a foot away from my ear.

"Will's been arrested. He'll be in jail tonight, so we'll be okay at home."

"Well, I'll be staying here with or without you."

"You're already there?"

"Uh-huh. Neil's got a great place. And I love the Harvilles. That Valerie—she is the sweetest. They've got a room all set up for us. I'm sitting on the bed right as we speak. You okay sharing a bed with me? It's a queen size. If you're not, I don't mind sleeping on the floor."

"Marcy, I'm not going to make you sleep on the floor."

"So, you're coming?"

"I don't think so. There's no reason to."

"Do you know what time it is? It's ten-thirty at night. Come back here. Valerie and I will be your chaperones."

"But—"

"We've already got it all worked out. I'll wait up for you, okay?"

"I don't think I'll be staying." As I say this, I notice a group of three male police officers standing at the door. They all turn their heads as soon as I look at them.

Marcy huffs. "Suit yourself."

I watch the officers as they turn to leave. If I'm hearing right, I think one of them says, "She ain't exactly da bomb I was thinking she'd be." Obviously, they were expecting the captain's date to be more attractive. It makes sense. Isn't it natural for a man to date a woman who is at least as attractive as he is?

Marcy's voice breaks through my thoughts. "Are you listening, Anne? I thought you wanted him back."

"I do, but—"

"But?"

I glance around at the door to make sure no one is listening, then I whisper into the phone. "He took me out to dinner, but once we got there, I found out that he wanted to apologize about something that happened last summer. I think he's trying to help me because he feels guilty. He said he's trying to forgive me. And, I'm also starting to wonder if he isn't more interested in catching Will than in being with me."

"He told you he's trying to forgive you?"

"Yeah."

"That's sweet."

Is it my imagination or has Marcy used the word "sweet" twice in one conversation? Valerie must be rubbing off on her already. "It's sweet, but I don't think he realizes he's torturing me."

Marcy sighs into the phone. "You have got to work it, girl. Take the situation, and use it to your advantage. Don't give up."

"I'll try. Just don't get too settled there. I'll need you to drive me home when I get out of here."

After I hang up, I realize that I'm completely alone. If Will finds me here, there'll be no way to escape—there's only one door to the room, and he'll be right there in front of it. Looking for a place where I can't be seen from the doorway, I scoot my chair over so it's hidden beside the last vending machine, then I arrange myself so my legs don't stick out. If Will finds me here, I plan to scream as loud as possible. I hold my keys in my right hand, prepared to gouge his eyes out with them.

Logically, there's no reason for me to be afraid. I'm sitting here on the third floor of police headquarters, surrounded by cops—why am I afraid? Besides that, Sergeant Hall told me Will was under arrest. Still, my heart pounds against my ribs.

I say a prayer, and then I listen. Occasionally, someone comes in to pour a cup of coffee or get a snack from the vending machine. I can see their reflections on the stainless steel trash can. None of them notices me—a good sign.

Sitting there, I have a long time to think about Neil. Yesterday, I was sure he was coming back to me. But today I'm not so sure. Today, I've been too much like a 911 call—the type of emergency he faces day after day at work. Why would a man date someone who is this much of a bother? Maybe I'm just a little box to check off on his to-do list: forgive Anne.

I slip off my shoes—better to run from Will that way—and pull my knees up toward my chest, checking to make sure the hem of my dress covers everything. In my mind, I try to figure out how I ever became the victim of a stalker. This is something I never thought I'd have to go through. Don't stalkers look for women who are shorter than I am, women who don't have to wear control-top panty hose? Aren't they the ones who write personal ads?

And how, come to think of it, did Will ever cross the line between being a nice guy that attends church in North Carolina to a creep who slithers underneath cars late at night? Did I drive him to this? I shuffle through my memory, looking for hints that something like this would happen. When I broke up with him, he didn't seem too angry or too sad, just casual as if he could take me or leave me. But there was a hint of arrogance, almost as if I was a two-year-old having a tantrum, and he was going to wait it out.

No matter how hard I try to convince myself to come out from behind the vending machine, I can't do it. I watch the trash can for about an hour before I see Neil approaching. "They called me and said they couldn't find you." I jump at the sound of his voice, even though I know it's him. "All they had to do was look in the break room where Chavez left you."

I try to smile as my fear drains away. Knowing he's here makes me feel safe. Not that I want to be dependent on him. He is, after all, only being nice. "I didn't mean to cause any trouble."

"I guess you heard we got him,"

I nod, wishing I could keep the tears from welling up in my eyes. "So it's all over?" My voice is so shaky it surprises me. How do I tell him that I'm not ready for it to be over? Yes, I want to be rid of Will, but do I have to lose Neil in the process?

"Why don't we go to my office? I'll explain there."

"Mind if I get some gum first?" I push the words out, hoping my voice will sound more normal, but it isn't working.

We stand in front of the vending machine, analyzing the choices, each of which is somehow unacceptable. The mint variety has sugar in it. The sugar-free type is green apple flavor—not exactly a breath freshener. And the cinnamon appears to be stuck in the machinery. I feed my dollar into the machine, but it spits it back out.

He takes the dollar from me, and feeds it back in, this time successfully. "Don't get the green apple. It's not you."

I smile and narrow my eyes at him. "What would you suggest?"

Standing beside me, he looks over the selections. "I think you're an A4—cinnamon."

Since I was going to get that one anyway, I push the buttons, and

Neil hits the machine so the pack of gum drops down without getting stuck. Then he bends over and retrieves the gum for me.

I fumble around with the gum wrapper while Neil gets my change out of the machine. I offer him a stick. He takes it. Why do I have to cry right now? I draw in my breath and follow him out of the break room and down a long hall, trying to put the change into my purse as I walk. The elevator at the end of the hall sinks down a little when we step onto it. Neil is quiet. I can tell he's wondering about the tears. I shrug my shoulders. He nods in acknowledgment.

Exiting the elevator, I follow him as he weaves through a maze of cubicles. His office is in the corner, a small room with one large window looking out on the cubicles and one window looking down on the city. The desk is piled high with papers, most in three stacks at the edge of his desk. A bookshelf under the outside window displays a world globe and a framed picture of his parents, along with some model airplanes. On the wall behind his desk is a poster of the Sacred Grove. There are various plaques and certificates hanging below the poster. A couple of dumb-bells sit on the floor in the corner.

He takes a box of tissues out of the bottom drawer of his file cabinet. "Your eyes are about to spill over."

That's what does it. Now, they're not just spilling, they're flooding. And what's worse, it's not a pretty cry—it's an ugly cry. My nose is running too. I shake my head as I grab a tissue.

As I blow my nose, he takes my purse out of my hands. "What do you have in this thing? It's at least five pounds."

I wipe my eyes with the tissue. "I like to be prepared."

His arms are around me, pulling me in. "You can't be prepared for everything." Then my face is pressed to his chest. Somehow my arms go around his neck without my even knowing that I moved them. He bends his head down, resting his chin on the top of my head. "You liked him a lot, didn't you?"

I don't want to move. I keep my face pressed up against his chest. "Why would I have broken up with him if I liked him a lot?" I can feel his body tense, and I realize what I've said. I look up into his face. "Not that I've never done that before." He stares down at me, and I turn back toward his chest, relieved that I finally said the right thing. "I know it's over, but I'm still scared."

He smooths my hair with his hand. "He's dangerous, Anne. You should be scared . . . I'm scared."

His words startle me enough that I pull away from his embrace. That's when I remember my worry about the bomb. "What did he do to your car?"

"Nothing. When we caught him, he was trying to duct-tape a GPS device to the chassis. That's how he tracked us down. Right now, I don't know if we have enough evidence to prosecute. The GPS was in his hand, not on my car. I think he was replacing the battery." He combs his fingers through his hair. "He's under arrest for failing to pay some tickets. He could be out on bail in a couple of hours." Turning his head to look out the window, he sighs. "I want so bad for this to be over for you."

And what will happen when it is over, I want to know. Will Neil walk back out of my life, considering his job done? I bite my bottom lip. "I'm sorry you've had to work on your day off. And I'm sorry about your car."

Someone knocks on the door. Neil reaches for the knob. "Forget about the car. If he'd done anything to you, it would have killed me." He opens the door and lets in a young woman in a uniform.

If there were ever an Officer Barbie, this woman could be the model for it—the long, sleek blond hair by itself could cause a five-car pile-up, and, as far as her body goes, those narrow hips can only be topped by what she carries on top. I watch as she sets her tight little behind down into the bench in front of the desk and lets her thick curtain of hair fall down across her face. Sweeping her hair back behind her shoulders, she opens up her laptop. Neil walks around to his desk, "Anne, this is Sergeant Murphy, our expert on stalking cases. She was kind enough to come in to talk to you."

Sergeant Murphy smiles at Neil in a way that makes her look a little too much like Lily. "It's really not a problem. You're welcome to call me anytime. Oh, and I keep meaning to thank you for the chocolates you brought by the other day. That was really sweet of you."

Chocolates? He gave her chocolates? As uncharitable as it is, I find myself wanting to yank out that beautiful hair of hers. Why would a woman with a body like hers choose a profession that's dominated by males? You'd think she'd already get too much attention.

Neil nods toward the bench. "Why don't you have a seat, Anne."

I sit down, suddenly aware of how wide my thighs look as they're pressed down against the seat. I shouldn't have eaten so much bread at dinner.

Sergeant Murphy swings her hair back. "Actually, it'd be better if we went somewhere else."

Neil leans back in his seat. "No, I can leave. I was just going to listen to her phone messages."

Sighing, I hand him my cell phone once again. "Why don't you stay? I don't have anything to hide."

He scoots his chair closer to me to get the phone. "I can tell that by looking at your face." Was that a compliment? Just in case it wasn't—or just in case it was another attempt to get me to blush— I refuse to believe it.

I maintain a business-like tone with Sergeant Murphy as she asks questions about my love life—including how I met Will, the extent of our physical relationship (nothing more than kissing), everything I know about his background, and anything threatening about his behavior. I give her information that's usually reserved for Marcy or Mary, but sharing it all with her, my mistakes seem so much more obvious. What was I thinking to date a guy who tracked me down at my office? I hadn't even given him my number. I was so caught up in his image—the flowers, the car, the designer clothes, his fancy job—that I didn't consider safety. The worst part is having to tell Sergeant Murphy that I let Will take my car to his mechanic. This is when I wish Neil isn't in the room—the way he looks at me is too sympathetic. I'd much rather see admiration or attraction in his eyes.

When the questioning is over, Sergeant Murphy decides she'll try to get in touch with Will's ex-wife before we plan out a strategy. While she steps out of the office, I wander over to look at the model airplanes on the bookshelf. Neil swivels his chair toward me. "Sergeant Murphy is really good. We're lucky she was willing to come in."

I spin his globe around, looking for no country in particular. It comes to a stop on India, and I trace its outline with my index finger. "She seems like someone who would know about stalkers."

Neil chuckles. "You'd be surprised."

"Try me?"

Leaning back in his chair, he scratches the back of his neck. "She hasn't always looked the way she does now. I'd say she's lost seventy or eighty pounds in the last year. Most of us think she should have stopped about ten pounds ago, but she keeps dieting."

"So you think she has an eating disorder?"

"I don't know. I saw her eat some chocolates this week. That's a good sign, isn't it?"

I walk my fingers across Africa and into the Atlantic Ocean. "I'd say she ate them because you gave them to her."

He folds his arms across his chest. "Maybe she ate them because she likes chocolate."

My fingers come to a stop at the Bahamas. "Or she likes you. That would be my opinion, based on observation." I'm trying not to sound jealous, but I've already opened the floodgate to that emotion. "Is this something you do often—giving women food when you think they aren't eating enough? Because you're sending the wrong message. Chocolates are for valentines, not coworkers."

"I was trying to help her." He stands and walks over to stand beside me. "I didn't mean to lead her on." He sticks his hands down deep into the pockets of his dress pants. "We've worked together for so long, I assumed she saw our relationship the same way I do."

I spin the globe backwards. "You shouldn't assume."

We stand in silence with him looking out the window and me staring down at the globe. After what seems like a long time, he asks, "So what should I do to let someone know I really like her?"

I meet his gaze. "That's the problem, Neil. You're so nice to everyone that it's hard for a woman to know when you're being considerate and when you're interested. I'm not saying you shouldn't be the way you are because I like you the way you are. I'm only saying . . . oh, I don't know what I'm saying."

A smile spreads across his face. "You and I have a lot in common, you know. I could say exactly the same thing about you." He holds up his hand to stop me from interrupting. "Before you argue with me, you should remember that I've been listening to messages from your ex-boyfriend all day, a man who still thinks you care about him.

And I know about you and Charlie. So I'm not the only one who's too nice." Ignoring the knock on his door, he takes a couple of steps so that he's standing right in front of me. "Promise me something?"

I swallow and look up into his blue eyes. "Yes?"

"Next time a man asks you out, don't assume he's just being considerate."

I giggle, sounding more nervous than I should. "All right." Sergeant Murphy's fingernails are tapping on the door again. "You'd better get that."

Neil leans in closer, making me think that he really meant what I hope he meant. For a couple of seconds, I think he's going to kiss me, but as I'm tipping my head back, he says, "It's better to reject someone sooner than later. Waiting only prolongs the agony."

The agony? It's better to reject someone sooner than later? By the time I recover, he's opened the door, and in walks Officer Barbie. This is definitely not the right time, but I can't leave that last part unanswered. I open my mouth before I'm even sure what I'm going to say. "Neil, I don't know what you're hearing on those messages, but I'm really not a cruel person. Maybe I take longer to sort through my feelings than some people. But aren't you the one that told me 'dating is a risk?' I thought you were on my side."

With his hand still on the doorknob, he looks up at the ceiling and rubs his other hand down the side of his face. That little hair at the crown of his head is sticking up again. "You're right. I was out of line."

Sergeant Murphy looks from Neil to me and then back to Neil. "Do you two need a minute?"

Neil shuts the door and looks down at my feet. "Do we need a minute, Anne?"

The tip of my nose tingles and my throat hurts from the tears I'm holding back. When his eyes move up to my face, I shake my head. We need much longer than a minute.

"This won't take long," Sergeant Murphy says as she takes a seat. "Basically, what you're going to do is avoid him. Don't talk to him, don't look at him, don't answer his calls. My guess is that he'll disappear in six weeks. He's just gone through a messy divorce. It's a classic case of a man who can't handle rejection. Give him a few more weeks, and he'll get over it."

Neal still grips the door handle. "I don't think this is a classic case, Sergeant. He practically kidnapped her. Then he used a GPS to track her down. This is not the average Joe with a crush. He's smart, and he's mentally unstable."

Sergeant Murphy slaps a stack of papers down on Neil's desk. "Either way, she'll need to read through this information. I recommend that she get a new phone, a locking gas cap, and keep a paper trail—that sort of thing. I wouldn't get a protective order if I were you—it'll only make him angry. If you'd called me earlier, I'd have advised you not to arrest him, but that's over now."

I can see the veins on Neil's neck. "The man was lying underneath my car with a GPS in his hand. He's been following us around all day. If I have to arrest him to protect Anne, then he'll have to be mad."

The sergeant shrugs her shoulders. "She should probably lie low for awhile, maybe get a dog. And you should keep her old phone to check all his messages. If he ever says or does anything threatening, we'll have a solid case against him."

A new phone? A dog? I haven't even paid the bill for that car repair yet. I don't even know how I'm going to get my car. And why is this woman talking about me as if I'm not in the room?

She draws in her breath, sticking out her chest and shaking her hair back like a model for a shampoo commercial. "Show his picture to all her neighbors, so they can report any unusual activity."

Neil reaches for the stack of papers. "We're not going anywhere near her apartment if I can help it. I'll find a place for her to stay around here."

Now they're planning my life as if I'm a child. I thrust my hand up like a kid in school, but I don't wait to be called upon. "I have a job. I have responsibilities. I can't spend the rest of my life hiding from Will. If I'm going to ignore him, I'm going to do it while I'm living my normal life." My voice is way too shaky.

Neil turns to face Sergeant Murphy. "Maybe we do need a minute."

Sergeant Murphy stands from her seat. "I was just leaving. I think I've told you all I can. If you think of anything else, you can call."

His eyes stay on my face as he thanks her and closes the door. Then he leans on the edge of his desk, his legs stretched out in front of him, almost touching mine. His blue eyes look so dark right now, staring out at me from bloodshot whites. His bottom lip juts out beneath his upper lip, giving the impression that he's very displeased. "What is this really about, Annie?"

"What is what really about?"

There's a deep crease between his eyebrows. "This 'I'm going to live my normal life' stuff."

"It means I'm going to live my normal life." I look down at my watch. It's close to midnight. Grabbing my purse, I stand up. "We'd better get going if I'm going to get home before two a.m."

Neil stays sitting on the edge of the desk and folds his arms across his chest. "It only takes fifteen minutes to get to my house."

Seeing his impatience, I talk faster. "I was thinking since Will's in jail tonight, it'd be better for me to go back to my apartment. Marcy will be with me, so I'll be okay."

He stands up, blocking my path. "Oh, no you don't. Did you call Marcy?"

"Yeah."

"So you know Val's got a room all ready for you. When I called Dave on the way back to the station, he said Marcy was already asleep, so I don't think she'll want to drive you back tonight."

Gripping my hands, I dig my fingernails into my palms. "I refuse to let Will have so much control over my life."

He clears his throat. "Too late." His tone isn't arrogant, but merciful.

I have no reply. He's right. It is too late. I feel him press his hand against the small of my back, leading me out the door of his office, through the maze of cubicles, into the bouncy elevator, then out into a parking garage, where we locate his car. It's only one of five or six cars parked on the floor.

Right as we step past his bumper, he grabs me by both shoulders. "Stay right here. I just had an idea."

"Is there something wrong?"

He walks over to the driver's side. "No."

"Will didn't do anything else to your car, did he?"

"No, I had the guys check it over. Everything's fine." He opens the door and sits down inside.

I crouch down to look underneath his car. But to really see anything at all, crouching isn't enough, I have to get down on my hands and knees. If it weren't for this dress I'm wearing, I'd lie down on the pavement. I never would have guessed Will was the kind of guy who'd be willing to lie down across oily asphalt, especially considering how expensive his clothes always looked.

I've got my head all the way under the car when I hear music—Enrique Iglesias singing "Hero." Wondering where it's coming from, I pop my head out to see Neil standing above me. He holds a hand out. "Care to dance?"

I reach for his hand. "What?"

He grabs my hand and pulls me up to stand. "Would you like to dance?"

"Here?" Somehow I've never thought of dancing in a concrete parking garage. Fluorescent lighting has never done much for me either.

He puts a hand to my waist. "The acoustics are great."

I let him pull me in, wondering if he's ever really listened to the lyrics of this song. Does he know it has kissing in it? "You don't have to do this, Neil. That whole thing at the dance last summer—it wasn't a big deal. You don't have to make up for it."

He smiles. "How about we relax and listen to the music?"

I reach my hand up to his shoulder, his very strong shoulder. He's told me to relax, but my heart is pounding in my chest. My brain says I can't yield to this feeling of attraction. I can't let myself be disappointed. At the same time, my hand feels at home in his. And the way he holds me, it's so natural, a perfect fit. How could he not notice?

He bends his head down and whispers in my ear. "Just like old times." Then he scans my face for a reaction. Is he teasing me?

If I only knew whether he was teasing or flirting, I would know what to say. I give him half a smile.

During the next verse of the song, he whispers to me again. "You're trembling . . . like the song says."

Leave it to my body to betray me. "At least I'm not blushing."

No laugh, only a look of concern. "You cold?"

"A little."

He pulls me in closer. "Is that better?"

I nod. Only a couple of inches separate us. Definitely better, but I don't think it's going to stop the trembling.

"Are you scared?" he asks a while later.

"No." The only thing I'm scared of right now is being too much in love with him. But I can't stop myself. That would be like telling a woman who's dehydrated not to drink from a glass of water you hand her—a glass of ice cold water. I have to steer the conversation away from my emotions to more rational thoughts. "Thanks so much for everything you've done for me today, Neil. I'm sorry it's been so much like another day at work for you."

"Not at all. I've enjoyed it." The song is winding down. He takes both my hands in his. "If you want to know the truth, today doesn't compare at all to a day at work. Anne, I . . ." He avoids my eyes as the last notes of the song trail off. "I can't think of anyone I'd rather spend the day with."

I force my mouth to shut. He can't think of anyone he'd rather spend the day with? That is not something a man says to be polite. I stammer. "Today's been wonderful . . . except the parts with Will."

Now would be the time for him to sweep me up in his arms and deliver that kiss I've been dreaming about. Instead, he checks his watch. "Wow! I didn't realize how late it was. We better get going." With a couple of steps, he reaches the passenger side door and helps me inside.

We ride home most of the way in comfortable silence, giving my mind the opportunity to replay what happened in the parking lot. As I start to fast-forward into the future, Neil interrupts my reveling. "You're not going to fall asleep on me again."

I fake a snore.

"Am I that boring?" he asks.

"No, but I could use a little boring." I squeeze his arm twice, stopping short of the third squeeze, our old signal for "I love you."

"Listen, Anne, if you really want to go back to your apartment, I can drive you down there."

Yes, I really wanted to go back to my apartment, but that was before the dancing. That was before he said he'd rather spend the day with me than anyone else.

He clears his throat. "Of course, that would mean I'd have to camp out in front of your door."

"Maybe we better go with Plan A. Everyone's expecting us."

He pulls to a stop along the side of the street. "Good, because we're here."

I look out at a well-lit brick townhouse with a narrow strip of lawn in front. It has a tidy, white front porch topped by a bay window on the second floor. "Is this your house?"

"This is it."

"I like it."

Neal turns his car into the narrow driveway that leads toward the back of the house, where Marcy and the Harvilles's cars are already parked in single file. "Built in 1927. It's small, but there are three bedrooms. The one with the bay window is for you and Marcy—it's right in front of you when you get to the top of the stairs. The Harvilles are in the other two."

"Where are you going to sleep?"

"I thought I'd bed down here," he says, pointing to the back of the car.

"You mean you're going to sleep in your car?"

He opens his door. "I'll be fine. I've got some camping gear inside that'll make it comfortable." His eyes flash toward my fingers on the door handle. "If you'll wait a second, I'll open it for you."

Bridling my independent streak, I watch him run around to get my door. He definitely moves with perfect, policeman form. I'm even starting to wonder if maybe he's seen a criminal when he swings open my door. "More like four seconds."

"Thanks."

He grabs my bag out of the trunk, then leads me through the gate to his back yard. The lights from the kitchen cast a glow on the tiny space that consists of a narrow deck, a square of lawn, a garbage can, a picnic table, two resin chairs, and something else—two little boxwoods planted on either side of the stairs leading to the deck. I catch my breath. "Are those boxwoods?"

"Yep. I decided I couldn't do without the smell. Planted them a few weeks ago."

I bend over to smell one while Neal unlocks the back door. "I have to warn you," he says, "I haven't gotten around to repainting the kitchen."

Stepping into the kitchen, I'm at once charmed by the cottage-like appeal of the small space and amused by the colors on the walls. The top half of the wall is a deep lavender while the bottom half is the color of split pea soup. Still, the place has charm with its diminutive refrigerator and stove, oak cabinets, and parquet floor. The floral draperies, obviously the choice of a former owner, fit right in.

Neil escorts me through the dining room, painted a pale yellow with shiny white moldings—the kind of millwork you only find in old houses. The floor is a dark, old hardwood, polished to a sheen. I stand beside the big, round table and turn a circle. "You've obviously repainted this room. It's beautiful."

He shrugs his shoulders, trying to conceal his pleasure in the compliment. "Thanks."

The living room is small with three tall, narrow windows, each draped with gauzy white curtains over privacy shades. There's barely enough room for his bookshelf, couch, and recliner. Still, it would be the perfect setting for a good night kiss. As he starts up the stairs with my suitcase, Neal tells me that he likes to read beside the windows in the morning, then he adds, "They're probably all asleep up there. We'd better be quiet."

I grab hold of the polished wooden stair rail and climb up behind him. At the top of the stairs, he sets down my suitcase and sticks his hands back in his pockets. His eyes flit around, checking the hallway, before landing on my face. "Let me know if you need anything, okay?" Again with the home teacher line.

I barely have time to utter a disappointed, "Okay," before he's heading back down the stairs.

25

Monday, July 18, 2005

*I've been here in Cape Verde for three months, and I'm finally get-
ting to the point where people understand what I'm saying. I never
thought I'd enjoy being a missionary so much. Sure, there are hard days
that I wouldn't want to live over, and I really am sick of eating fish. But
it's so wonderful to see people change their lives. Last week, we started
teaching Tote. He wanted to change so badly that he stopped drinking
before we even taught him about the Word of Wisdom.*

*The members here are so happy. I really never expected that. They're
so poor. I think I've sat on maybe one sofa since I got on the island. Most
people have metal folding chairs and card tables for furniture. Running
water, refrigerators, and toilets are all luxuries that a lot of people do
without. I guess, as an American, I always thought happiness had a
lot to do with money and possessions and security. These people have
taught me that I was completely wrong. The days of me saying "I can't"
are over.*

I have no sensation of being lost when I wake, though the place is
unfamiliar. The sun is streaming in through the edges of the curtains
at the window, lighting up the dark, hardwood floor beside the bed.
The smell of something baking wafts through the air. Rising up on
my elbows, I look around for a clock, which isn't so easy to do without my contacts.

Beside me, on the bedside table is a box of tissues, a reading lamp, and a large wooden bowl that contains three autographed baseballs. Taking a ball in my hand, I read the signatures—all of them are unfamiliar until I reach Neil's name. Deciding it must be a team ball, I set it down and examine the other two, which also seem to be team balls. Underneath the balls in the wooden bowl is an assortment of small items, among which I notice a guitar pick, a fishing weight, a super ball, a Duty to God award, two arrowheads, and a pocketknife.

Marcy comes in from the adjoining bathroom as I'm replacing the guitar pick. Her hair and makeup are done, and she's wearing an orange wrap dress.

"Is it time for church already?" I ask.

"That depends whether you're going home with me or staying. I have to give a prayer in sacrament."

"Oh." It never occurred to me that Marcy wouldn't be attending Neil's ward.

She looks at her watch. "I'll probably be leaving here in an hour or so. I think Val said Neil's ward starts at one."

I reach for my suitcase, which is right beside the bed. "Are they expecting me to go to church with them?"

Marcy zips her suitcase up while I unzip mine. "If by 'they' you mean Neil, all I can say is I don't think he knows what to expect."

I groan. "I want to tell him how I feel, but I'm not sure how he feels. I hate this uncertainty."

Marcy starts to straighten the sheets on the bed. "From my vantage point, there isn't much uncertainty. He spent all day yesterday with you, took you to a five-star restaurant, and slept out in his car so you'd have a safe place to stay. You do know this is his bedroom?"

I guess I should have known that. "I thought the mattress was really comfortable for a guest room."

She yanks up the bedspread. "Girl, you have got to open your eyes. He is totally into you."

I put a finger to my mouth, reminding her to be quiet. "If you knew him the way I know him, you wouldn't be so sure. He's a nice guy. He sacrifices for people all the time."

She smooths the covers on the bed. "Yeah, I'll bet he takes all his charity cases out to fancy Italian restaurants."

"I didn't tell you about the dancing either. We danced in the parking garage at the police station."

"Don't tell me—he kissed you good night too."

I shake my head. "No kissing. Every time I feel like it's about to happen, he says something completely unromantic."

"That's only because he doesn't know how you feel. He's nervous."

"Don't you think if we're both still in love that we'll eventually understand each other? I mean, it's not like we're in high school, trying to interpret every little word or action as if it has some huge significance. I think we're both mature enough to take things slow."

"What you forget is that you've put him through pain in the past. The less you show your feelings, the more he's gonna wonder if it's worth it."

I catch my breath and grab the toiletry bag out of my suitcase. Maybe she's right. "I better get dressed."

When I make my way downstairs, Valerie Harville is sitting in Neil's recliner putting her long red hair in hot rollers. "How'd you sleep?"

"It was the best sleep I've had in a long time, thanks."

The morning light streaming in from the windows makes her hair glow bright orange. "Neil will be happy to hear that. He was real anxious for you to have a nice, clean room."

"Thanks for fixing it up for me."

She laughs. "Oh, it wasn't me. Neil did it when he was here yesterday afternoon."

So that's what he was doing. He had it all planned out. For a moment, I waver between taking offense and feeling flattered. How could he assume I would stay here? Then again, he drove all the way out here just to clean up for me. "Where is he?"

"He's out on the back porch, watching the girls and working on a lesson he has to teach. You should get yourself some of Dave's pecan waffles on the way. They're the best."

I make my way through the dining room and into the kitchen, where Dave is pouring the last of the batter into the waffle iron. "You're just in time to eat with me," he exclaims. "Around here, the cook always eats last."

I peek out the window to see Neil at the far corner of the backyard with his cell phone to his ear. Set against the backdrop of three or four townhouses and standing in front of a graying, wooden fence, he seems so small, even with the Harville children running back and forth in front of him. His white shirt is untucked, the collar unbuttoned.

Dave sets down a plate and silverware for me on the tiny kitchen table. "Have a seat," he calls with the easy manner of an old friend. "It's already been blessed." As I start on my waffle, Dave removes his wallet from his back pocket and takes out a picture. "Here's something you might want to see. It's a picture of my sister, Wendy."

I look down at a snapshot of a brunette, who appears to be the complete opposite of Jay Bentley. Her smile is exuberant. Her clothing is bold—she wears a silky red kimono top with gold accents. Her hair is meticulously styled with a cascade of curls falling from an up-do. Her skin glows with health. "She's beautiful," I say, almost wishing I didn't sound so surprised. "I'm so sorry."

"It's been a year. Val and I are going to the temple this week to do her work. I'd hoped—we'd always planned that Jay would come with us. But—poor Wendy, I don't think she would have forgotten him so soon."

He remains silent while I swallow my food. "No. I don't think she would," I finally mutter.

Dave shakes his head. "She was so attached to him. She wasn't the type of person to get over him so fast."

"I don't think any woman who was really in love could get over it in less than a year."

Dave smiles a little. "So you think it's because he's a man?"

"All I can say is we don't forget you as soon as you forget us. We tend to brood over things, always wondering what might have been, while you—well, it seems to me that men don't spend a lot of time thinking about relationships."

Dave laughs and points his fork at me. "I suppose you could say that about men in general, but it doesn't apply to Jay. If any man is a thinker, he is. You've talked to him. You know how he is. He's constantly thinking."

I nod. "You're right. I forgot about that."

Dave slowly chews his food before he speaks again. "In my profession, I deal with a lot of emotion. Granted, it's mostly violent emotion. But I can say from my own experience that men's emotions are as strong as women's. If anything, men have stronger emotions. You look in any prison. I don't have to argue with you that it's mostly men in there—men who couldn't control their emotions."

"Yes, but, like you say, we're talking about an entirely different kind of emotion. People who love too much probably aren't going to end up in prison. For some, prison might be an easier punishment than their own feelings."

Dave rubs the stubble on his chin. "You talk like you have experience, Anne, like you lost someone you loved."

I smooth the napkin on my lap. "I didn't exactly lose him. I let him get away." I grab my fork and cram another piece of waffle in my mouth, hoping it'll keep me from revealing any more. What is it about Dave that makes me want to tell him my secrets? I hardly know the guy. If he has this kind of power over criminals, I can only imagine the kind of confessions he can drag out of them.

I'm relieved to hear the click-clack of Valerie's heels approaching on the hardwood floor. "Didn't I tell you those waffles are to die for?"

My mouth full, I nod while she heads out the back door. Within a few seconds, we hear her asking Neil about his lesson. When he answers, it's obvious he's sitting on the back porch—right underneath the open kitchen window. Why didn't I notice that the window was open before? And how long has Neil been sitting there?

"I'm fine out here, Val," I hear him say. "You go ahead and relax inside. The kids are behaving themselves."

"All right, but you let me know when you're through and I'll come get them." With that, Valerie opens the door again and retraces her steps to the living room.

Dave watches her with a sort of admiration. "I don't suppose I can win this argument, Anne. But if I could just let you know how much a man suffers when he can't be with the woman he loves. Let me tell you, back when I was in the reserves and I had to serve in Iraq, taking that last look at Val and the kids as I boarded the plane, wondering if I'd see them again in this life. Then if I could explain to you how I felt when I was coming home—trying to count the hours, the minutes until I could hold them again. I'll tell you, I would figure in every possible delay, just so I wouldn't be disappointed, but all the while I'd hope to get there as soon as possible. Then, finally being with them again, I don't think heaven could be any better."

"Okay, you've proven your point there. Men can be as faithful as women."

"Then we're in agreement."

"Except in one point."

"What's that?"

"Well, we're talking about Jay's situation, right? I think, in a way, it's a great compliment to your sister that Jay could fall in love again so fast. He had a good relationship with Wendy, and he wanted something like that with someone else."

Dave shrugs his shoulders. "Maybe."

"In the case of women, I think it's harder for us to transfer our love to someone else." I take a breath and force out the last few words. "We're more likely to keep loving when there's no hope."

Dave squeezes my forearm. "You're too sweet to argue with, Anne. Besides, when I think of Jay, my tongue is tied."

Our conversation turns to less serious topics, and I find myself scheming and wondering about Neil. Why doesn't he come inside? He knows I'm here. Should I go out there? When I stand at the sink, doing dishes with Dave, I peak through the window. Neil is completely absorbed in writing. Could he really be that engrossed in preparing a Sunday lesson to completely ignore me?

Bewildered, I go back upstairs to find my toothbrush. As I'm opening the bedroom door, I hear the quick, light steps of a child and turn to see the oldest Harville, a girl, approaching me. "Are you Anne?" she asks in a whisper.

"Yes."

Her hands are behind her back. "Are you alone?"

I look around. "Yes."

"Good." She holds out a folded piece of yellow, legal paper. "Neil says it's a secret for you. I'm not supposed to let anyone else see."

I take the paper, daring to hope that this is the kind of note I want to get from him. My name is scrawled on the outside in writing that's hardly legible. So this is what was keeping him busy while

I talked with Dave. I close the door to the room—his room—and unfold it. My eyes race over its words.

Dear Anne, I hate to admit I've been eavesdropping. How could I not listen when you're all I think about anymore? I've been holding off, knowing the last thing you need is another admirer. But the things you've said to Dave about how it's hard to forget, how women love longer. You're torturing me, Anne, and, at the same time, giving me a reason to hope. Do I have a chance or am I too late? Is there anything left of the feelings you once had for me? Because I haven't forgotten. If anything, I love you more now than I did eight and a half years ago. Don't tell me a man can't love as long as a woman. You're the only woman I've loved. I'll admit I've been selfish and unforgiving, but I've never replaced you in my heart.

I think by now you could have guessed my intentions in dropping by your apartment, calling you, and so on. I've tried to make my feelings clear. Yet I still wonder about yours. Last night, driving home, you were so quiet. I thought for sure I'd come on too strong. I can hardly write. Not knowing is agony. One way or the other, I need to know how you feel. Will you give me another chance? Love, Neil

I read it over again before I'm ready to believe it's real, that I've understood exactly what he's said. Then, my hands shaking and my heart racing, I fling open the door and run straight into Dave, who's just come up the stairs. Excusing myself and grasping the yellow paper to my chest, I try my best to pretend that everything is normal because there is no way I'm going to submit to curious questions on my way to the back porch. Luckily, Valerie and Marcy are so occupied in conversation downstairs that I pass by them unnoticed. Before I know it, I'm tripping over a chair leg in the kitchen and twisting the handle of the back door. "Anne," I hear Marcy's voice behind me, "have you decided whether you want to drive home with me?"

Twisting to face Marcy, I feel oddly out of balance and have to pull a little on the door to steady myself. "I think I'll be staying, thanks."

Marcy wiggles her neck. "Now you're talking."

Turning back to the door, I notice that it's already open and Neil is watching me with straight lips. Sitting on the porch steps with Dave's youngest daughter on his lap, he seems almost terrified by my presence. I encountered that expression only once before—at the hospital in North Carolina. I smile at him and he hurries to stand up, jostling the little Harville a bit in the process. She holds her hands up to him and bounces, begging to be picked up, but he doesn't notice. His eyes drift to the yellow paper I still hold against my chest. He points to it. "Did you—"

I let the screen door slam behind me. "Yes." My breath steams white in the outside air, but I don't feel cold.

He takes my hand and steps closer, searching my face. Then all at once, I'm in his arms, tilting back my head. And even with the little Harville girl crying to be picked up, he takes my cue. His lips brush mine, then press down, and it seems we're back in my front yard beside the boxwoods. I can even smell them. Every nerve in my body is firing off, sensing his closeness, the smell of his freshly shampooed hair, the taste of cinnamon on his breath—everything about him is exactly the way it should be.

I feel his whiskers against my cheek as he whispers, "Does this mean you're giving me another chance?"

Valerie comes through the door to grab the crying child from between our legs. Neil doesn't even seem to notice. Valerie gives me a knowing smile before departing.

I laugh. "You had me at the garage sale."

He grins, obviously surprised, then shakes his head. "I should have asked you out as soon as I found out you were still single. I've been an idiot." Glancing through the window into his house, where an audience of tiny Harvilles is gathering, he reaches for my hand. "Why don't we go for a walk?"

He leads me past the baby boxwoods, across his tiny backyard and out through the gate. Our feet crinkle the autumn leaves as we walk. "This sidewalk isn't the best," Neil warns, grabbing hold of my elbow. "People trip all the time."

I look down the row of brick townhomes, all with old-fashioned front porches, some looking slightly dilapidated. "I love your street. It almost feels like we've gone back in time. The houses have such character."

Neil clears his throat and laughs at the same time. "Much as I want to talk about the real estate around here, I've got something else I need to get off my chest. Not that anything can excuse my behavior last summer."

I should interrupt with an offer of forgiveness, but Neil doesn't pause. "When Jack brought me to your dad's house, I didn't think I'd feel anything being around you again. You were exactly the same as I remembered. But it was like opening up an old wound. It hurt so much. I promised myself then and there that I wouldn't fall for you again."

Another attack of regret—to know I caused so much suffering. I wish he knew I hurt myself as much as I hurt him. "I'm really sorry," I begin, but we turn a corner and I almost run into an old lady with two fluffy, black dogs.

After untangling me from the leash, Neil keeps talking. "I guess the turning point was at that dance, seeing the comparison between you and Lily. You were a real woman, exactly what I've always wanted—mature, patient, taking things in stride, completely cool when you should have been angry. Then you gave me that hint that you were still a little attracted to me."

"When was that?"

"You don't remember? You said I was the best looking guy in the room." He squeezes my hand—three times—I'm sure I'm not imagining. "Going to the beach only made it more obvious. Just when I'd made up my mind, Lily had her accident. I couldn't exactly break up with her when she was lying there in the hospital."

He puts his arm around my shoulder and I lean into him. I take a moment to digest what he said. Of course he couldn't break up with Lily while she was in the hospital. Why didn't I see that before? It's like I've been wearing a blindfold. "You were right to wait," I stammer. "She might not have recovered as well."

We stop next to a brick wall that doesn't seem to belong to anyone in particular. Neal sits down on it, then dusts off a place for me to sit. "Once I knew she was going to be okay, I avoided talking to her. I thought it might help her lose interest in me. I called when I thought she'd be asleep. And since I had no vacation time left anyway, I used that as an excuse to avoid visiting. It was a lucky break when she fell in love with Jay. I just wish she'd told me sooner."

I sit down and pick at a dandelion that's gone to seed. "Me too," I say. "When she announced her engagement, I thought she was engaged to you, not Jay."

Laughing, Neil plants his hand on the ground behind me. "If you hadn't been dating Will, I would have come over and told you myself. But Liz had me pretty much convinced—"

I lean back on my arms so my right arm crisscrosses his left. "Liz doesn't take the time to figure out what I think. She just shares her own opinions and attributes them to me. If I'd known how you felt—"

"I thought it over on the way home from North Carolina—while you were sleeping. You were practically related to Lily. If I told you how I felt before I broke up with her, I risked alienating Mary and Charlie and all the rest of the Musgroves. I didn't think you'd be happy with that kind of thing."

I pick a dandelion and blow the seeds, then watch them float through the air, some landing on pavement, others catching the breeze toward fertile ground. "And you didn't think I could keep a secret?"

"That would have been the biggest risk of all. I already messed up with you once by going too fast. This time I thought I'd better take things slow. Besides that, I was such a jerk last summer, I couldn't see how you'd ever take me back."

I smooth down his cowlick. "I wouldn't say you were a jerk . . . stand-offish maybe, but not a jerk."

Wrapping an arm across my shoulders, he laughs. "I would say it's a good thing you're forgiving."

I love the strength of his arm across my back and, for once, knowing what it means. Leaning into him, I feel a surge of satisfaction. I lack nothing. This is exactly where I belong.

His arm is still draped across my shoulders hours later as we sit in sacrament meeting. And with every female eye in the room drifting our way, I wish we'd thought to sit in the back. Even the bishop and his two counselors lean forward in their seats to get a better view past the podium. Checking to make sure Neil isn't too embarrassed, I discover a triumphant smile on his face, the look you see on soldiers who've arrived home from long assignments.

26

Sunday, November 23, 2008

The stock market keeps going down. No one knows when it's going to stop. My clients have all lost a lot of money. Everyone is scared. My job is to give them hope, but sometimes I feel a little hopeless. It doesn't help to talk to the other brokers—some of them are more upset than my clients.

I sometimes wonder, is this all there is to my life? Working through all the daylight hours and coming home to an empty apartment? Is this loneliness a punishment for rejecting an offer of marriage when I was nineteen? When I really think about it, I know that loneliness is not what Heavenly Father plans for me. I'm holding on to every bit of hope that things will get better. The light at the end of the tunnel seems very far away, but I might as well keep walking toward it. At least in my personal life, I can know that Heavenly Father is in control. The scriptures are all about second chances, and I want to be ready when my second chance comes along.

I tell my clients that we're going to use this market to our advantage. High quality stocks are as affordable as the lower quality stocks now. It's a great time to upgrade their portfolios.

I'm doing the same kind of upgrading in my personal life. Though it's hard to admit, once I turn off the TV and computer, I have more free time than I've had in the past. I might as well use that time to improve myself and prepare for a brighter future.

The night of Daniel's second birthday party probably isn't the best time to introduce my new boyfriend to my family, but this is how it's going to be. Seeing as how Mary is pregnant, I let myself in without knocking. We find Mom sitting in between Liz and Mary on the old blue couch. Liz has her head on Mom's shoulder while Mary leans back, rubbing her belly. Though I probably never would have chosen them as friends, these women are the constant ones in my life. Yes, we irritate and disagree and deviate from each other. But looking at my sisters and mother right now, I know I belong, no matter what.

It takes them a while to notice us and when they do, they all sit straight up and their eyes go from me to Neil. I grab Neil's hand. The room is silent with the shock of it all. "You remember Neil," I begin.

Mom gives Neil a half smile. "How could I forget? It's nice to see you, Neil."

Neil extends his hand to hers. "Nice to see you too."

Mom shakes his hand. "I had a feeling you two would get back together."

Mary hasn't taken her eyes off of us. "Back together? When were they ever together?"

Mom leans back into the couch cushion. "They had a little fling—how long ago was it?"

"Eight years ago," I say, trying both to ignore the words "little fling" and to avoid the glare in Mary's eyes. "It was the summer you spent with Grandma. I would have told you, but—"

"Anne always thinks of others before herself," Neil breaks in. "She didn't want to embarrass Lily."

Mary rolls her eyes. "I'd be surprised if anything ever embarrasses Lily."

We sit down in two straight-back chairs facing the sofa, and I feel almost as if we've been placed before the judge and jury.

Liz stretches her hair out in front of her face, checking for split ends. "You really should check your phone more often, Anne. I've been trying to call you all day."

"Me too," Mary chimes in, her voice sounding especially irritated. "I guess you're too good to talk to us anymore."

"Sorry."

Mary rubs her six-months-pregnant belly and makes an effort to get up. "Can you believe I haven't frosted the cake yet?" With her legs wide apart, she hinges forward, unable to rise from the soft cushion.

I stand and reach out a hand for her. She takes it. "Thanks."

"I'll help you."

Once she's on her feet, she puts both hands at her waist and pushes out her chest. "I can do it myself. You don't have to worry about me. I don't have any imaginary stalkers."

As much as I want to sit back down, I know that Mary's insults are only a front. "I don't have an imaginary stalker either. Mine is real. And you might as well let me help. I know what happens when you try to frost a cake by yourself." At Charlie's last birthday party, the cake was a mound of crumbs. The two of us laughed so hard that Mary had to run to the bathroom right in the middle of the "Happy Birthday" song.

This time, she doesn't laugh at all. "That is just like you, Anne, to point out my flaws and ignore your own. You're like that man in the bible with the big telephone pole in his eye."

Whatever I do, I cannot look at Neil because laughing right now would really seal my fate. "I was kidding," I say as I follow her into the kitchen.

As soon as we step off the carpet and onto the linoleum, she lets loose. "What is wrong with you, Anne? Can't you think of anyone but yourself? You know Dad was terrified he was going to lose his job because of you? You couldn't have chosen a worse time for this stalker baloney. And I don't suppose you know that Felicia broke up with him? How could you? You never answer your phone. Liz and I have been playing therapists all week. And you know what's really ironic? Will—your supposed stalker—has been more help than you have. He's made it clear that he really cares about the family. He's been over to Dad's apartment every night. He's even been in touch with Felicia, trying to convince her that Dad wants her back. So, after all this—finally—you come waltzing in with your new boy-friend as if you're on a date. Do you know how much stress you've caused us?"

Stunned, I grab the dishrag and start to wipe off Mary's sticky kitchen countertop. If I'm going to defend myself, I'd better start now.

"What I don't understand is why you can trust Will more than you trust your own sister. What is he to you? I'm the one who's helped you every time you've had a baby. I'm the one who's babysat your kids and weeded your garden and taken you to get your driver's license and done almost everything a good sister should do. You know I'm not a liar. And you know I care about Dad."

"Why didn't you tell me about Neil?"

"I don't know. It was easier not to. I should have told you."

"But I asked you about him. You should have told me."

"It was so awkward with him dating Lily."

"Why would Lily care? This was how many years ago?"

"Eight."

"Didn't you think I could keep a secret?"

"I guess I just didn't want to talk about it."

"So you didn't tell anybody?"

"I told Marcy a little, but that was before."

"Before what?"

"Before he started dating Lily and I had to see them together every day."

Mary is silent. Then she laughs, a sound that brings at least partial relief to the granny knot that's been growing in my stomach. "You have it really bad for this guy, huh?"

"Yeah."

"It's about time." She puts the cake on the counter in front of me, and then opens the cabinet to grab a can of frosting. "So are you going to fill me in on your little fling?"

There's that word again—fling. "It wasn't a fling. It was real, Mary."

"Don't let him hurt you, okay? I mean he's younger than you and on the rebound."

"He's two years older than I am, Mary."

"Well, he looks so young and hip."

"Hip?" I can't believe she used that word.

"Just don't let him hurt you, okay?" Mary stares at me. The doorbell rings. "I better get that. Charlie's in the backyard." But she doesn't move. "Don't let him hurt you again, okay?"

"I have a lot I need to explain to you," I say, as Liz opens the door for Dad, then Felicia, and then Will. Who invited him?

"What's wrong?" I hear Mary say.

Then Neil's voice somewhere behind me: "I'm afraid we have to get going, Mary. I got your coat, Anne. Annie?"

I can't take my eyes off of Will. I have to watch his every move. If I take my eyes off of him, even to put on my coat—

"We're leaving, Anne," Neil whispers. He pulls me by the arm to the sliding glass door. "Don't worry about him. I've got you."

I can't see Will anymore, only Mary following us out onto the back porch. She pulls the door shut behind us. "I'm so sorry. I didn't realize."

Charlie, who's tossing a ball with Joseph, raises a hand to Neil. "Hey, Wentworth, long time no see. How you doin', Anne? You guys leaving already?"

"They're leaving because Will showed up," Mary answers.

Charlie drops the ball. "Will? Who let him in? Wait a minute and I'll throw him out." He grabs the handrail and climbs the stairs to the back door.

Such determination on Charlie's part—completely out of character—gives me hope that at least one person in the family is on my side.

"Don't bother," Neil calls to him. "It's better for us to leave."

"What's wrong with kicking him out?" I ask.

By this time, Charlie is heading for the door. "Nothing's wrong with it. I'll do it right now."

Neil stops. "Hold off a minute, Charlie. Anne, why don't we discuss this? We can take a drive around the block and think this through."

He escorts me out the back gate and across the side yard to where I parked my recently recovered car. My hands are still shaky as I fumble around in my purse for the keys. They're much easier to find when Neil, always prepared, whips out his flashlight and aims it down into my purse.

Something about driving the car on that clear autumn night slows down my thoughts. It's so close to Halloween, and the memory of walking these streets with my Dad and sisters holding bags of candy overshadows my agitation at seeing Will. Of course, it helps that Neil is right beside me, brandishing a gun on his calf. Funny that all those times I worried about him becoming a police officer, I never considered the advantages of it.

After I've driven the same streets three or four times, I figure I'm calm enough to discuss things. "I don't see why Charlie's idea is so bad. It would give us a chance to talk to Dad. You could show him those papers about Will's divorce."

Neil waits a long time before he answers. "It isn't a good idea to make people angry when you don't need to, Annie. Your dad will come around. He'll see through Will's charade soon enough. We'll be patient and pray for him to see what's really happening."

I glance over at him, trying to scan his face for signs of aging. Maybe Mary is right. He does look younger than I do. He might have a receding hairline, but not much of one.

He pats my shoulder. "Let's give him some time."

The truth is, he could have any woman he wants, even if he had a receding hairline or a bald spot. Now that he has me back, it's possible he'll realize I wasn't worth the chase. That's what men like—the chase.

Neil's phone rings. As he starts to dig it out of his pocket, I catch sight of the Jaguar coming around the corner. I take my foot off the gas pedal. "Keep driving," Neil tells me.

I hit the gas harder, as Neil answers the phone. I can't help looking at Will when I pass by. What makes it easier is that he's not alone. A woman—I think it's Felicia—is riding beside him in the front seat.

Neil puts down his phone. "That was Charlie letting us know that Will left. Wasn't that your father's girlfriend in the car with Will?"

"Yeah."

"They were sitting pretty close."

"Were they?"

"She had her arm around him."

"Really?"

Neil chuckles. "This problem between you and your dad is going to resolve itself faster than I thought."

"Poor Dad."

"He's better off—believe me."

27

*T*hings are going really great with Neil. It's been six months since
we started dating again, and I'm so sure and confident and happy
about being in love with him. I sometimes wonder if he's as sure as I am,
though. He says he loves me. But he is going so slow. I wonder if he has
doubts, or if maybe he isn't as attracted to me. Or maybe he's bored. Or
maybe he's scared that I'll reject him again. I know, he's right not to rush
something so important, but when you're as sure as I feel right now, why
should you wait? Marcy says I'm going to have to propose to him. I'm
beginning to wonder if she's right.

I made it on time despite having to wake up at 7:00 a.m. on a Saturday and brave the Beltway traffic. The temple is beautiful. Azaleas
are blooming all over the grounds. Lily and Jay—along with Hannah
and Barry—couldn't have chosen a better day for their wedding. I'm
waiting beside the fountain, hardly caring that Neil is a half hour
late. At this rate, we may not make it to the sealing. I close my eyes
and lean back on the bench, my face turned up to the warm sun.

If I'd moved to Baltimore like Neil wanted me to, I wouldn't
be waiting for him now. We'd be driving together. Of course, then
I'd have a killer commute every workday—three hours at least, considering rush hour traffic. But it strikes me how silly I've been to let
those three hours come between us. I should have moved months
ago. "That's what I'm going to do," I mutter to myself.

"And what is that?" I hear Neil's voice coming from my right.

Opening my eyes, I see him sitting right beside me on the bench. "How long have you been here?"

"Just a minute." He lets his words hang there, as if he has something else to say.

I jump up from the bench. "I was thinking I should move to Baltimore, but we'll have to talk about that later. We're late."

Neil is still sitting there, a sly smile growing on his face. "I think we can work that out."

"Come on. We were supposed to be there thirty minutes ago."

He rises slowly and takes my hand, "Next month, it'll be nine years." Then he leans in and gives me a kiss that shows no regard for us being late. In fact, time seems to be dissolving around us. "I think we should do something special."

I take a step toward the temple. "Okay. When?"

"A month from today—for our nine-year anniversary. I've made reservations. You think you could keep the day open?"

I squeeze his hand three times. "Of course." That Italian place would be nice.

Passing the recommend desk, I feel the immediate sense of relief that comes from being in the temple. The Spirit has swept away any sense of worry, regret, or nervousness I had before. Here in the temple I am happier than I deserve. Thanks to the miracle of forgiveness, I can forget my imperfect past. And with gratitude, I walk into the sealing room, my hand in Neil's.

This sealing room is the largest in the temple, and it's filled to capacity with the Musgroves' relatives. There are also a few members of Jay's family tucked in here and there—I can tell from their pallid complexions. Barry, being a convert, has a few friends sitting on the other side of the room. Neil and I slip into the last two available seats beside Mary and Charlie. Mary hands me a tissue as the sealer instructs Lily and Jay to kneel down at the altar. Though I've never cried at a wedding before, I have reason to think that might change today.

The words of the sealing ceremony have a way of making all everyday concerns shrink away. The magnitude of eternal marriage—knowing we can be together forever with our families—has always seemed out of reach for me, but right now, it's something I want, something I think might actually happen to me.

Though I should keep my eyes on the happy couple, I sneak a glance at Neil, who must have had the same idea. He winks. That's when I have to dab away a tear. Thank you, Heavenly Father, for second chances.

Barry and Hannah are next. They are beautiful, the two of them, dressed in white and holding hands. I've never seen Barry look happier. The sealer, a different one, takes his time, making sure that Barry and Hannah's ceremony is special and separate from the one we just witnessed.

It ends quietly. All I want to do is sit here, holding Neil's hand and gazing at the chandelier. Neil has other plans, though. We slowly file through the line, congratulate the two couples, then exit to the hallway. Instead of following the others downstairs, Neil asks if I can wait a minute while he checks on something. I sit down on one of the chairs in the hallway, happy to stay in the temple a moment longer.

Neil returns, looking as if he's trying not to smile. "I want to show you something."

He takes me down the hall to a small sealing room, one that has only about fifteen chairs surrounding the altar. We stand in the middle of the room, facing the mirrors. Our reflections go on and on. I am looking at Neil's reflection. He is looking at mine.

He speaks to me through the mirror. "What do you think?" He says it with enough nervousness in his voice to spark my curiosity.

I turn from his reflection to the real man. What do I say? Do I say what I'm thinking? That what I want more than anything else is to marry him.

He speaks before I respond. "What I meant was what do you think of the room?"

The room? No reason to get carried away—he's talking about the room. I take a quick scan of the chairs and walls around us, wondering where he's going with this. "It's beautiful."

"Do you think it's big enough?"

I hope that this is heading where I think it's heading. "Of course."

"And," he points to the mirror, "what do you think of this?"

Again, I look at our reflections. He pulls me closer beside him. "Because, to tell you the truth, Anne—" He pauses to catch his breath.

I jump in. "I want to marry you if that's what you're asking. Even if you're not asking, I might as well tell you."

His smile spreads as far as his cheeks can take it. "I hope you're not going to tell our children that you proposed to me."

"I might have to if you don't."

"What I was going to say is that whenever you're not around, I miss you. All I think about is the next time I get to see you. Eternity would be intolerable if I couldn't have you with me. So," here he lifts his eyebrows, "I've already reserved this room."

"What?"

"How about it? Will you marry me?"

"Yes."

I am in a trance of joy as we walk down the long set of stairs and out into the beams of April sunshine. No bride could be happier than I am right now. We follow a little path that circles down behind the temple. Neil stops halfway down beside a flowering crepe myrtle tree and faces me, holding both my hands in his. There's a glimmer of amusement in his eyes. "You haven't asked me when I reserved that room for."

"Okay, what day did you reserve it for?"

He bends down so his face is level with mine. "Four weeks from today—our nine year anniversary."

At first I think he must be kidding, but I can tell by his expression that he isn't. "Don't you think that's a little soon? I mean, we'll have to order the invitations and plan the reception and I have to get a dress."

"I've waited almost nine years, Anne."

"You couldn't have asked me a little sooner? I would have said yes last month or two months ago."

He gives me a short kiss. "It's taken me a while to get your parents on board."

"What do you mean?"

"Your mom is working on the invitations, and your dad is helping to get the garden ready for the reception. Jack said we can have the reception at his house if you're okay with that. Marcy said she'll help plan the menu, that is if you don't mind having a vegetarian menu."

I reach up to smooth the cowlick on the back of his head. "Wait a minute. Are you saying that you've already talked to my parents and Jack and Marcy and you haven't said a word about it to me?"

He squints. "I thought it'd make it easier for you."

I let out my breath and fold my arms.

"Uh-oh," Neil mutters, running his hand through the cowlick I just smoothed.

"I would think that by now you would know that I'll marry you no matter what my parents think. I'm not going to—" I'm going to come out and say it, even though Neil appears to be more interested in looking through the pockets in his suit coat. "There is no way I'm going to call off the engagement this time."

Still fumbling through his pockets, he smiles in my direction. "Glad to hear it." He removes his suit coat and checks the pockets again.

"You didn't need to get my parents' permission."

"I thought it'd make it easier for you. I didn't want you to have to worry about anything." He feels along the bottom edge of his coat. "I forgot about the hole in this pocket."

I smooth down the cowlick. "We can fix that later."

Mary is calling to us from the top of the hill. "Where have you two been? We've been looking all over for you. I need you to hold the baby, so I can be in the pictures."

"We've been getting engaged," Neil shouts back at her.

Mary takes a few steps down the hill. "What did you say?"

Neil looks at me. "Anne is going to marry me in four weeks." He says it just loud enough for me to hear.

Mary is still yelling at us. "What?"

He looks back down at his pocket. "I should have remembered about this hole."

It starts to dawn on me. "Don't tell me you had a ring in your pocket?"

He shrugs.

I can't help it. I have to laugh. Here's a guy who usually has it all together—the type of guy who fixes holes in his pockets. I've turned him into—well, I've turned him into someone like me.

By now, Mary is a few feet away. "What's so funny?"

Neil, now double-checking all his pockets, says, "I lost Anne's engagement ring."

Mary gives me a crusty stare. "It's not funny, Anne. Now, I don't know what to do—be in the picture or help you look for the ring."

Now I'm laughing even harder. "I guess you'd better help us find the ring."

With Neil in the lead, we retrace our steps. Mary runs ahead to ask the temple workers if anyone has turned in a ring. Janet Musgrove overhears Mary's question and immediately takes charge. Within seconds, everyone, even the brides and grooms, are walking around with their eyes on the ground, looking for my ring. The photographer, not quite knowing what to do, is snapping shots of Lily and Jay as they bend over the flower beds, searching in vain for a little sparkle. Charlie is running over with Neil's keys to check his car. Joseph and Daniel are reaching—almost falling—into the fountain.

I run over to get the boys, but I'm too late. Daniel is already in. I pull him out of the fountain, then I get Joseph, who's wet up to his elbows.

That's when Neil grabs my wet hand. "I've got something that belongs to you." He slides the ring on my finger. Janet Musgrove and the photographer are right behind him.

I stare down at my left hand and there it is—the ring, the one with three diamonds in a row. The one I wore eight and a half years ago. I throw my arms around him. "You saved it all these years?"

"I guess that would have been romantic—if I'd saved it all these years."

I look at the ring again. "It's beautiful. I hope you didn't have to spend too much. The price of gold has gone up so much."

"Now who's being romantic?"

I'd forgotten about Janet Musgrove being so close until she reaches out to hug me and then Neil. "Congratulations, you two. You make such a cute couple. I barely figured out you were dating. It's only been two or three months, hasn't it? That's almost as fast as Lily and Jay."

225

Neil lets out a little chuckle. "When a man finds the right woman, he might as well hurry up and get engaged."

Janet pokes her finger at Neil's arm. "You're lucky Anne isn't as hard-hearted as my Hannah. It took Barry two years to win her over. Funny how things turn out, isn't it—first Lily and Jay, then you two. I guess you've heard about Will Grandin?"

Neil glances at me as I shake my head. "Let me guess—he's marrying my dad's ex-girlfriend."

"You've got that right. You should see the ring. It is the most enormous—well, I guess I've seen bigger, but not often. If I didn't know better, I'd say she's after his money. But, then again, she's older— maybe he's after her money. Listen to me—I'm really sounding like a gossip, aren't I? It was such a sight to see. I ran into them at the mall. They had shopping bags from the most expensive places. I never look at people's shopping bags, but they had so many, I couldn't help it."

Neil raises his eyebrow at me.

Janet pats my arm. "Well, I couldn't be happier for you two. You make a great couple. Now, I best be getting back to the wedding party. After all, I am the mother of the brides."

As we watch Janet head over toward the photographer, a thought surfaces that I have to share with Neil. "I wonder if Felicia knows Will declared bankruptcy. Do you suppose I should tell her?"

Neil winces. "She needs to know, but you don't need to be the messenger."

"Maybe we could slip a few papers into the mail for her? Do you still have the stuff you found in public records?"

"As long as you don't send her a wedding invitation." He checks his watch. "That reminds me. We'd better get going. I told your mom we'd meet her for lunch to start the planning."

28

T oday is our first anniversary. Looking back, I couldn't have planned a more perfect wedding day if I'd had ten years to work on it. I guess Neil would say I did have ten years—almost.

The weather on the day we were sealed was gray and stormy, but it didn't matter. How else would I have gotten all those great pictures of us under umbrellas in front of the temple? The food didn't matter. We hardly got a chance to taste it. The invitations, the dress, the colors—they were beautiful. But they're all over and done with. What does matter is that we're married and sealed for all eternity.

I can't say marriage has been completely without challenges. There've been financial things and getting-used-to-each-other things. On the whole, though, I'm really happy. I'm so blessed to be married to Neil. Yes, he forgets to hang up his clothes and leaves the toilet seat up and eats too much junk food. But those are such minor things. He is the kind of husband I always knew he could be. He is kind, considerate, loving, and faithful. Better yet, I seem to be the kind of wife I wished I could be. And, yes, I'm not perfect either. I burn pancakes, snore, and get grouchy occasionally.

It's been a year now, and I'm writing this as I sit at our little kitchen table. Out the window, I can see Neil holding our two-week-old baby boy on the back porch. The moon is coming out, and the baby (of course) is waking up. But whether the baby's awake or asleep, Neil is holding him every chance he gets. It doesn't get any better than this.

Discussion Questions

1. How does Anne's family background affect her relationships? How does she overcome her insecurities regarding marriage?

2. Compare this book with Jane Austen's *Persuasion* (either the book or the movie). What are the similarities and differences between Regency England and modern culture, particularly LDS culture?

3. How does Anne cope with the stressful situation of a reunion with Neil? What attitudes and behaviors help her get through? How do you get through stressful situations?

4. How do the characters differ in their attitudes toward money and debt?

5. At the dance in chapter six, Neil says that Anne needs to learn to stand up for herself. Do you think he's right? Does Anne learn to stand up for herself? How have you learned to stand up for yourself?

6. What does Anne's relationship with Will Grandin show about the hazards of dating?

7. How are the characters shaped by traumatic events in their lives, such as accidents, medical emergencies, or health problems?

8. What role does forgiveness play? Which characters must forgive each other? How are they able to forgive?

9. What methods does Anne use to attract Neil? In the end, what is it that really attracts him?

Anne suggests you choose from among the following treats for your book club meeting: cinnamon rolls, rice cakes, whole wheat blueberry muffins, raspberry smoothies or, if all else fails, brownie batter emergency ice cream.

Glossary of Terms

used in The Church of Jesus Christ
of Latter-day Saints

Apostle: One of twelve leaders of the Church who are special witnesses of Christ. When an apostle dies, the other apostles choose a new apostle through inspiration.

Baptism for the Dead: A vicarious baptism in the temple. Members of the Church are baptized in behalf of the deceased. They believe that the dead person's spirit has the opportunity to accept or reject the baptism.

Blessing: A prayer of healing or counsel given by a man who holds the priesthood. Most adult male members of the Church hold the priesthood, and, if worthy, they can give blessings to other members.

Calling: An assignment to do specific volunteer work in the Church.

Fireside: An evening get-together, where members listen to an inspirational speaker.

General Conference: A twice-yearly conference, where Church leaders speak to all members of the worldwide Church. Members usually watch conference on TV or the Internet.

Home Teacher: A man who is assigned to visit a family regularly and help with their needs. Each member or family has a home teacher assigned to serve them.

Relief Society: The women's organization of the Church, which organizes service and holds regular meetings.

Scriptures: Sacred books, which consist of the Bible, the Book of Mormon, the Doctrine and Covenants, and the Pearl of Great Price.

Sealing: A temple marriage ceremony. Members believe that a sealed marriage does not end at death, as long as each person remains worthy. Their children can also be sealed to them.

Stake Center: A larger church building, which can accommodate a meeting of several wards.

Ward: A group of people in a specific geographic area who attend church together.

Word of Wisdom: A law of health that encourages healthy eating and forbids the use of coffee, alcoholic beverages, tobacco, and harmful drugs.

About the Author

Photo by Rachael Nelson

Rebecca Jamison hopes that her ex-boyfriends don't get any ideas from this book. She wants them to know that she is happily married to her husband, another writer. Her only regret is that her husband doesn't like to dance as much as she does. Rebecca grew up in Vienna, Virginia. She attended Brigham Young University, earning a BA and MA in English. In between college and grad school, she served a mission to Portugal and the Cape Verde islands. Rebecca and her husband have six children, so there is never any emergency ice cream to be found in her house. She enjoys running, making jewelry, reading, and watching chick flicks. You can learn more about Rebecca at **www.RebeccaHJamison.com**.